AP中文
仿真试题集

[美] 谢碧霞（Bih-hsya Hsieh）
[美] 于晓华（Sunny X. Yu） ◎编著
[美] 张相华（Hsiang-hua Chang）

（第二版）

AP CHINESE LANGUAGE AND CULTURE SIMULATED TESTS (SECOND EDITION)

图书在版编目(CIP)数据

AP中文仿真试题集 /(美)谢碧霞,(美)于晓华,(美)张相华编著. —2版. —北京:北京大学出版社,2021.10
ISBN 978-7-301-32440-0

Ⅰ.①A… Ⅱ.①谢…②于…③张… Ⅲ.①汉语–高等学校–入学考试–美国–习题集 Ⅳ.①H193.9

中国版本图书馆CIP数据核字(2021)第192512号

书　　　名	AP中文仿真试题集(第二版) AP ZHONGWEN FANGZHEN SHITIJI (DI-ER BAN)
著作责任者	[美]谢碧霞　[美]于晓华　[美]张相华　编著
责任编辑	孙艳玲
特约编辑	徐玲华
标准书号	ISBN 978-7-301-32440-0
出版发行	北京大学出版社
地　　　址	北京市海淀区成府路205号　100871
网　　　址	http://www.pup.cn　　新浪微博:@北京大学出版社
电子信箱	zpup@pup.cn
电　　　话	邮购部 010-62752015　发行部 010-62750672　编辑部 010-62753334
印　刷　者	三河市博文印刷有限公司
经　销　者	新华书店
	889毫米×1194毫米　16开本　23.5印张　460千字 2021年10月第2版　2023年11月第4次印刷
定　　　价	198.00元(含试题集、录音文本及参考答案)

未经许可,不得以任何方式复制或抄袭本书之部分或全部内容。
版权所有,侵权必究
举报电话: 010-62752024　电子信箱: fd@pup.pku.edu.cn
图书如有印装质量问题,请与出版部联系,电话: 010-62756370

AP中文仿真试题集（第二版）
网络版

个人订阅

学校订阅

第二版前言

随着AP中文考试的不断发展，美国大学理事会于2019年出版了最新的《AP中文课程与考试手册》，并强调AP中文考试的大方向、内容和题型基本不变，但未来出题方向会和其他外语更加一致。这表明，AP中文将会和其他AP外语一样，更加注重学生的社会关怀和批判性思维。

举例来说，其他AP外语近年已有许多考题着眼于现代社会生活的挑战，比如AP西班牙文作文题曾考过"使用社交媒体的好坏""公司应该允许雇员在家工作吗"等。而目前AP中文的文化演说题大多仍围绕传统节日、人物、生活等，与社会生活紧密结合的题目似乎不多。未来的考试趋势实际上对AP老师和学生提出了更高的要求，意味着学生要对六大主题，即个人与社会认同、家庭社区、现代生活、科学技术、美与美学和全球挑战，有更全面的认识。

2010年，美国CLERC出版社（iChineseEdu公司前身）出版了由谢碧霞和于晓华执笔的模拟试题集（第一版），共八套试题。该试题集以美国大学理事会颁布的AP中文课程与考试大纲为依据，严格控制词汇、语法以符合AP考试水平，从考题形式到内容完全仿真。试题集深受AP中文师生的欢迎，被视作考前复习宝典，不但在出版后多次重印，而且应师生的需求开发了网络版。但如上所述，随着社会和科技的变迁，该试题集也到了重新修订的时候。

第二版在第一版试题集的基础上进行了两大改善：一是在保持主体内容大致不变的前提下，由原作者对原来的八套题进行内容上的更新，使其更符合新的考试要求；二是由张相华老师在对原来八套题的主题和内容统计分析的基础上，针对尚需补充内容的主题编写了第九、十套题，以使这十套题的听说读写各类题型和内容能够更加全面、平衡地涵盖AP中文六大主题。

《AP中文仿真试题集》（第二版）网络版在美国iChineseEdu公司旗下的iChineseAPlus平台发布。该平台是一个功能完备的中文考试一站式服务网站，有如下功能：支持考试模式和练习模式做题，学生可以获得高度仿真的AP中文模拟考试体验；学生做完一套题后，听力和阅读部分由系统自动判分，口语和写作由老师手动判分；系统可根据得分自动生成统计图表，方便师生掌握学习情况。欲知更多详情，可浏览www.

iChineseAPlus.com。

  第二版得以问世，特别感谢 iChineseEdu 公司的孟凌老师及徐玲华老师多方面的协助、鼓励和宝贵的建议，并感谢北京大学出版社孙艳玲老师对出版纸书的热心支持。谨以此书献给在 AP 中文第一线辛勤努力的老师和同学们！

谢碧霞	于晓华	张相华
San Francisco University High School	Piedmont High School	Oakland University
bihhsya.hsieh@sfuhs.org	xsunnyyu@aol.com	chang23@oakland.edu

第一版前言

自2007年5月美国大学理事会首次举办AP中文考试以来，全美很多学校都相继开设了中文项目，一些已成立中文项目的高中也增设了AP中文课程。学生人数的增加、学生学习中文兴趣的提升，以及学生中文水平的逐年提高，更激发了中文教师从事教学工作的热情和干劲。在过去数年的实际教学中，我们意识到目前针对AP中文考试形式及内容编写的材料非常有限，我们也十分了解一线教师工作的繁忙以及AP中文教学的需求，因此我们不恤野人献曝，以大学理事会所颁布的AP中文教学大纲为范畴，以大学理事会所公布的AP部分中文考试的样题为尺度，以2009年最新AP考试形式为准绳，编写了这本AP中文模拟试题练习册，以供学生平时练习及考前准备之用。

本册共有八套模拟试题，其中第一、三、五、七套题由于晓华负责，第二、四、六、八套题由谢碧霞负责，初步编写完竣，再共同推敲、改写及定稿。在编写过程中，我们既考虑到AP中文考试为水平考试的性质，又顾及目前各校中文课程使用教材不一的特点，尽可能地包括常用的、难易程度适中的词汇与语法，并有意识地穿插少量较难的词汇，以期对学生理解生词有所助益。在文化知识方面，我们把常识性的文化知识融入阅读之中，对于一些较重要的文化知识，学生有机会在文化演绎表达部分充分发挥。在听力对话部分，我们尽可能注意语言情境内容的真实自然及实用性。

虽然我们的初衷是希望本册模拟试题能够兼具内容丰富、程度适中、涵盖面广的特性，并与实际的AP考题题型及内容同步，但囿于个人经验、水平及时间，本书定有不足及需改正之处，尚祈诸位先进多所包涵并不吝指教。对于诸多曾经给予我们建议及宝贵意见的同行与学生，我们在此一并致谢。此外，此书得以问世，我们也由衷感谢CLERC出版社的鼎力支持及张晓江先生的鞭策与协助，以及刘湘燕小姐的编辑与校对。

谢碧霞
San Francisco University High School
bihhsya.hsieh@sfuhs.org

于晓华
Piedmont High School
xsunnyyu@aol.com

目 录

AP Chinese Language and Culture Test 1 ·· 1

AP Chinese Language and Culture Test 2 ·· 23

AP Chinese Language and Culture Test 3 ·· 42

AP Chinese Language and Culture Test 4 ·· 63

AP Chinese Language and Culture Test 5 ·· 83

AP Chinese Language and Culture Test 6 ·· 104

AP Chinese Language and Culture Test 7 ·· 124

AP Chinese Language and Culture Test 8 ·· 148

AP Chinese Language and Culture Test 9 ·· 170

AP Chinese Language and Culture Test 10 ·· 194

AP Chinese Language and Culture Test 1

listening

Section I: Multiple Choice

Part A: Listening (Rejoinders and Listening Selections)

> **Listening Part Directions**
>
> You will answer two types of questions: rejoinders and questions based on listening selections.
>
> For all tasks, you will have a specific amount of response time. When the response time has ended, you will automatically go on to the next question. You cannot return to previous questions.

> **Listening Part Directions: Rejoinders (10%, 10 minutes)**
>
> You will hear several short conversations or parts of conversations followed by four choices, designated A, B, C, and D. Choose the one that continues or completes the conversation in a logical and culturally appropriate manner. After you have decided which of the suggested answers is best, COMPLETELY fill in the corresponding circle on the answer sheet. You will have 5 seconds to answer each question.
>
> YOU WILL NOW BEGIN THIS PART.

1. Mark your answer on your answer sheet.
2. Mark your answer on your answer sheet.
3. Mark your answer on your answer sheet.
4. Mark your answer on your answer sheet.
5. Mark your answer on your answer sheet.
6. Mark your answer on your answer sheet.
7. Mark your answer on your answer sheet.
8. Mark your answer on your answer sheet.
9. Mark your answer on your answer sheet.
10. Mark your answer on your answer sheet.
11. Mark your answer on your answer sheet.
12. Mark your answer on your answer sheet.
13. Mark your answer on your answer sheet.
14. Mark your answer on your answer sheet.
15. Mark your answer on your answer sheet.

Listening Part Directions: Listening Selections (15%, 10 minutes)

You will listen to several selections in Chinese. For each selection, you will be told whether it will be played once or twice. You may take notes as you listen. Your notes will not be graded. After listening to each selection, you will see questions in English. For each question, choose the response that is best according to the selection. You will have 12 seconds to answer each question.

YOU WILL NOW BEGIN THIS PART.

Selection 1: Announcement (Selection plays two times.)

16. The donation is for the benefit of

    A) the school

    B) the students

    C) the homeless

    D) the low-income families

17. How will the food be collected?

    A) Students shall drop the food at the Student Center.

    B) Students need to send the food directly to a non-profit organization.

    C) Students can leave the food in the boxes outside the classrooms.

    D) Volunteers will collect the food during the fourth class.

18. What kinds of food are NOT accepted?

    A) Fresh meat and vegetables

    B) Canned food

    C) Rice and flour

    D) Cooking oil and salt

19. How long will this event last ?

    A) Until the end of the month

    B) Until the end of the semester

    C) Until enough food has been collected

    D) For one week

Selection 2: Conversation (Selection plays one time.)

20. The boy asks the girl to go to a

    A) volunteer event

    B) dance party

    C) birthday party

    D) movie theatre

21. Why does the girl NOT want to go with the boy?

    A) She has to do homework.

    B) She has to volunteer at an event.

    C) She does not enjoy dancing.

    D) She thinks the boy is too aggressive.

22. What is the outcome of the boy's invitation?

    A) The girl will go to the party with someone else.

    B) The girl accepted the boy's invitation.

    C) The girl will not go to the party with the boy.

    D) The girl would like to think about it some more.

Selection 3: Voice Message (Selection plays two times.)

23. Where did the boy stay with his uncle?

    A) San Francisco

    B) Los Angeles

    C) Beijing

    D) Shanghai

24. The boy visited his uncle during

    A) the summer

    B) spring break

    C) Christmas break

    D) Chinese New Year

25. Why is the boy worried about going to school the next day?

    A) He has a lot of homework to do.

    B) He is tired of going to school.

    C) He is experiencing jet lag.

    D) He is still very excited about his recent trip.

26. Which of the following is TRUE about the boy's return flight?

   A) It arrived on time.

   B) It arrived thirty minutes early.

   C) It was delayed by thirty minutes.

   D) It was delayed by one hour.

Selection 4: Instructions (Selection plays one time.)

27. Can the user upload their personal books to this device?

   A) Yes, but there is a fee involved.

   B) Yes, they can do that.

   C) No, the user will have to buy directly from the e-store.

   D) No, but there are free books they can download.

28. The Kindle eBook Reader has become popular because

   A) it has been heavily marketed

   B) the price of the reader is affordable

   C) it is convenient to use

   D) e-books have become affordable

29. How does the user turn it on?

   A) Press the "on" button on the top of the device

   B) Press a button on the device or touch the screen

   C) Type in the product serial code on the receipt

   D) Use the password and log-in ID

30. What can the user do on the device?

   A) To watch a movie

   B) To listen to music

   C) To send a fax

   D) To purchase books

31. Which of the following can it NOT do?

   A) To read cartoons

   B) To make calls

   C) To wirelessly connect to the internet

   D) To read documents with pictures

Selection 5: Report (Selection plays one time.)

32. What will happen tonight?

    A) It will get warmer.

    B) It will get colder.

    C) It will continue to rain.

    D) It will begin to snow.

33. What will happen in the next few days?

    A) It will get warmer.

    B) It will get colder.

    C) It will continue to rain.

    D) It will begin to snow.

34. The forecast advises to

    A) apply sunblock when going outside

    B) carry an umbrella

    C) wear multiple layers

    D) stay indoors

35. What is the scope of the forecast?

    A) Nationwide

    B) Citywide

    C) Statewide

    D) Worldwide

Part B: Reading Selections

Note: In this part of the exam, you may move back and forth among all the questions.

Reading Part Directions: Reading Selections (25%, 60 minutes)

You will read several selections in Chinese. Each selection is accompanied by a number of questions in English. For each question, choose the response that is best according to the selection. After you have decided which of the suggested answers is best, COMPLETELY fill in the corresponding circle on the answer sheet. Chinese tests appear here in both traditional and simplified characters. You will have 60 minutes to answer all questions.

YOU WILL NOW BEGIN THIS PART.

Read this e-mail.

(Traditional characters)

發件人：小紅

收件人：媽媽

郵件主題：在中國旅遊

發件日期：7月18日

親愛的媽媽：

　　您好！今天是我在北京的第四天。前兩天，我去了天安門、故宮、長城和十三陵，昨天我逛了王府井。據說王府井是北京最有名的一條商業街，但是我最感興趣的不是那些賣各種世界名牌的商店，也不是被稱作中華老字號的商店，更不是街頭表演，而是王府井的小吃街。在王府井商業街裡有一條小胡同，裡面全都是專賣各種小吃的店鋪。每個店鋪所賣的食品都具有獨特的地方風味。比如，新疆的烤羊肉串兒、陝西的羊肉泡饃、四川的麻辣粉兒，還有上海的小籠包，等等，多得吃不過來。我想，將來有機會，我一定要帶您來品嚐這裡的美食。

　　明天我就要離開北京去昆明、廣州、珠海等城市了，大約一週後到香港。您在家安心養病，不要擔心我，我會隨時給您寫信或打電話。

　　再見！

女兒 小紅上

(Simplified characters)

发件人：小红

收件人：妈妈

邮件主题：在中国旅游

发件日期：7月18日

亲爱的妈妈：

　　您好！今天是我在北京的第四天。前两天，我去了天安门、故宫、长城和十三陵，昨天我逛了王府井。据说王府井是北京最有名的一条商业街，但是我最感兴趣的不是那些卖各种世界名牌的商店，也不是被称作中华老字号的商店，更不是街头表演，而是王府井的小吃街。在王府井商业街里有一条小胡同，里面全都是专卖各种小吃的店铺。每个店铺所卖的食品都具有独特的地方风味。比如，新疆的烤羊肉串儿、陕西的羊肉泡馍、四川的麻辣粉儿，还有上海的小笼包，等等，多得吃不过来。我想，将来有机会，我一定要带您来品尝这里的美食。

明天我就要离开北京去昆明、广州、珠海等城市了，大约一周后到香港。您在家安心养病，不要担心我，我会随时给您写信或打电话。

再见！

女儿 小红上

1. What was the most memorable location of her trip?

    A) The Forbidden City

    B) The Great Wall

    C) Tian'anmen Square

    D) Wangfujing Snack Street

2. Which of the following statements is TRUE?

    A) Spicy bean noodles are from Beijing.

    B) Steamed pork dumplings are from Shanghai.

    C) Lamb kabobs are from Sichuan.

    D) There are various snacks from the world at Wangfujing Snack Street.

3. What aspect of Wangfujing Street does Xiaohong like the most?

    A) Eating the snacks of Wangfujing

    B) Shopping in internationally known brand name stores

    C) Shopping in traditional Chinese stores

    D) Watching street performances

4. What part of China will Xiaohong visit next?

    A) The North

    B) The South

    C) The East

    D) The West

5. Which of the following statements about Xiaohong's mother is TRUE?

    A) She met with Xiaohong in Hong Kong the following week.

    B) She was sick at home.

    C) She continued to stay in Beijing after Xiaohong left.

    D) She was waiting for Xiaohong to come to Kunming the next day.

Read this public sign.

(Traditional characters)　　　　　　　(Simplified characters)

此處危險！請勿靠近！　　　　　　　此处危险！请勿靠近！

6. What does the warning on the sign suggest?

   A) Do not approach!

   B) Security check needed!

   C) Enter with caution!

   D) Watch both sides of the street before crossing!

7. Where would this sign most likely appear?

   A) On a high-voltage electric fence

   B) Beside a swimming pool

   C) On a children's play structure

   D) In a parking lot

Read this public sign.

(Traditional characters)　　　　　　　(Simplified characters)

平時注入一滴水　　　　　　　　　　平时注入一滴水
難時擁有太平洋　　　　　　　　　　难时拥有太平洋

8. Where is the sign most likely seen?

   A) On a school bus

   B) Near the sink of the public restrooms

   C) Near the beach

   D) In a restaurant

9. The purpose of the sign is to

   A) tell people that travelling across the Pacific Ocean is dangerous

   B) encourage people to save water

   C) say that the Pacific Ocean is the best source for drinking water

   D) remind people to always have plenty of drinking water

Read this advertisement on a poster.

(Traditional characters)

汽車拍賣會

　　本市最盛大的汽車拍賣會，有三百多輛豪華型和經濟型的各式汽車可供挑選。

具體事宜如下：

一、汽車種類：
- 各式轎車
- 各式輕型卡車
- 政府沒收車
- 銀行回收車

二、看車日期：1月1日（星期五）上午十點至下午五點

三、拍賣日期：1月7日（星期四）上午九點至下午三點

四、拍賣地點：江南市市政府東區停車場

　　聯繫電話：（956）300-4000

五、注意事項：
- 風雨無阻，免費入場
- 自由出價，提供貸款
- 買方需支付10%的費用給拍賣行
- 此次拍賣與任何政府機構無關

(Simplified characters)

汽车拍卖会

　　本市最盛大的汽车拍卖会，有三百多辆豪华型和经济型的各式汽车可供挑选。

具体事宜如下：

一、汽车种类：
- 各式轿车
- 各式轻型卡车
- 政府没收车
- 银行回收车

二、看车日期：1月1日（星期五）上午十点至下午五点

三、拍卖日期：1月7日（星期四）上午九点至下午三点

四、拍卖地点：江南市市政府东区停车场

　　联系电话：（956）300-4000

五、注意事项：
- 风雨无阻，免费入场
- 自由出价，提供贷款
- 买方需支付10%的费用给拍卖行
- 此次拍卖与任何政府机构无关

10. Which of the following car categories will NOT be offered at the auction?

    A) Sports cars

    B) Light trucks

    C) Bank owned cars

    D) Government repossessed cars

11. According to the notice, which of the following statements is TRUE?

    A) Buyers must pay a 10% fee to the seller.

    B) Auction participants must pay an entrance fee.

    C) The auction will be canceled if there is rain.

    D) This auction is organized by a government agency.

12. Where is the auction going to be held?

    A) At an auto dealership

    B) In a parking lot next to city hall

    C) In the eastern part of the city

    D) In a parking lot in front of a bank

13. Which of the following statements is FALSE?

    A) The buyer can view the cars prior to the auction.

    B) The buyer can name their own price.

    C) The buyer must have good credit.

    D) The buyer can obtain loans.

Read this advertisement.

(Traditional characters)

德州州立大學女留學生，找人合租一套兩室一廳一浴獨立單元。月租五百美元，兩人平分。單獨睡房，共用客廳及廚浴。合租人須是在校大學生，不吸菸，無寵物，男女不限。有意者請下午三點鐘後電（111）123-4567聯繫。

(Simplified characters)

> 德州州立大学女留学生，找人合租一套两室一厅一浴独立单元。月租五百美元，两人平分。单独睡房，共用客厅及厨浴。合租人须是在校大学生，不吸烟，无宠物，男女不限。有意者请下午三点钟后电（111）123-4567联系。

14. Who puts up this advertisement?

    A) An international student

    B) The apartment owner

    C) A real estate agent

    D) The college's housing service

15. What type of roommate is preferred?

    A) Female college student

    B) Male college student

    C) Non-smoking college student

    D) College student with pets

16. How much is the rent?

    A) $500 per person

    B) $250 per person

    C) $1,000 per person

    D) It depends on the size of the room.

17. What is the preferred contact time?

    A) Before 3:00 pm

    B) After 3:00 pm

    C) At 3:00 pm

    D) Around 3:00 pm

18. Where is the apartment located?

    A) California

    B) Oregon

    C) Washington

    D) Texas

Read this letter.

(Traditional characters)

大偉：

你好！

隨父母從北京遷居紐約已經快一週了，我非常想念你和其他的同學。

這是我第一次來紐約，對這裡的一切都感到新奇。紐約是一座1624年建立的城市，是世界金融和貿易中心，非常繁華。紐約也有很多世界級的畫廊和演藝比賽場地，是西半球文化和娛樂的中心之一，芭蕾、古典音樂、歌劇、音樂會等各種表演應有盡有，很多都是世界一流的水平。世界級藝術和歷史展品的博物館也令人目不暇接。我逛了舉世聞名的時代廣場和帝國大廈，看了自由女神像，還參觀了被譽為美國的"復活標誌"的新世貿大廈。希望將來你有機會來紐約的時候，我可以做你的導遊，帶你看演出、參觀博物館，一起去新世貿大廈，在那兒的觀景平臺上，觀賞紐約迷人的夜景。

祝好！

小明

10月16日

(Simplified characters)

大伟：

你好！

随父母从北京迁居纽约已经快一周了，我非常想念你和其他的同学。

这是我第一次来纽约，对这里的一切都感到新奇。纽约是一座1624年建立的城市，是世界金融和贸易中心，非常繁华。纽约也有很多世界级的画廊和演艺比赛场地，是西半球文化和娱乐的中心之一，芭蕾、古典音乐、歌剧、音乐会等各种表演应有尽有，很多都是世界一流的水平。世界级艺术和历史展品的博物馆也令人目不暇接。我逛了举世闻名的时代广场和帝国大厦，看了自由女神像，还参观了被誉为美国的"复活标志"的新世贸大厦。希望将来你有机会来纽约的时候，我可以做你的导游，带你看演出、参观博物馆，一起去新世贸大厦，在那儿的观景平台上，观赏纽约迷人的夜景。

祝好！

小明

10月16日

19. Why did Xiaoming come to New York?

    A) To visit his father and mother

    B) His family moved to New York.

    C) He works in New York.

    D) To visit a friend with his parents

20. Which of the following statements is NOT TRUE?

    A) Xiaoming has been in New York before.

    B) Xiaoming visited Time Square and the Empire State Building.

    C) Xiaoming hopes to give his friend a tour.

    D) Xiaoming misses his friend very much.

21. Why does Xiaoming want Dawei to visit the new World Trade Center?

    A) Because the building is a landmark.

    B) To admire the beautiful night view of New York

    C) To visit world-class museums

    D) To taste various kinds of cuisine

22. How long has Xiaoming been in New York?

    A) Less than a week

    B) More than a week

    C) At least a month

    D) Almost a year

Read this article.

(Traditional characters)

問路

馬克第一次到中國旅遊，遊覽了中國的兩個城市：北京和哈爾濱。他有一個非常有趣的發現。在北京，當他問路時，當地人都是答向東、向西、向南或者向北，總是以東南西北來指示方向。但是在哈爾濱，當地人都是以向左、向右、向前或者向後來指示方向。他對此感到非常好奇。

他參考了北京和哈爾濱的地理位置和城市發展歷史後發現，北京地處內陸華北平原，以紫禁城為中心，街道像一個個方塊向外層層擴展，主要街道佈局為東西或南北方向。而哈爾濱緊鄰松花江，由於河道彎曲，哈爾濱的街道像蜘蛛網一樣由江邊向兩岸擴展，城市的主要街道彎彎曲曲。馬克想，也許城市規劃的不同就是那些土生土長的北京人和哈爾濱人指路時方法不同的主要原因吧。

(Simplified characters)

问路

马克第一次到中国旅游，游览了中国的两个城市：北京和哈尔滨。他有一个非常有趣的发现。在北京，当他问路时，当地人都是答向东、向西、向南或者向北，总是以东南西北来指示方向。但是在哈尔滨，当地人都是以向左、向右、向前或者向后来指示方向。他对此感到非常好奇。

他参考了北京和哈尔滨的地理位置和城市发展历史后发现，北京地处内陆华北平原，以紫禁城为中心，街道像一个个方块向外层层扩展，主要街道布局为东西或南北方向。而哈尔滨紧邻松花江，由于河道弯曲，哈尔滨的街道像蜘蛛网一样由江边向两岸扩展，城市的主要街道弯弯曲曲。马克想，也许城市规划的不同就是那些土生土长的北京人和哈尔滨人指路时方法不同的主要原因吧。

23. Beijing locals like to give directions using

    A) street signs

    B) "Left, right, forward, backward"

    C) "East, west, north, south"

    D) maps

24. Which of the following is the best description of the streets of Beijing?

    A) They are twisted like a spider's web.

    B) They are narrow.

    C) They are straight and orderly.

    D) They are twisted like a bird's nest.

25. Why do local people of Beijing and Harbin give directions in different ways?

    A) Beijing is an older city than Harbin.

    B) Harbin's population is larger.

    C) The layout of the streets of the two cities is different.

    D) Beijing is the capital of China.

Read this poster.

(Traditional characters)

大學申請指導系列講座

如何正確選擇大學專業和職業道路

時間：4月1日下午2點至5點

地點：東北科技學院第一教學樓

主講人：李景新教授

　　大學是人生的重要發展階段，選擇合適的專業對於一個人今後的職業起到非常重要的作用，然而常常很難抉擇。

　　李教授在這方面有著長期的研究和豐富的經驗。在講座中，李教授將對學科和專業方向、就業市場現狀及發展進行較爲全面的分析，使同學們對如何選擇專業有進一步的瞭解。李教授講解後，有一個測評表需要你來填寫。你要誠實回答表上的20個問題。完成後，你將收到一個評估報告。這份報告是根據你的個人興趣、專業偏好進行客觀分析和評估後得出的。報告會對你的專業選擇給出建議。講座最後一個環節是10分鐘的一對一的個人輔導。李教授團隊的專家們會對你個人的實際情況進行評估，并幫你權衡專業選擇。希望這次講座對你的大學申請以及專業選擇有指導作用。

(Simplified characters)

大学申请指导系列讲座

如何正确选择大学专业和职业道路

时间：4月1日下午2点至5点

地点：东北科技学院第一教学楼

主讲人：李景新教授

　　大学是人生的重要发展阶段，选择合适的专业对于一个人今后的职业起到非常重要的作用，然而常常很难抉择。

　　李教授在这方面有着长期的研究和丰富的经验。在讲座中，李教授将对学科和专业方向、就业市场现状及发展进行较为全面的分析，使同学们对如何选择专业有进一步的了解。李教授讲解后，有一个测评表需要你来填写。你要诚实回答表上的20个问题。完成后，你将收到一个评估报告。这份报告是根据你的个人兴趣、专业偏好进行客观分析和评估后得出的。报告会对你的专业选择给出建议。讲座最后一个环节是10分钟的一对一的个人辅导。李教授团队的专家们会对你个人的实际情况进行评估，并帮你权衡专业选择。希望这次讲座对你的大学申请以及专业选择有指导作用。

26. What is the purpose of the seminar?

    A) To inform students about possible financial aid opportunities

    B) To discuss with students about the college major and its future career path

    C) How to fill out the college application

    D) To discuss available college scholarships

27. What will Professor Li address at the seminar?

    A) His personal college experience

    B) Sporting events at college

    C) Analysis of current job market and college major selection

    D) What student clubs are offered at college

28. Attendees will need to fill out

    A) a survey about the seminar content

    B) a personal preference quiz

    C) a question form for Professor Li

    D) an evaluation of Professor Li's speech

29. At the end of the seminar, attendees will

    A) choose their preferred college major

    B) select a club that suits the major they are interested in

    C) consult with a college admission officer about college major choice

    D) have an individual consultation meeting with Professor Li's team of college advisors

30. Where is the seminar held?

    A) At an admissions office building

    B) In a building at the Northeastern University of Technology and Science

    C) In a building on the north east side of campus

    D) At a university of technology and science

Read this story.

(Traditional characters)

> 4月的一天，爺孫二人牽著一頭小毛驢去趕集。集市上人山人海，有說書唱戲的，有打拳賣藝的，也有賣燒餅的，非常熱鬧。逛了半天，他們有些累了。爺爺心疼孫子，就讓他騎著驢走，自己在後面跟著。沒走多遠，聽見有人說："那孩子真不懂事兒，他自己騎在驢上，讓爺爺在後面跟著走。"聽了這話，孫子馬上跳下來，把爺爺扶上驢，自己在後面趕著驢走。
>
> 沒走多遠，又有人說："這個老頭兒真可笑，自己騎在驢上，倒讓小孫子給他趕驢，不疼愛孩子。"聽了這話，爺爺又忙跳下驢來。孫子在前面牽著，爺爺在後面趕著向前走。沒走多遠，看見的人又嘲笑說："你看這一老一小，真是一對大傻瓜，有驢不騎，卻在地上走。"聽了這話，爺爺趕忙又把孫子扶到驢上，然後自己也爬上去。祖孫倆一前一後，同時騎在驢上，壓得小毛驢直冒汗。沒走多遠，又有人批評說："哼！這兩個人簡直是在虐待小驢。"聽了這話，祖孫二人一塊兒跳下驢來，心想，這驢到底怎麼騎纔好？
>
> 爺孫倆對視了半天，爺爺說："孩子，只有一個辦法了，咱們乾脆抬著驢子走吧。"說完，兩個人把驢子的四條腿綁起來，用一根棍子抬著走了。孫子累得要死，生氣地說："這頭驢好麻煩，沒有它就好了。"爺爺上氣不接下氣地說："驢子不會說話，不能怨它。就是那些多事兒的人，鬧得咱們不知所措，纔抬著驢子走的。"

(Simplified characters)

> 4月的一天，爷孙二人牵着一头小毛驴去赶集。集市上人山人海，有说书唱戏的，有打拳卖艺的，也有卖烧饼的，非常热闹。逛了半天，他们有些累了。爷爷心疼孙子，就让他骑着驴走，自己在后面跟着。没走多远，听见有人说："那孩子真不懂事儿，他自己骑在驴上，让爷爷在后面跟着走。"听了这话，孙子马上跳下来，把爷爷扶上驴，自己在后面赶着驴走。
>
> 没走多远，又有人说："这个老头儿真可笑，自己骑在驴上，倒让小孙子给他赶驴，不疼爱孩子。"听了这话，爷爷又忙跳下驴来。孙子在前面牵着，爷爷在后面赶着向前走。没走多远，看见的人又嘲笑说："你看这一老一小，真是一对大傻瓜，有驴不骑，却在地上走。"听了这话，爷爷赶忙又把孙子扶到驴上，然后自己

也爬上去。祖孙俩一前一后，同时骑在驴上，压得小毛驴直冒汗。没走多远，又有人批评说："哼！这两个人简直是在虐待小驴。"听了这话，祖孙二人一块儿跳下驴来，心想，这驴到底怎么骑才好？

爷孙俩对视了半天，爷爷说："孩子，只有一个办法了，咱们干脆抬着驴子走吧。"说完，两个人把驴子的四条腿绑起来，用一根棍子抬着走了。孙子累得要死，生气地说："这头驴好麻烦，没有它就好了。"爷爷上气不接下气地说："驴子不会说话，不能怨它。就是那些多事儿的人，闹得咱们不知所措，才抬着驴子走的。"

31. Which of the following statements is TRUE?

   A) The story took place during the spring.

   B) A grandfather and his grandson went to visit their relatives.

   C) People were selling books at the market.

   D) A father and son went shopping with a donkey.

32. Why did the townspeople complain when they saw the boy riding the donkey?

   A) The boy was too heavy.

   B) The boy should let his grandfather ride the donkey.

   C) The donkey was tired.

   D) The grandfather was upset.

33. The grandfather got on the donkey because

   A) he was tired

   B) he was upset with the boy

   C) he thought that was what the townspeople wanted him to do

   D) he thought the donkey was strong enough to carry him

34. Why did both the boy and the grandfather get on the donkey?

   A) The donkey was refreshed from a rest.

   B) The townspeople wanted to take the donkey away.

   C) The townspeople complained that nobody was using the donkey.

   D) Both the boy and grandfather were tired.

35. What did the boy and grandfather do with the donkey in the end?

   A) They sold it on the market.

   B) They walked the donkey home.

   C) They carried the donkey home by a stick.

   D) They both rode the donkey home.

END OF SECTION I
YOU MAY REVIEW WORK IF THERE IS TIME LEFT.
DO NOT GO ON TO SECTION II UNTIL YOU ARE TOLD TO DO SO.

Section II: Free Response

Part A: Writing (Story Narration and E-mail Response)

Note: In this part of the exam, the student may NOT move back and forth among questions.

Writing Part Directions

You will be asked to perform two writing tasks in Chinese. In each case, you will be asked to write for a specific purpose and to a specific person. You should write in as complete and as culturally appropriate a manner as possible, taking into account the purpose and the person described.

Presentational Writing: Story Narration (15%, 15 minutes)

The four pictures present a story. Imagine you are writing the story for a friend. Narrate a complete story as suggested by the pictures. Give your story a beginning, a middle, and an end.

Interpersonal Writing: E-mail Response (10%, 15 minutes)

Read this e-mail from a friend and then type a response.

(Traditional characters)

發件人：小強

郵件主題：玩兒電子遊戲

　　最近我非常著迷電子遊戲。每天放學後一回到家，作業都還沒做，就急著打電子遊戲，而且每天都玩兒到深夜。第二天上學常常遲到，上課沒精神，學習成績也下降了。爸爸和媽媽經常跟我生氣，但我還是管不住自己。你說我該怎麼辦？

(Simplified characters)

发件人：小强

邮件主题：玩儿电子游戏

　　最近我非常着迷电子游戏。每天放学后一回到家，作业都还没做，就急着打电子游戏，而且每天都玩儿到深夜。第二天上学常常迟到，上课没精神，学习成绩也下降了。爸爸和妈妈经常跟我生气，但我还是管不住自己。你说我该怎么办？

Part B: Speaking (Conversation and Cultural Presentation)

Note: In this part of the exam, you may NOT move back and forth among questions.

speaking

Speaking Part Directions: Conversation

You will participate in a simulated conversation. Each time it is your turn to speak, you will have 20 seconds to record. You should respond as fully and as appropriately as possible. There will be six times when it is your turn to speak.

Interpersonal Speaking: Conversation (10%, 4 minutes)

You will have a conversation with Xiaofan, your classmate, about your plan of SAT study during the summer vacation.

Speaking Question 1 of 7

1. Record your answer. (20 seconds)

Speaking Question 2 of 7

2. Record your answer. (20 seconds)

Speaking Question 3 of 7

3. Record your answer. (20 seconds)

Speaking Question 4 of 7

4. Record your answer. (20 seconds)

Speaking Question 5 of 7

5. Record your answer. (20 seconds)

Speaking Question 6 of 7

6. Record your answer. (20 seconds)

Speaking Part Directions: Cultural Presentation

You will be asked to speak in Chinese on a specific topic. Imagine you are making an oral presentation to your Chinese class. First, you will read and hear the topic for your presentation. You will have 4 minutes to prepare your presentation. Then you will have 2 minutes to record your presentation. Your presentation should be as complete as possible.

Presentational Speaking: Cultural Presentation (15%, 7 minutes)

Speaking Question 7 of 7

7. Name a Chinese movie that has left a lasting impression on you. What aspects of Chinese culture did it present? Why did you find this movie memorable? In your presentation, describe this movie and explain its significance.

You have four minutes to prepare your presentation. (240 seconds)
You have two minutes to record your presentation. (120 seconds)

YOU HAVE FINISHED THIS PART OF THE EXAM.
END OF EXAM

AP Chinese Language and Culture Test 2

listening

Section I: Multiple Choice

Part A: Listening (Rejoinders and Listening Selections)

> **Listening Part Directions**
>
> You will answer two types of questions: rejoinders and questions based on listening selections.
>
> For all tasks, you will have a specific amount of response time. When the response time has ended, you will automatically go on to the next question. You cannot return to previous questions.

> **Listening Part Directions: Rejoinders (10%, 10 minutes)**
>
> You will hear several short conversations or parts of conversations followed by four choices, designated A, B, C, and D. Choose the one that continues or completes the conversation in a logical and culturally appropriate manner. After you have decided which of the suggested answers is best, COMPLETELY fill in the corresponding circle on the answer sheet. You will have 5 seconds to answer each question.
>
> YOU WILL NOW BEGIN THIS PART.

1. Mark your answer on your answer sheet.
2. Mark your answer on your answer sheet.
3. Mark your answer on your answer sheet.
4. Mark your answer on your answer sheet.
5. Mark your answer on your answer sheet.
6. Mark your answer on your answer sheet.
7. Mark your answer on your answer sheet.
8. Mark your answer on your answer sheet.
9. Mark your answer on your answer sheet.
10. Mark your answer on your answer sheet.
11. Mark your answer on your answer sheet.
12. Mark your answer on your answer sheet.
13. Mark your answer on your answer sheet.
14. Mark your answer on your answer sheet.
15. Mark your answer on your answer sheet.

Listening Part Directions: Listening Selections (15%, 10 minutes)

You will listen to several selections in Chinese. For each selection, you will be told whether it will be played once or twice. You may take notes as you listen. Your notes will not be graded. After listening to each selection, you will see questions in English. For each question, choose the response that is best according to the selection. You will have 12 seconds to answer each question.

YOU WILL NOW BEGIN THIS PART.

Selection 1: Announcement (Selection plays two times.)

16. This announcement would be broadcast

    A) at the railroad station

    B) at the airport

    C) at the subway station

    D) on the plane

17. This announcement is to remind the passengers

    A) to get ready for departure

    B) where to claim baggage

    C) to go to the counter to check in

    D) where to buy the ticket

Selection 2: Conversation (Selection plays one time.)

18. Xiaowen is dressed up because

    A) she is going to work

    B) she is going for a job interview

    C) she is going to apply for a job

    D) she is going on a date

19. What is good about the coffee shop for Xiaowen?

    A) It is close to school.

    B) It has very good coffee.

    C) Her friends like to hang out there.

    D) The coffee there is inexpensive.

20. Based on this conversation, Xiaowen's mother tried to

    A) encourage her to get some working experience

    B) prevent her from going out today

    C) take her to the coffee shop herself

    D) tell her to study hard

21. Xiaowen was worried about being late because

    A) she had spent too much time dressing up

    B) she did not want her boyfriend to wait too long

    C) she did not want the employer to have a bad impression of her

    D) she just missed the bus

22. Xiaowen would like to have a job because

    A) she wants to be independent

    B) she thinks making extra money is important

    C) she regards having working experience to be beneficial to her college application

    D) she thinks working is funny

Selection 3: Instructions (Selection plays one time.)

23. The voice mail instructions are most likely for

    A) a childcare center

    B) a library

    C) an athletic center

    D) a school

24. If you would like to talk to the head of the organization, you are asked to press

    A) 0

    B) 1

    C) 2

    D) 3

25. If you would like to inquire about the location of a certain game, you are asked to press

    A) 0

    B) 1

    C) 4

    D) 5

26. You need to press "0", if you would like to

   A) leave a message for your child

   B) renew a book

   C) report an absence

   D) donate books to the library

Selection 4: Voice Message (Selection plays two times.)

27. According to the passage, which of the following statements is TRUE?

   A) Lili was late for school this morning.

   B) Her English class is the last class of the day.

   C) She has an English test today.

   D) She does not have an English class today.

28. Lili's homework was left on

   A) the right side of her desk

   B) the top shelf of the bookcase to the left of her desk

   C) her bed

   D) the top shelf of the bookcase to the right of her desk

29. When Lili's mother arrives at school, she is supposed to

   A) go directly to Lili's class

   B) give the homework to the teacher

   C) give the homework to Ms. Li

   D) ask to see Lili

30. Why doesn't Lili want her mother to call her?

   A) She left the cell phone at home.

   B) She has classes all afternoon.

   C) She won't have time to come out to see her.

   D) It would take too much of her time.

Selection 5: Report (Selection plays one time.)

31. The survey was NOT done

   A) in the shopping center

   B) in front of schools

   C) in front of movie theaters

   D) in the parks

32. This survey was done by

    A) high school students

    B) a parents' association

    C) a TV journalist

    D) an official at a public policy institute

33. What is the percentage of the students who spend more than five hours on the internet every evening?

    A) 5%

    B) 15%

    C) 18%

    D) 80%

34. Parents are opposed to their kids spending too much time on the internet because they would rather see them spend more time on

    A) communicating with parents

    B) helping parents with housework

    C) working on their homework

    D) sleeping

35. According to this survey, which of the following statements is TRUE?

    A) Students feel they indeed spend too much time on the internet.

    B) When students talk to friends on the internet, it's not necessarily chatting.

    C) In addition to internet shopping, students also utilize the resources on the internet to do research.

    D) Students spend the majority of their internet time on playing computer games and chatting

Part B: Reading Selections

Note: In this part of the exam, you may move back and forth among all the questions.

Reading Part Directions: Reading Selections (25%, 60 minutes)

You will read several selections in Chinese. Each selection is accompanied by a number of questions in English. For each question, choose the response that is best according to the selection. After you have decided which of the suggested answers is best, COMPLETELY fill in the corresponding circle on the answer sheet. Chinese tests appear here in both traditional and simplified characters. You will have 60 minutes to answer all questions.

YOU WILL NOW BEGIN THIS PART.

Read this e-mail.

(Traditional characters)

> 發件人：白大衛
> 收件人：李京
> 郵件主題：共度感恩節邀請
> 發件日期：11月18日
>
> 李京：
>
> 　　感恩節快到了，我想請你來我家跟我們全家一起過感恩節。我媽媽每年都會烤一隻大火雞，再做幾樣拿手的好菜，還會烤又香又好吃的蘋果餅和南瓜餅。我知道你從來沒在美國過過感恩節，非常希望你能來我家看看典型的美國家庭是怎麼過節的。我父母常常聽我提起你，他們很想認識你，對你為什麼遠離親人來美國上高中都非常好奇，也想知道中國人有什麼年節、怎麼慶祝。你不用擔心到我家來怎麼走，我可以開車去接你。另外，你什麼東西都不用帶，帶上個好胃口就行了。儘早給我回個電郵吧！
>
> 　　　　　　　　　　　　　　　　　　　　　　　　大衛

(Simplified characters)

> 发件人：白大卫
> 收件人：李京
> 邮件主题：共度感恩节邀请
> 发件日期：11月18日
>
> 李京：
>
> 　　感恩节快到了，我想请你来我家跟我们全家一起过感恩节。我妈妈每年都会烤一只大火鸡，再做几样拿手的好菜，还会烤又香又好吃的苹果饼和南瓜饼。我知道你从来没在美国过过感恩节，非常希望你能来我家看看典型的美国家庭是怎么过节的。我父母常常听我提起你，他们很想认识你，对你为什么远离亲人来美国上高中都非常好奇，也想知道中国人有什么年节、怎么庆祝。你不用担心到我家来怎么走，我可以开车去接你。另外，你什么东西都不用带，带上个好胃口就行了。尽早给我回个电邮吧！
>
> 　　　　　　　　　　　　　　　　　　　　　　　　大卫

1. Dawei invited Li Jing to celebrate

   A) Christmas with his family

   B) Thanksgiving with his family

C) Easter with his family

D) Halloween with his family

2. Which of the following statements is TRUE?

   A) Dawei's parents have met Li Jing before.

   B) Li Jing knows how to get to Dawei's house.

   C) Li Jing's parents do not live in America.

   D) Li Jing likes the food Dawei's mother makes.

3. Which of the following statements is FALSE?

   A) Dawei's parents are not familiar with Chinese festivals.

   B) Li Jing has a good appetite.

   C) Li Jing is not supposed to take any gifts with him to Dawei's house.

   D) Dawei's parents are curious about Li Jing.

Read this public sign.

(Traditional characters)

保持校園清潔
請勿亂丟紙屑果皮

(Simplified characters)

保持校园清洁
请勿乱丢纸屑果皮

4. Where would this sign most likely appear?

   A) In a park

   B) At a school

   C) In a concert hall

   D) In a movie theater

5. What is the purpose of this sign?

   A) To educate people to recycle

   B) To encourage people to save energy

   C) To tell people to take good care of their property

   D) To ask people to keep the environment clean

Read this public sign.

(Traditional characters)

隨手關燈一小步
節約能源一大步

(Simplified characters)

随手关灯一小步
节约能源一大步

6. Where would this sign most likely appear?

    A) By a light switch

    B) By a faucet

    C) By a window

    D) On a refrigerator

7. The purpose of this sign is to

    A) remind people to save water

    B) remind people to save electricity

    C) remind people not to waste food

    D) remind people to save money

Read this letter.

(Traditional characters)

> 小易：
>
> 　　你好！我可以借用你的《西洋文明小史》嗎？我自己有一本，可是十天前被小張借走了，他這個週末跟父母到東部參觀大學，所以我拿不回來。我西洋文明史課下星期四有個口頭報告，我有幾個論點還需要參考一下《西洋文明小史》。如果你這兩天不會用到這本書的話，可不可以借給我？我三天後一定歸還，感激不盡！我做完報告後，請你喝奶茶。
>
> 　　　　　　　　　　　　　　　　　　　　　　　　　麗明
>
> 　　　　　　　　　　　　　　　　　　　　　　　　　10月21日

(Simplified characters)

> 小易：
>
> 　　你好！我可以借用你的《西洋文明小史》吗？我自己有一本，可是十天前被小张借走了，他这个周末跟父母到东部参观大学，所以我拿不回来。我西洋文明史课下星期四有个口头报告，我有几个论点还需要参考一下《西洋文明小史》。如果你这两天不会用到这本书的话，可不可以借给我？我三天后一定归还，感激不尽！我做完报告后，请你喝奶茶。
>
> 　　　　　　　　　　　　　　　　　　　　　　　　　丽明
>
> 　　　　　　　　　　　　　　　　　　　　　　　　　10月21日

8. According to this note, what does Liming want to do?

   A) She wants Xiao Yi to give her copy of *A Short History of Western Civilization* to Xiao Zhang.

   B) She wants Xiao Zhang to lend her *A Short History of Western Civilization*.

   C) She would like Xiao Yi to lend her *A Short History of Western Civilization*.

   D) She would like Xiao Yi to return *A Short History of Western Civilization* to her.

9. According to the note, which of the following statements is TRUE?

   A) Xiao Zhang went to visit colleges after he borrowed a book from Liming.

   B) Xiao Zhang needed the book for college visiting.

   C) Xiao Zhang promised to treat Liming to milk tea.

   D) Xiao Yi would not lend the book to Liming unless she agrees to return in three days.

10. What does Liming need *A Short History of Western Civilization* for?

    A) She is preparing for a translation exam.

    B) She is preparing for an oral presentation.

    C) She does not know certain English words.

    D) She is writing a paper for her western civilization class.

Read this advertisement on a poster.

(Traditional characters)

美美服飾店結束營業大減價
女裝六五折（名牌外套除外），
男士襯衫一律七折，長褲八折，
童裝一律對折。
現金、支付寶、微信支付皆可。
恕不代客更改長短大小。

(Simplified characters)

美美服饰店结束营业大减价
女装六五折（名牌外套除外），
男士衬衫一律七折，长裤八折，
童装一律对折。
现金、支付宝、微信支付皆可。
恕不代客更改长短大小。

11. The store is having a sale because

    A) it is a pre-season sale

    B) it is going out of business

    C) it is an end of the year sale

    D) it is an anniversary sale

12. What are NOT on sale?

    A) Ladies designer jackets

    B) Ladies designer dresses

    C) Children's pants

    D) Men's clothes

13. What clothes have the biggest discount?

    A) Children's clothes

    B) Ladies clothes

    C) Men's shirts

    D) Men's pants

14. Which of the following statements is TRUE?

    A) If you cannot find the right size, they can order for you.

    B) If you cannot find the right size, they can alter for you.

    C) They don't provide alteration service.

    D) They accept credit card payment.

Read this advertisement.

(Traditional characters)

中文社急徵中文報義工

義工的工作範圍主要包括兩部分：一是從中文報紙、雜誌及互聯網上選擇適合學生閱讀的文章；二是編選同學們的來稿。應徵者的中文、美術都要有一定的水平，能熟練使用電腦繪圖軟件與工具，工作時間為一週四至六小時。有興趣的同學請於本週五前與學生活動中心的李老師電郵聯繫：lqz@abc.edu。

(Simplified characters)

中文社急征中文报义工

义工的工作范围主要包括两部分：一是从中文报纸、杂志及互联网上选择适合学生阅读的文章；二是编选同学们的来稿。应征者的中文、美术都要有一定的水平，能熟练使用电脑绘图软件与工具，工作时间为一周四至六小时。有兴趣的同学请于本周五前与学生活动中心的李老师电邮联系：lqz@abc.edu。

15. This advertisement is to solicit

    A) subscription to a school Chinese newspaper

    B) reporters for school activities

    C) volunteers for a school Chinese newspaper

    D) application for computer work

16. The students who are interested need to

    A) have a computer

    B) know Teacher Li

    C) have certain art skills

    D) be native Chinese speakers

17. Which of the following statements is FALSE?

    A) The work requires computer skills.

    B) Any applications submitted after this Friday won't be accepted.

    C) The work requires writing articles in Chinese.

    D) The work involves reading a lot of articles from various sources.

Read this letter.

(Traditional characters)

大山表哥：

　　你好！謝謝你前幾天給我寄來的生日禮物，那個光盤裡的歌曲真好聽，我邊聽邊學，一下子就學會了好幾首。昨天我們學校有個才藝表演，你絕對想不到，內向的我居然也抱著吉他上臺了，邊彈邊唱，表演的就是那個光盤裡的兩首歌。唱完以後，臺下的老師和同學都為我熱烈鼓掌，還大叫"再來一個！再來一個"，我興奮得滿臉通紅，因為這是我第一次上臺表演，唱的還是中國民謠呢。說來也許你不相信，表演之前，我甚至緊張得全身發抖！我要再次謝謝你，因為是你為我精心挑選的禮物，使我克服了不敢在大家面前表演的心理障礙。

　　最後祝你健康快樂！

毛毛

10月24日

(Simplified characters)

大山表哥：

　　你好！谢谢你前几天给我寄来的生日礼物，那个光盘里的歌曲真好听，我边听边学，一下子就学会了好几首。昨天我们学校有个才艺表演，你绝对想不到，内向的我居然也抱着吉他上台了，边弹边唱，表演的就是那个光盘里的两首歌。唱完以后，台下的老师和同学都为我热烈鼓掌，还大叫"再来一个！再来一个"，我兴奋得满脸通红，因为这是我第一次上台表演，唱的还是中国民谣呢。说来也许你不相信，表演之前，我甚至紧张得全身发抖！我要再次谢谢你，因为是你为我精心挑选的礼物，使我克服了不敢在大家面前表演的心理障碍。

　　最后祝你健康快乐！

毛毛

10月24日

18. What birthday present did Dashan give Maomao?

   A) A CD

   B) MP3 files

   C) A guitar

   D) Sheet music

19. Why did Maomao's face turn red?

   A) Because she forgot one line while singing.

   B) Because she played one note wrong and felt embarrassed.

   C) Because her teacher complimented her in front of everyone.

   D) Because her performance was well received.

20. Which of the following statements is TRUE?

   A) Dashan gave the present to Maomao in person.

   B) Maomao has a lot of experience performing for others.

   C) Maomao learns to sing songs very fast.

   D) Maomao chose the present herself.

21. Which of the following statements is FALSE?

   A) Maomao knows how to play the guitar.

   B) Dashan taught Maomao how to overcome psychological handicaps.

   C) The audience urged Maomao to sing more songs.

   D) This is Maomao's first performance in public.

22. The songs that Maomao sang

   A) were the ones that she had practiced for a long time

   B) were the ones that she was familiar with from childhood

   C) are Chinese popular songs

   D) are Chinese folk songs

23. Maomao regards herself to be quite

   A) introverted

   B) outgoing

   C) cheerful

   D) passionate

Read this article.

(Traditional characters)

中文演講比賽

今天學校舉辦了題為"學中文的苦與樂"的中文演講比賽，參加的學生漢語都說得非常流利。我因為每天課後都得參加足球隊的訓練，沒時間準備，所以只去當聽眾。他們演講的內容都十分生動有趣，聽眾不時爆出笑聲。比方說，有個同學說她剛學漢語時，四聲搞不清楚，本來要說"你真酷"，結果說成了"你真苦"。還有同學說，很多詞語不會用中文表達，就直接從英文翻譯成中文，像是把"帶狗出去散步"——也就是"遛狗"——說成了"走狗"，或者是"載人一程，到了目的地，先把人放下車"，說成了"丟人"。我聽了他們的演講以後，覺得獲益良多，中文水平無形中提升了不少。

(Simplified characters)

中文演讲比赛

今天学校举办了题为"学中文的苦与乐"的中文演讲比赛，参加的学生汉语都说得非常流利。我因为每天课后都得参加足球队的训练，没时间准备，所以只去当听众。他们演讲的内容都十分生动有趣，听众不时爆出笑声。比方说，有个同学说她刚学汉语时，四声搞不清楚，本来要说"你真酷"，结果说成了"你真苦"。还有同学说，很多词语不会用中文表达，就直接从英文翻译成中文，像是把"带狗出去散步"——也就是"遛狗"——说成了"走狗"，或者是"载人一程，到了目的地，先把人放下车"，说成了"丢人"。我听了他们的演讲以后，觉得获益良多，中文水平无形中提升了不少。

24. The Chinese speech contest is

   A) for students who speak Chinese fluently

   B) for students to tell about their own experiences in learning Chinese

   C) for students to tell the difference among the four tones

   D) for students to tell some Chinese jokes

25. According to this passage, the narrator

   A) was very polite and applauded every speaker

   B) went there to improve his level of Chinese proficiency

   C) participated in the speech contest

   D) understood Chinese very well

26. What do you think "丢人" means?

   A) Losing face

   B) Losing people

C) Dropping someone off

D) Throwing people

27. The example given on the mess-up of the tones in one of the speeches involves

    A) the second tone and the third tone

    B) the third tone and the fourth tone

    C) the first tone and the third tone

    D) the second tone and the fourth tone

Read this poster.

(Traditional characters)

武術課更改通知
因王大中老師應美國加州大學邀請出國訪問，王老師所授週一、三、五下午四點的武術課暫停，週二、四下午五點的課暫由李平老師代課。所有課程等王老師回國後恢復原來上課時間。至於王老師何時返校授課，將另貼海報通知。

中國武術社

(Simplified characters)

武术课更改通知
因王大中老师应美国加州大学邀请出国访问，王老师所授周一、三、五下午四点的武术课暂停，周二、四下午五点的课暂由李平老师代课。所有课程等王老师回国后恢复原来上课时间。至于王老师何时返校授课，将另贴海报通知。

中国武术社

28. This poster is intended for

    A) the general public

    B) the martial arts class students

    C) the students at the University of California

    D) American students

29. Which of the following statements is TRUE?

    A) Teacher Wang has classes every weekday.

    B) None of Teacher Wang's students can continue classes during his absence.

    C) Teacher Wang is going to America to visit relatives.

    D) Teacher Wang has informed the students of his return date.

30. During Teacher Wang's absence

    A) his Wednesday class will be canceled

    B) Teacher Li will be subbing in his Thursday morning class

C) Teacher Li will be subbing in his Friday afternoon class

D) all of his students can continue their classes

31. Upon Teacher Wang's return, students will be notified by

    A) e-mail

    B) text message

    C) poster announcement

    D) none of the above

Read this story.

(Traditional characters)

2月14日情人節，依照西方的習俗，可以贈送玫瑰花或巧克力給喜歡的人。農曆的七月初七則是中國傳統習俗中的情人節，有許多關於牛郎和織女的傳說。其中有一個傳說是牛郎和織女本來都住在天上，後來他們墜入愛河，展開了一段美麗的愛情。從此牛郎放牛不盡力，織女也不專心織布，惹得玉皇大帝非常生氣，就把他們分別放逐到銀河兩岸。一年當中只有七月初七晚上，有喜鵲飛來築成一座橋，他們纔能在鵲橋上相會，天亮時又要各自回到銀河的兩岸去，日日夜夜隔著銀河思念愛人。這是一個淒美的傳說，也引發了許多詩人無窮的想象，寫下了不少傳誦古今的篇章。

(Simplified characters)

2月14日情人节，依照西方的习俗，可以赠送玫瑰花或巧克力给喜欢的人。农历的七月初七则是中国传统习俗中的情人节，有许多关于牛郎和织女的传说。其中有一个传说是牛郎和织女本来都住在天上，后来他们坠入爱河，展开了一段美丽的爱情。从此牛郎放牛不尽力，织女也不专心织布，惹得玉皇大帝非常生气，就把他们分别放逐到银河两岸。一年当中只有七月初七晚上，有喜鹊飞来筑成一座桥，他们才能在鹊桥上相会，天亮时又要各自回到银河的两岸去，日日夜夜隔着银河思念爱人。这是一个凄美的传说，也引发了许多诗人无穷的想象，写下了不少传诵古今的篇章。

32. According to this passage, which of the following statements is TRUE?

    A) Chinese give chocolate to people they like on the seventh day of the seventh month in the lunar calendar.

    B) There are a lot of writings about Valentine's Day in China.

    C) The story of 牛郎 and 织女 (織女) is well known among the school kids.

    D) The romance of 牛郎 and 织女 (織女) has inspired the Chinese poets to write about it.

33. Why were 牛郎 and 织女 (織女) separated by the Jade Emperor?

   A) The Jade Emperor was jealous of their love.

   B) They became irresponsible about their respective work duties.

   C) They did not ask for the Jade Emperor's approval.

   D) They were slandered by other people.

34. According to this story, 牛郎 and 织女 (織女) were banished to opposite banks of

   A) the Milky Way

   B) the Yellow River

   C) the Yangtze River

   D) the Love River

35. What animals help build a bridge for 牛郎 and 织女 (織女) to meet once a year?

   A) Cows

   B) Rabbits

   C) Fish

   D) Magpies

END OF SECTION I

YOU MAY REVIEW WORK IF THERE IS TIME LEFT.

DO NOT GO ON TO SECTION II UNTIL YOU ARE TOLD TO DO SO.

Section II: Free Response

Part A: Writing (Story Narration and E-mail Response)

Note: In this part of the exam, the student may NOT move back and forth among questions.

Writing Part Directions

You will be asked to perform two writing tasks in Chinese. In each case, you will be asked to write for a specific purpose and to a specific person. You should write in as complete and as culturally appropriate a manner as possible, taking into account the purpose and the person described.

Presentational Writing: Story Narration (15%, 15 minutes)

The four pictures present a story. Imagine you are writing the story to a friend. Narrate a complete story as suggested by the pictures. Give your story a beginning, a middle, and an end.

Interpersonal Writing: E-mail Response (10%, 15 minutes)

Read this e-mail from a friend and then type a response.

(Traditional characters)

發件人：謝明

郵件主題：暑期活動

　　今年暑假我有兩個學習的機會，一個是去夏令營當輔導員，有六個星期，另一個是去我家附近的大學上兩門跟電腦有關的課程，要上兩個月的課。我沒法兒同時參加兩項活動，你覺得我選哪項活動比較好？請你給我一些具體的建議。謝謝！

(Simplified characters)

发件人：谢明

邮件主题：暑期活动

　　今年暑假我有两个学习的机会，一个是去夏令营当辅导员，有六个星期，另一个是去我家附近的大学上两门跟电脑有关的课程，要上两个月的课。我没法儿同时参加两项活动，你觉得我选哪项活动比较好？请你给我一些具体的建议。谢谢！

speaking

Part B: Speaking (Conversation and Cultural Presentation)

Note: In this part of the exam, you may NOT move back and forth among questions.

Speaking Part Directions: Conversation

You will participate in a simulated conversation. Each time it is your turn to speak, you will have 20 seconds to record. You should respond as fully and as appropriately as possible. There will be six times when it is your turn to speak.

Interpersonal Speaking: Conversation (10%, 4 minutes)

You will have a conversation with Wang Zhong, your host parent, about dining at a local Chinese restaurant.

Speaking Question 1 of 7

1. Record your answer. (20 seconds)

Speaking Question 2 of 7

2. Record your answer. (20 seconds)

Speaking Question 3 of 7

3. Record your answer. (20 seconds)

Speaking Question 4 of 7

4. Record your answer. (20 seconds)

Speaking Question 5 of 7

5. Record your answer. (20 seconds)

Speaking Question 6 of 7

6. Record your answer. (20 seconds)

> **Speaking Part Directions: Cultural Presentation**
>
> You will be asked to speak in Chinese on a specific topic. Imagine you are making an oral presentation to your Chinese class. First, you will read and hear the topic for your presentation. You will have 4 minutes to prepare your presentation. Then you will have 2 minutes to record your presentation. Your presentation should be as complete as possible.

> **Presentational Speaking: Cultural Presentation (15%, 7 minutes)**

Speaking Question 7 of 7

7. Choose ONE historical or contemporary Chinese figure. In your presentation, describe this person's background, what he/she has done, and explain his or her significance in China.

You have four minutes to prepare your presentation. (240 seconds)

You have two minutes to record your presentation. (120 seconds)

YOU HAVE FINISHED THIS PART OF THE EXAM.
END OF EXAM

AP Chinese Language and Culture Test 3

listening

Section I: Multiple Choice

Part A: Listening (Rejoinders and Listening Selections)

Listening Part Directions

You will answer two types of questions: rejoinders and questions based on listening selections.

For all tasks, you will have a specific amount of response time. When the response time has ended, you will automatically go on to the next question. You cannot return to previous questions.

Listening Part Directions: Rejoinders (10%, 10 minutes)

You will hear several short conversations or parts of conversations followed by four choices, designated A, B, C, and D. Choose the one that continues or completes the conversation in a logical and culturally appropriate manner. After you have decided which of the suggested answers is best, COMPLETELY fill in the corresponding circle on the answer sheet. You will have 5 seconds to answer each question.

YOU WILL NOW BEGIN THIS PART.

---

1. Mark your answer on your answer sheet.
2. Mark your answer on your answer sheet.
3. Mark your answer on your answer sheet.
4. Mark your answer on your answer sheet.
5. Mark your answer on your answer sheet.
6. Mark your answer on your answer sheet.
7. Mark your answer on your answer sheet.
8. Mark your answer on your answer sheet.
9. Mark your answer on your answer sheet.
10. Mark your answer on your answer sheet.
11. Mark your answer on your answer sheet.
12. Mark your answer on your answer sheet.
13. Mark your answer on your answer sheet.
14. Mark your answer on your answer sheet.
15. Mark your answer on your answer sheet.

Listening Part Directions: Listening Selections (15%, 10 minutes)

You will listen to several selections in Chinese. For each selection, you will be told whether it will be played once or twice. You may take notes as you listen. Your notes will not be graded. After listening to each selection, you will see questions in English. For each question, choose the response that is best according to the selection. You will have 12 seconds to answer each question.

YOU WILL NOW BEGIN THIS PART.

Selection 1: Conversation (Selection plays one time.)

16. What is the main topic of the conversation?

    A) How to look for information on the internet

    B) How to apply to colleges

    C) Attending a college seminar

    D) Meeting friends

17. What is the benefit of attending the meeting?

    A) Networking with college admissions staff

    B) Having fun with friends

    C) Obtaining answers unavailable on the internet

    D) Learning how to use the internet

18. Why can't the girl go to the seminar?

    A) Because the boy can bring her all the information.

    B) Because she can get all the information online.

    C) Because she has another arrangement.

    D) Because she is not interested.

19. How will the boy pass on the information to the girl?

    A) He will mail it to her.

    B) He will call her.

    C) He will fax it to her.

    D) He will give it in person or e-mail it.

Selection 2: Announcement (Selection plays two times.)

20. What's the purpose of this announcement?

    A) To remind the students about Teachers' Day

B) To inform the students that there will be a Teachers' Day celebration

C) To tell everyone to bring a gift for their teachers

D) To announce that there will be no lunch served on Teachers' Day

21. What will happen on Teachers' Day?

    A) Donations will be collected for teachers.

    B) The teachers will sing for the students.

    C) There will be a performance to watch.

    D) All teachers will take the day off.

22. For Teachers' Day, the students are going to

    A) dance and sing

    B) prepare a lunch for teachers

    C) receive a gift from teachers

    D) write a thank you card to their favorite teacher

Selection 3: Voice Message (Selection plays two times.)

23. Why did Xiaomei call her teacher?

    A) To complain that the museum is too far

    B) To suggest a field trip to the museum

    C) To say that her mom can drive students to the museum

    D) To say that her mom's car needs repairs

24. Why can't Xiaomei's mom drive the students back from the museum?

    A) She needs to go to work.

    B) She has a doctor's appointment.

    C) She will have to meet another parent.

    D) She needs to pick up someone at the airport.

25. What did Xiaomei suggest to resolve the problem?

    A) To take the bus

    B) To only take six students

    C) To ask other parents for help

    D) To take the subway

Selection 4: Instructions (Selection plays one time.)

26. The fire drill route is changed because

    A) the new route is shorter

    B) there is construction going on

    C) the new route is safer

    D) the gathering location was changed

27. What do the students do right after exiting from the back door?

    A) Walk straight

    B) Take the path on the left

    C) Turn right

    D) Wait until everyone gets there

28. Where do the students gather?

    A) On a footpath behind the school

    B) Inside the community center

    C) In the backyard of the school

    D) On the lawns

29. What should the teacher do after gathering?

    A) To ask the students to sit down and stay quiet

    B) To take roll call

    C) To get the first aid kits ready

    D) To go back to the classroom to make sure everyone is out

Selection 5: Report (Selection plays one time.)

30. The report is about

    A) a job fair

    B) the college selection process

    C) an alumni reception

    D) career pathways

31. Who gave the speeches?

    A) Counselors at the college center

    B) School counselors

    C) Former graduates

    D) Career specialists

32. How often does the school organize this activity?

   A) Twice a year

   B) Once a year

   C) Once a month

   D) Not mentioned

Selection 6: Conversation (Selection plays one time.)

33. The man is going to get a visa himself because

   A) his parents think he needs to learn the process

   B) his friend told him how to obtain one

   C) he has experience from a previous trip

   D) his parents are both away on business trips

34. How many documents will the man need to present to obtain a visa?

   A) 2

   B) 3

   C) 4

   D) 5

35. What is the fee for triple entries to China?

   A) $65

   B) $90

   C) $130

   D) $165

Part B: Reading Selections

Note: In this part of the exam, you may move back and forth among all the questions.

> **Reading Part Directions: Reading Selections (25%, 60 minutes)**
>
> You will read several selections in Chinese. Each selection is accompanied by a number of questions in English. For each question, choose the response that is best according to the selection. After you have decided which of the suggested answers is best, COMPLETELY fill in the corresponding circle on the answer sheet. Chinese tests appear here in both traditional and simplified characters. You will have 60 minutes to answer all questions.
>
> YOU WILL NOW BEGIN THIS PART.

Read this e-mail.

(Traditional characters)

發件人：大明
收件人：小剛
郵件主題：北京旅遊指南
郵件日期：6月3日

小剛：

聽說你近期要到北京去學習三個月，真是太好了！北京是世界上著名的旅遊城市之一，有數百個非常吸引人的觀光景點，包括長城、故宮、天安門廣場、頤和園、天壇公園、奧運會場館等。除了去這些有名的景點參觀以外，我建議你到北京市區居民住的地方走走，這樣你會對北京人及北京的文化有更為真切的感受。我手上有一本非常好的《北京旅遊指南》。該指南除了介紹旅遊景點，還對150個特色商店、市場、老街和北京傳統的胡同分別做了介紹。該指南標明了一些北京有名的購物區，并附有街道圖以及商店地址、電話、營業時間等資料。該指南還附有地鐵和公交車的交通圖以及其他非常實用的自助旅遊資訊。我現在馬上快遞給你，希望能對你有幫助。

　　祝你在北京愉快！

　　　　　　　　　　　　　　　　　　　　　　　　　　　　　　大明

(Simplified characters)

发件人：大明
收件人：小刚
邮件主题：北京旅游指南
邮件日期：6月3日

小刚：

听说你近期要到北京去学习三个月，真是太好了！北京是世界上著名的旅游城市之一，有数百个非常吸引人的观光景点，包括长城、故宫、天安门广场、颐和园、天坛公园、奥运会场馆等。除了去这些有名的景点参观以外，我建议你到北京市区居民住的地方走走，这样你会对北京人及北京的文化有更为真切的感受。我手上有一本非常好的《北京旅游指南》。该指南除了介绍旅游景点，还对150个特色商店、市场、老街和北京传统的胡同分别做了介绍。该指南标明了一些北京有名的购物区，并附有街道图以及商店地址、电话、营业时间等资料。该指南还附有地铁和公交车的交通图以及其他非常实用的自助旅游资讯。我现在马上快递给你，希望能对你有帮助。

　　祝你在北京愉快!

大明

1. Which tourist attraction of Beijing is NOT mentioned in this e-mail?

    A) The Great Wall

    B) The Summer Palace

    C) The Forbidden City

    D) Beihai Park

2. Which place in particular did Daming suggest Xiaogang to visit?

    A) The famous shopping centers

    B) Universities

    C) Areas where common people live

    D) Beijing's popular subways

3. What information is NOT included in the *Travelers' Handbook*?

    A) A map of the transportation system

    B) Stores

    C) Schools

    D) Traditional alleys

Read this advertisement.

(Traditional characters)

美中青少年領導才能訓練營

活動時間：8月2日至8月15日

活動地點：北京、上海

活動費用：$3,600（含國際機票、食宿和國內交通，但簽證自理）

　　　　　在4月15日前報名者可享受$100優惠

活動內容：領導才能訓練課程（8課時）

　　　　　中國文化學習（8課時）

　　　　　參觀北京和上海的名勝古跡

　　　　　品嚐中國美食

報名資格：

1. 14～18歲高中生

2. 初級以上中文說寫能力

3. 在校平均成績B以上

4. 一篇300～500字的短文，簡單介紹個人教育背景、語言能力及參加活動的目的

5. 家長同意書

欲知詳情請與美中青年文化辦事處聯繫

電話：(321)123-4567

(Simplified characters)

美中青少年领导才能训练营

活动时间：8月2日至8月15日

活动地点：北京、上海

活动费用：$3,600（含国际机票、食宿和国内交通，但签证自理）

在4月15日前报名者可享受$100优惠

活动内容：领导才能训练课程（8课时）

中国文化学习（8课时）

参观北京和上海的名胜古迹

品尝中国美食

报名资格：

1. 14～18岁高中生

2. 初级以上中文说写能力

3. 在校平均成绩B以上

4. 一篇300～500字的短文，简单介绍个人教育背景、语言能力及参加活动的目的

5. 家长同意书

欲知详情请与美中青年文化办事处联系

电话：(321)123-4567

4. What is this advertisement for?

   A) A youth leadership training program

   B) A cultural exchange program

   C) A trip abroad

   D) A scholarship competition for college students

5. Which of the following expenses is NOT included in the fee?

    A) International air ticket

    B) Domestic transportation

    C) Food and hotel

    D) Visa application

6. Which of the following qualifications is NOT required?

    A) One must be a college student

    B) A GPA above a "B" average

    C) Parental consent

    D) Knowledge of the Chinese language

Read this public sign.

(Traditional characters)　　　　　　　(Simplified characters)

　　　腳下留青　　　　　　　　　　　脚下留青

7. The sign is to tell people

    A) that walking maintains health

    B) to be careful while walking

    C) that there are trees down the hill

    D) not to step on the grass

8. Where would this sign most likely appear?

    A) In a hospital

    B) At a school

    C) On the lawns

    D) At the base of a mountain

Read this article.

(Traditional characters)

> 京杭大運河是世界上最長的一條人工開鑿的運河，北起北京，南到杭州，經北京、天津兩直轄市及河北、山東、江蘇、浙江四省，貫通海河、黃河、淮河、長江、錢塘江五大水系。運河全長約1,750千米，是蘇伊士運河的16倍，巴拿馬運河的33倍。

京杭大運河也是世界上最古老的運河之一。我們今天所說的大運河開掘於大約2,500年前的春秋時期，公元1293年全綫通航，前後共持續了1,779年。京杭大運河和萬里長城并稱爲中國古代的兩項偉大工程，聞名於全世界。

(Simplified characters)

京杭大运河是世界上最长的一条人工开凿的运河，北起北京，南到杭州，经北京、天津两直辖市及河北、山东、江苏、浙江四省，贯通海河、黄河、淮河、长江、钱塘江五大水系。运河全长约1,750千米，是苏伊士运河的16倍，巴拿马运河的33倍。

京杭大运河也是世界上最古老的运河之一。我们今天所说的大运河开掘于大约2,500年前的春秋时期，公元1293年全线通航，前后共持续了1,779年。京杭大运河和万里长城并称为中国古代的两项伟大工程，闻名于全世界。

9. When did the construction of the Great Jing-Hang Canal begin?

    A) 1,750 years ago

    B) 1,293 years ago

    C) 1,779 years ago

    D) 2,500 years ago

10. Which river does the Great Jing-Hang Canal NOT link up with?

    A) Songhua River

    B) Yangtze River

    C) Yellow River

    D) Huai River

11. How many provinces does the Great Jing-Hang Canal pass through?

    A) Two

    B) Three

    C) Four

    D) Five

12. Where is the north end of the Great Jing-Hang Canal?

    A) Tianjin

    B) Jinan

C) Shanghai

D) Beijing

13. How much longer is the Great Jing-Hang Canal than the Panama Canal?

   A) 16 times longer

   B) 33 times longer

   C) 61 times longer

   D) 49 times longer

Read this notice.

(Traditional characters)

足球賽

　　由本校學生會主辦的足球賽將於4月24日（星期六）下午5點在學校足球場舉行，參賽隊伍分別爲我校校隊和香港大學校隊。令人高興的是，中國足球協會的教練和國家隊的隊員將到場觀看比賽，并在賽後與參賽的雙方隊員舉行座談。歡迎同學們屆時觀看。

　　　　　　　　　　學生會

　　　　　　　　　　4月21日

(Simplified characters)

足球赛

　　由本校学生会主办的足球赛将于4月24日（星期六）下午5点在学校足球场举行，参赛队伍分别为我校校队和香港大学校队。令人高兴的是，中国足球协会的教练和国家队的队员将到场观看比赛，并在赛后与参赛的双方队员举行座谈。欢迎同学们届时观看。

　　　　　　　　　　学生会

　　　　　　　　　　4月21日

14. Who organized this soccer game?

   A) Hong Kong University

   B) Chinese Soccer Association

   C) Chinese Soccer Team

   D) The School Student Union

15. Which two teams is the soccer match between?

   A) Hong Kong University soccer team and the home team

   B) Hong Kong University soccer team and the National Soccer Team

   C) The National Soccer Team and the home team

   D) None of the above

16. What will follow after the game?

    A) A celebration dinner

    B) A discussion

    C) A chance for students to meet the players

    D) Another soccer game

Read this advertisement.

(Traditional characters)

北京人文大學2021年暑期中文班招生

一、強化中文學習4週（6月28日至7月25日）

　　1. 小班上課

　　2. 閱讀、口語和寫作練習

　　3. 提供一對一語言訓練

　　4. 週三晚觀看文藝演出，週六遊覽歷史文化景點

　　5. 住本校學生宿舍，兩人間，設備齊全，安全舒適

二、語言實習文化旅遊12天（7月26日至8月6日），所去城市包括北京、西安、曲阜和上海

三、費用$3,980，包括學費、吃住、教材、參觀景點和觀看演出，以及文化旅遊的相關費用，不含國際機票和簽證費

四、報名資格：大學生、研究生及年滿18歲的高中生。即日起接受報名至4月20日止，名額爲50人，額滿爲止

詳情請洽金山大學中文系。

電話：(456)654-4567

(Simplified characters)

北京人文大学2021年暑期中文班招生

一、强化中文学习4周（6月28日至7月25日）

　　1. 小班上课

　　2. 阅读、口语和写作练习

　　3. 提供一对一语言训练

　　4. 周三晚观看文艺演出，周六游览历史文化景点

　　5. 住本校学生宿舍，两人间，设备齐全，安全舒适

二、语言实习文化旅游12天（7月26日至8月6日），所去城市包括北京、西安、曲阜和上海

三、费用$3,980，包括学费、吃住、教材、参观景点和观看演出，以及文化旅游的相关费用，不含国际机票和签证费

四、报名资格：大学生、研究生及年满18岁的高中生。即日起接受报名至4月20日止，名额为50人，额满为止

详情请洽金山大学中文系。

电话：(456)654-4567

17. Which of the following subjects is NOT offered in this summer program?

    A) Drawing

    B) Reading

    C) Speaking

    D) Writing

18. Which of the following statement is NOT TRUE?

    A) The class size will be small.

    B) There will be two students per bedroom.

    C) College students cannot apply for the program.

    D) Students can watch a show on every Wednesday night.

19. Which of the following expenses is NOT covered in the fee?

    A) Tuition

    B) Food and living

    C) Domestic transportation

    D) International airfare

Read this letter.

(Traditional characters)

敬愛的李老師：

您好！您的身體還好嗎？一年一度的教師節就要到了，這讓我想起您教我們中文時的一些事。我知道您為我們班的同學做了大量的工作，付出了很多的心血，特別是您還常用自己的時間輔導我們，組織一些課外活動。同學們都說您是一位認真負責、親切和藹的老師。現在我雖然轉學了，但是還常常想念您和中文班的同學。

我現在這所學校也有許多讓我尊敬的老師，不過我還是覺得您是最好的老師。一個學期都快過去了，對這裡的環境我還是覺得很陌生，大概還得再過一段時間纔能適應。您以前對我的教誨會一直激勵著我努力學習的。

　　祝您節日快樂！

　　　　　　　　　　　　　　　　　　　　　　　　您的學生　何京
　　　　　　　　　　　　　　　　　　　　　　　　4月20日

(Simplified characters)

敬爱的李老师：

　　您好！您的身体还好吗？一年一度的教师节就要到了，这让我想起您教我们中文时的一些事。我知道您为我们班的同学做了大量的工作，付出了很多的心血，特别是您还常用自己的时间辅导我们，组织一些课外活动。同学们都说您是一位认真负责、亲切和蔼的老师。现在我虽然转学了，但是还常常想念您和中文班的同学。我现在这所学校也有许多让我尊敬的老师，不过我还是觉得您是最好的老师。一个学期都快过去了，对这里的环境我还是觉得很陌生，大概还得再过一段时间才能适应。您以前对我的教诲会一直激励着我努力学习的。

　　祝您节日快乐！

　　　　　　　　　　　　　　　　　　　　　　　　您的学生　何京
　　　　　　　　　　　　　　　　　　　　　　　　4月20日

20. When did He Jing write the letter?

　　A) Upon transferring to a new school

　　B) Before Teachers' Day

　　C) On his birthday

　　D) Around the New Year

21. What do the students think of Teacher Li?

　　A) He is very knowledgeable and kind.

　　B) He is conscientious, responsible, and amiable.

　　C) He is hardworking and tough.

　　D) He is sensitive and inspiring.

22. How does He Jing describe the new environment?

　　A) Bizarre

B) Pleasant

C) Unfamiliar

D) Similar to his previous environment

23. How long has He Jing been at his new school?

   A) Almost one week

   B) Almost one month

   C) Almost one semester

   D) Almost one year

Read this poster.

(Traditional characters)

緊急通知

根據氣象部門的天氣預報，本市明後天將有暴風雨。學校已經收到電力局的通知，本市將有部分地區停電48個小時，停電時間從星期六（明天）早晨4點至星期一早晨4點。我校屬於停電範圍之內，爲此學校決定，原定於星期六晚上7點的家長會，改在下星期六的同一時間召開，請同學們互相轉告。

校長辦公室

(Simplified characters)

紧急通知

根据气象部门的天气预报，本市明后天将有暴风雨。学校已经收到电力局的通知，本市将有部分地区停电48个小时，停电时间从星期六（明天）早晨4点至星期一早晨4点。我校属于停电范围之内，为此学校决定，原定于星期六晚上7点的家长会，改在下星期六的同一时间召开，请同学们互相转告。

校长办公室

24. This poster announces that

   A) the parents' meeting of tomorrow will be changed to next Saturday

   B) there will be a rainstorm for the next two days

   C) there will be no electricity in the school the following week

   D) the parents' meeting will be canceled

25. What does "明后天" (明後天) mean?

   A) Tomorrow

   B) After tomorrow

   C) Two days

   D) Tomorrow and the day after tomorrow

26. Which of the following statements is NOT TRUE?

    A) There will be a rainstorm tomorrow.

    B) There will be no parents' meeting tomorrow.

    C) There will be no electricity across the city.

    D) The parents' meeting will be held next Saturday.

27. For how long will there be no electricity?

    A) One day

    B) Two days

    C) One weekend

    D) One week

Read this story.

(Traditional characters)

有一個非常有趣的小故事，叫作《太陽從西邊升起》。它最初刊登在一個叫《故事會》的雜誌上。故事講一個十一二歲的小姑娘畫了一幅畫兒，參加全省少兒美術比賽。她的那幅畫兒畫得很好，但最終卻因犯了個常識性錯誤，把初升的太陽畫到了西邊而落選。老師不解地去問小姑娘，怎麼會把太陽畫到西邊了呢？小姑娘哭著說："我就是要讓太陽從西邊升起……"原來，她爸爸和媽媽吵架了，爸爸出走了，臨走時說，要他重回這個家，除非太陽從西邊升起。所以小姑娘就天天盼望西邊出太陽了。

(Simplified characters)

有一个非常有趣的小故事，叫作《太阳从西边升起》。它最初刊登在一个叫《故事会》的杂志上。故事讲一个十一二岁的小姑娘画了一幅画儿，参加全省少儿美术比赛。她的那幅画儿画得很好，但最终却因犯了个常识性错误，把初升的太阳画到了西边而落选。老师不解地去问小姑娘，怎么会把太阳画到西边了呢？小姑娘哭着说："我就是要让太阳从西边升起……"原来，她爸爸和妈妈吵架了，爸爸出走了，临走时说，要他重回这个家，除非太阳从西边升起。所以小姑娘就天天盼望西边出太阳了。

28. What mistake did the little girl make in her picture?

    A) She did not draw the picture well.

    B) She did not draw a sun in the sky.

    C) The sun is rising from the west.

    D) She did not finish the picture.

29. Where was the story initially published?

   A) In a newspaper

   B) In a magazine

   C) At a meeting

   D) On the radio

30. What did the little girl's father say before he left the house?

   A) He will come home when the sun rises the next day.

   B) He will be back soon.

   C) He will come home only if the sun rises from the west.

   D) The sun rises from the west.

31. What kind of competition did the girl attend?

   A) Adult art competition

   B) Children's art competition

   C) City-wide art competition

   D) School-wide art competition

Read this passage.

(Traditional characters)

梁實秋是一位中國現代著名作家。他曾寫過一篇文章來勸告人們從小就要養成良好的習慣。在那篇文章中，他寫到人們的天性大致是差不多的，但是在習慣上卻各有不同。習慣是慢慢養成的，在幼小的時候最容易培養，一旦養成之後，要想改變過來卻不容易。比如說清晨早起是一個好習慣，這也要從小培養。很多人從小就貪睡懶覺，一遇假日便要睡到太陽高照還遲遲不起，平時也是不肯早起，上學經常遲到。這樣的人長大了之後，多半不能有什麼成就。好的習慣很多，他勸大家從小就要有意識地在各方面培養良好的習慣。

(Simplified characters)

梁实秋是一位中国现代著名作家。他曾写过一篇文章来劝告人们从小就要养成良好的习惯。在那篇文章中，他写到人们的天性大致是差不多的，但是在习惯上却各有不同。习惯是慢慢养成的，在幼小的时候最容易培养，一旦养成之后，要想改变过来却不容易。比如说清晨早起是一个好习惯，这也要从小培养。很多人从小就贪睡懒觉，一遇假日便要睡到太阳高照还迟迟不起，平时也是不肯早起，上学经常迟到。这样的人长大了之后，多半不能有什么成就。好的习惯很多，他劝大家从小就要有意识地在各方面培养良好的习惯。

32. What is the main message of the passage?

    A) Cultivate good habits early.

    B) Get up early.

    C) Do not go to school late.

    D) Do not go to sleep late.

33. Which of the following statements is TRUE?

    A) The author is a modern writer.

    B) People all have the same habits.

    C) People do not change their habits.

    D) The author suggests children sleep more on weekends or during holidays.

34. Liang Shiqiu thinks that a man who sleeps a lot

    A) will have a great future

    B) will be more intelligent

    C) will need to eat less

    D) will not be successful

35. Liang Shiqiu believes that people are born

    A) relatively the same and change over time

    B) different and do not change

    C) different and change over time

    D) similar to their parents

END OF SECTION I
YOU MAY REVIEW WORK IF THERE IS TIME LEFT.
DO NOT GO ON TO SECTION II UNTIL YOU ARE TOLD TO DO SO.

Section II: Free Response

Part A: Writing (Story Narration and E-mail Response)

Note: In this part of the exam, the student may NOT move back and forth among questions.

> **Writing Part Directions**
>
> You will be asked to perform two writing tasks in Chinese. In each case, you will be asked to write for a specific purpose and to a specific person. You should write in as complete and as culturally appropriate a manner as possible, taking into account the purpose and the person described.

> **Presentational Writing: Story Narration (15%, 15 minutes)**
>
> The four pictures present a story. Imagine you are writing the story to a friend. Narrate a complete story as suggested by the pictures. Give your story a beginning, a middle, and an end.

Interpersonal Writing: E-mail Response (10%, 15 minutes)

Read this e-mail from a friend and then type a response.

(Traditional characters)

發件人：康健
郵件主題：大學選擇
大衛：
　　告訴你一個好消息，我已經被你們學校錄取了，同時我還收到了全國最好的一所公立大學的錄取通知書。到底應該去哪所大學，我感到很難決定。你們學校當然是全美最好的大學之一，可是這所公立大學也很有名。在我做最後決定之前，我非常想聽聽你的看法和建議。請你給我介紹一下你們學校的情況，包括校園生活和當地氣候等。謝謝！

(Simplified characters)

发件人：康健
邮件主题：大学选择
大卫：
　　告诉你一个好消息，我已经被你们学校录取了，同时我还收到了全国最好的一所公立大学的录取通知书。到底应该去哪所大学，我感到很难决定。你们学校当然是全美最好的大学之一，可是这所公立大学也很有名。在我做最后决定之前，我非常想听听你的看法和建议。请你给我介绍一下你们学校的情况，包括校园生活和当地气候等。谢谢！

Part B: Speaking (Conversation and Cultural Presentation)

Note: In this part of the exam, you may NOT move back and forth among questions.

speaking

Speaking Part Directions: Conversation

You will participate in a simulated conversation. Each time it is your turn to speak, you will have 20 seconds to record. You should respond as fully and as appropriately as possible. There will be six times when it is your turn to speak.

Interpersonal Speaking: Conversation (10%, 4 minutes)

You have been invited to have dinner with a Chinese family. You will have a conversation with a member of the family at the dinner table.

Speaking Question 1 of 7

1. Record your answer. (20 seconds)

Speaking Question 2 of 7

2. Record your answer. (20 seconds)

Speaking Question 3 of 7

3. Record your answer. (20 seconds)

Speaking Question 4 of 7

4. Record your answer. (20 seconds)

Speaking Question 5 of 7

5. Record your answer. (20 seconds)

Speaking Question 6 of 7

6. Record your answer. (20 seconds)

Speaking Part Directions: Cultural Presentation

You will be asked to speak in Chinese on a specific topic. Imagine you are making an oral presentation to your Chinese class. First, you will read and hear the topic for your presentation. You will have 4 minutes to prepare your presentation. Then you will have 2 minutes to record your presentation. Your presentation should be as complete as possible.

Presentational Speaking: Cultural Presentation (15%, 7 minutes)

Speaking Question 7 of 7

7. The concept of "一日为师，终身为父" (一日爲師，終身爲父) ("A teacher for one day, and a father forever") has always been valued in China. In your presentation, share your thoughts on this concept and explain its significance, compare and contrast it with the Western cultural attitudes toward the role of teachers, and toward education as a whole.

You have four minutes to prepare your presentation. (240 seconds)
You have two minutes to record your presentation. (120 seconds)

YOU HAVE FINISHED THIS PART OF THE EXAM.
END OF EXAM

AP Chinese Language and Culture Test 4

listening

Section I: Multiple Choice

Part A: Listening (Rejoinders and Listening Selections)

> **Listening Part Directions**
>
> You will answer two types of questions: rejoinders and questions based on listening selections.
>
> For all tasks, you will have a specific amount of response time. When the response time has ended, you will automatically go on to the next question. You cannot return to previous questions.

> **Listening Part Directions: Rejoinders (10%, 10 minutes)**
>
> You will hear several short conversations or parts of conversations followed by four choices, designated A, B, C, and D. Choose the one that continues or completes the conversation in a logical and culturally appropriate manner. After you have decided which of the suggested answers is best, COMPLETELY fill in the corresponding circle on the answer sheet. You will have 5 seconds to answer each question.
>
> YOU WILL NOW BEGIN THIS PART.

1. Mark your answer on your answer sheet.
2. Mark your answer on your answer sheet.
3. Mark your answer on your answer sheet.
4. Mark your answer on your answer sheet.
5. Mark your answer on your answer sheet.
6. Mark your answer on your answer sheet.
7. Mark your answer on your answer sheet.
8. Mark your answer on your answer sheet.
9. Mark your answer on your answer sheet.
10. Mark your answer on your answer sheet.
11. Mark your answer on your answer sheet.
12. Mark your answer on your answer sheet.
13. Mark your answer on your answer sheet.
14. Mark your answer on your answer sheet.
15. Mark your answer on your answer sheet.

Listening Part Directions: Listening Selections (15%, 10 minutes)

You will listen to several selections in Chinese. For each selection, you will be told whether it will be played once or twice. You may take notes as you listen. Your notes will not be graded. After listening to each selection, you will see questions in English. For each question, choose the response that is best according to the selection. You will have 12 seconds to answer each question.

YOU WILL NOW BEGIN THIS PART.

Selection 1: Announcement (Selection plays two times.)

16. The flight is delayed because

   A) there are mechanical problems

   B) it has to wait for some passengers from another flight

   C) the weather condition is not suitable for taking off

   D) there are some problems with the check-in procedure

17. The passengers are told to

   A) take the next available flight

   B) exit the aircraft

   C) go to the counter to get vouchers for meals and lodging

   D) wait in the waiting room

Selection 2: Conversation (Selection plays one time.)

18. The man and the woman came to this restaurant because

   A) the man frequently patronizes the place

   B) the restaurant received lots of good reviews

   C) the woman's roommate recommends it

   D) the man's roommate suggested to them that they go there

19. It's most likely that this restaurant specializes in

   A) Sichuan cuisine

   B) Shanghai cuisine

   C) Cantonese cuisine

   D) Beijing cuisine

20. The woman prefers to have

    A) vegetarian dishes

    B) light dishes

    C) spicy food

    D) tofu dishes

21. The woman initially showed some doubt about the restaurant because

    A) she did not really like spicy food

    B) she was concerned that the restaurant adds MSG to their food

    C) the man's roommate did not recommend it

    D) the restaurant advertises too much on TV and the newspapers

Selection 3: Instructions (Selection plays one time.)

22. Who is giving the instructions?

    A) The nurse

    B) The pharmacist

    C) The mother

    D) The doctor

23. The recipient of the instructions was most likely concerned about having

    A) H1N1 flu

    B) a seasonal cold

    C) persistent coughs

    D) an unabated fever

24. The recipient of the instructions needs to take the bigger tablets

    A) as needed

    B) in six-hour intervals

    C) before meals

    D) twice a day, three tablets each time

25. The smaller tablets are for

    A) unabated fever

    B) persistent coughs

    C) sore throat

    D) a severe case of running nose

Selection 4: Voice Message (Selection plays two times.)

26. What made the telephone caller wonder if Xiaopeng had been busy?

    A) Xiaopeng did not pick up the phone for quite a few times.

    B) Xiaopeng's phone was busy for quite a long while.

    C) Xiaopeng's voice mailbox message indicated that he was busy.

    D) Xiaopeng did not return his phone calls.

27. Xiaopeng is a high school

    A) freshman

    B) sophomore

    C) junior

    D) senior

28. Why did the telephone caller wish to speak to Xiaopeng?

    A) Because he would like to go to a sports game with Xiaopeng.

    B) Because he would like to discuss with Xiaopeng about the graduation ceremony.

    C) Because he would like to perform with Xiaopeng at the school's talent show.

    D) Because he would like to go to a "Xiangsheng" performance.

29. The school put out the announcement

    A) in early March

    B) in mid-March

    C) at the end of April

    D) in mid-April

30. The caller mentioned Teacher Wang, because

    A) Teacher Wang can provide information about "Xiangsheng"

    B) Teacher Wang has the tickets to the "Xiangsheng" performance

    C) Teacher Wang has the costumes that they need

    D) Teacher Wang can help them rent the costumes that they need

Selection 5: Report (Selection plays one time.)

31. The survey was conducted

    A) in person

    B) by filling out the questionnaire on paper

    C) online

    D) by telephone interviews

32. What groups of students were surveyed?

    A) The entire school

    B) The upper classmen

    C) The lower classmen

    D) 10th, 11st, and 12nd grade students

33. We may conclude that most of the students who work for more than 15 hours a week do so in order to

    A) help with the family finance

    B) have more money to spend

    C) have more working experience

    D) save for college tuition

34. Among the students surveyed, how many students have had some working experience?

    A) 234 students

    B) 60% of the students

    C) 70% of the students

    D) 74% of the students

35. If the part-time job has a negative impact on school work, what would the students do?

    A) All of them would quit the job.

    B) All of them would cut down their working hours and keep the job.

    C) Some of them would try to look for less demanding work.

    D) Some of them would quit the job.

Part B: Reading Selections

Note: In this part of the exam, you may move back and forth among all the questions.

> **Reading Part Directions: Reading Selections (25%, 60 minutes)**
>
> You will read several selections in Chinese. Each selection is accompanied by a number of questions in English. For each question, choose the response that is best according to the selection. After you have decided which of the suggested answers is best, COMPLETELY fill in the corresponding circle on the answer sheet. Chinese tests appear here in both traditional and simplified characters. You will have 60 minutes to answer all questions.
>
> YOU WILL NOW BEGIN THIS PART.

Read this e-mail.

(Traditional characters)

發件人：林曉莉
收件人：全班同學
郵件主題：畢業典禮的門票
發件日期：5月8日

大家好！

　　不知道誰有多出來的畢業典禮門票啊？本來學校發給我們每人的五張票夠了，因爲我們家就我爸媽、爺爺、奶奶和我哥哥參加，五張正好。可是昨天我的籃球教練跟我說，他也很想參加我的畢業典禮。我高中四年都是跟這個教練練的籃球，因爲他對我的教導，我纔得到了州立大學的籃球獎學金。我問學校能不能多給我一張，可他們說票都發完了。媽媽看我很爲難，決定留在家裡，把票給籃球教練。我們一輩子纔一次的高中畢業典禮，要是媽媽不能參加，我會很難過的。所以，拜託你們，誰能給我一張票？我一定請你看電影、吃飯。先謝了！

　　　　　　　　　　　　　　　　　　　　　　　　　　　　曉莉

(Simplified characters)

发件人：林晓莉
收件人：全班同学
邮件主题：毕业典礼的门票
发件日期：5月8日

大家好！

　　不知道谁有多出来的毕业典礼门票啊？本来学校发给我们每人的五张票够了，因为我们家就我爸妈、爷爷、奶奶和我哥哥参加，五张正好。可是昨天我的篮球教练跟我说，他也很想参加我的毕业典礼。我高中四年都是跟这个教练练的篮球，因为他对我的教导，我才得到了州立大学的篮球奖学金。我问学校能不能多给我一张，可他们说票都发完了。妈妈看我很为难，决定留在家里，把票给篮球教练。我们一辈子才一次的高中毕业典礼，要是妈妈不能参加，我会很难过的。所以，拜托你们，谁能给我一张票？我一定请你看电影、吃饭。先谢了！

　　　　　　　　　　　　　　　　　　　　　　　　　　　　晓莉

1. How many admission tickets does Xiaoli need altogether?

   A) One

   B) Five

C) Six

D) Seven

2. What are the tickets for?

   A) Basketball games

   B) Movie

   C) College tour

   D) Graduation ceremony

3. To whom is the e-mail sent?

   A) The entire school

   B) The entire class

   C) Her best friends

   D) Basketball teammates

4. What is the reason that Xiaoli's mother considers staying home?

   A) She is not interested in the event.

   B) She has seen it before.

   C) She would like to give her ticket to the basketball coach.

   D) She will be busy that day.

5. What word best describes Xiaoli's attitude toward her coach?

   A) Grateful

   B) Resentful

   C) Indifferent

   D) Mixed feeling

Read this public sign.

(Traditional characters)

海水無情
若無救生員在場
請勿戲水

(Simplified characters)

海水无情
若无救生员在场
请勿戏水

6. Where would this sign most likely appear?

   A) On the deck of a swimming pool

   B) By a river

C) On the beach

D) By a lake

7. What is the purpose of this sign?

   A) To warn people of the danger of water

   B) To encourage people to swim

   C) To remind people of wearing life jackets when entering the water

   D) To warn people that swimming is prohibited there

Read this public sign.

(Traditional characters)

> 欣賞演出時，
> 請將手機及其他電子產品暫時關閉，
> 并嚴禁拍照

(Simplified characters)

> 欣赏演出时，
> 请将手机及其他电子产品暂时关闭，
> 并严禁拍照

8. This sign is most likely to be displayed

   A) in the library

   B) on an airplane

   C) in a concert hall

   D) in a gym

9. According to this sign, which of the following statements is FALSE?

   A) Pagers are not allowed to be on.

   B) All the electronics should be turned off, except for cameras.

   C) Cell phones are not allowed to be on.

   D) Taking pictures is forbidden.

Read this note.

(Traditional characters)

> 文文：
> 　　剛剛小平打電話來，說你們明天洗車募款的活動因爲學校不同意，必須取消。他要你先去跟王老師聯絡一下，看看學校爲什麼反對這項活動，能不能讓學校改變他們的決定。他會先發短信給那些已報名參加活動的同學，告訴他們活動已經取消，免得他們明天白跑一趟，等學校答復了，再做安排，另行通知。他要你儘快跟

王老師聯繫，然後給他打個電話，或發個電郵。

新華
3月4日中午12點

(Simplified characters)

文文：
　　刚刚小平打电话来，说你们明天洗车募款的活动因为学校不同意，必须取消。他要你先去跟王老师联络一下，看看学校为什么反对这项活动，能不能让学校改变他们的决定。他会先发短信给那些已报名参加活动的同学，告诉他们活动已经取消，免得他们明天白跑一趟，等学校答复了，再做安排，另行通知。他要你尽快跟王老师联系，然后给他打个电话，或发个电邮。

新华
3月4日中午12点

10. Because of the school's opposition, the fundraising event has to

　　A) be postponed until they can convince the school to change their position

　　B) be cancelled for the time being

　　C) be postponed until tomorrow

　　D) be postponed until they talk to Teacher Wang

11. Which of the following statements is TRUE?

　　A) Xiaoping knows the reasons why the school is opposed to their ideas.

　　B) Xiaoping still hopes that the school would change their position.

　　C) Xiaoping is expecting Wenwen to send him a text message.

　　D) Xiaoping would like Teacher Wang to have some influence on the school's decision-making process.

12. Which of the following statements is FALSE?

　　A) All of the students who signed up for the event will be informed of the change of plan by Xiaoping.

　　B) Some of the students who signed up for the event will be informed of the change of plan via e-mail.

　　C) Xiaoping would like Wenwen to contact Teacher Wang as soon as possible.

　　D) All of the students who signed up for the event will be informed of the change of plan so that they won't have to show up for nothing.

Read this advertisement.

(Traditional characters)

大衆書店
慶祝本店成立三十週年
所有圖書、文具一律大減價
圖書八折，文具七五折
營業時間：每日上午10時30分至晚上9時，週一休息
活動日期：本月月初四日及月末三日
您也可以隨時訪問我們的網站購書：
www.everyonebookstore.com

(Simplified characters)

大众书店
庆祝本店成立三十周年
所有图书、文具一律大减价
图书八折，文具七五折
营业时间：每日上午10时30分至晚上9时，周一休息
活动日期：本月月初四日及月末三日
您也可以随时访问我们的网站购书：
www.everyonebookstore.com

13. The sale at the bookstore is

    A) a 30-year anniversary sale

    B) to celebrate the bookstore's being established for 30 weeks

    C) a closeout sale

    D) a grand opening sale

14. When is the sale held?

    A) Every day of the week except Monday

    B) The last three days of the month

    C) The fourth of the month and the last three days of the month

    D) The first four days and the last three days of the month

15. If you would like to buy a dictionary, the discount is

    A) 80% off

    B) 75% off

    C) 20% off

    D) 25% off

16. If the original price of a calculator is $100, you can get it on the sale days for

    A) $70

    B) $75

    C) $80

    D) $85

Read this announcement.

(Traditional characters)

親愛的同學們：
　　學生會將於4月的第二週在學生活動中心大禮堂舉辦音樂週活動。活動內容包括演唱中外流行歌曲、演奏中國古典音樂或西洋古典音樂，每人以參加兩項為限。如果你想演奏中國古典音樂或西洋古典音樂，除了鋼琴，請自備樂器。如果你對此活動感興趣，請於3月22日前帶學生證到學生會辦公室報名或電郵學生會，電郵中請寫明姓名、年級、手機號碼與學生證號碼，以及想要參加的項目。學生會辦公室在學生活動中心二層，電郵地址是abc@xyz.edu。歡迎大家參加。謝謝！
　　　　　　　　　　　　　學生會
　　　　　　　　　　　　　3月1日

(Simplified characters)

亲爱的同学们：
　　学生会将于4月的第二周在学生活动中心大礼堂举办音乐周活动。活动内容包括演唱中外流行歌曲、演奏中国古典音乐或西洋古典音乐，每人以参加两项为限。如果你想演奏中国古典音乐或西洋古典音乐，除了钢琴，请自备乐器。如果你对此活动感兴趣，请于3月22日前带学生证到学生会办公室报名或电邮学生会，电邮中请写明姓名、年级、手机号码与学生证号码，以及想要参加的项目。学生会办公室在学生活动中心二层，电邮地址是abc@xyz.edu。欢迎大家参加。谢谢！
　　　　　　　　　　　　　学生会
　　　　　　　　　　　　　3月1日

17. Which of the following statements is TRUE?

   A) The music activity will last two weeks.

   B) The music activity will be held in the theater.

   C) Students do not have to register in person.

   D) Students can participate in as many events as they wish.

18. Which of the following music is not mentioned in this announcement?

   A) Chinese popular songs

   B) Traditional Chinese music

   C) Classical music

   D) Opera

19. Which of the following statements is FALSE?

   A) Regardless of what type of music you would like to perform, you need to bring your own instrument.

   B) When registering for the event in person, students need to take the student ID with them.

C) The student activity center has more than one storey.

D) It's still three weeks away from the deadline to register for the event.

20. What information is needed to register for the event?

    A) The exact music piece

    B) The cell phone number

    C) The length of the music piece

    D) The composer of the music

Read this letter.

(Traditional characters)

小寧：

　　你好，好久沒給你寫信了。你一定覺得我這個筆友太懶了，是不是？其實不是我懶，而是前些時候，我老是生病，整天流鼻涕、咳嗽，甚至還發高燒，全身都疼，胃口也相當差。媽媽帶我去看了醫生，醫生說我一天到晚坐在教室裡上課，回家不是打電腦，就是看電視，生活習慣非常不好，再這麼下去，身體肯定會越來越糟。聽了醫生的話以後，現在我每天早上都到附近的公園去跑步。早晨的公園人還真多呢，有騎車的，有遛狗的，有打太極拳的，還有人跟我一樣，戴著耳機，邊跑邊聽音樂。跑了兩三個星期以後，我現在身體好多了。你平常都做些什麼運動呢？

　　祝好！

　　　　　　　　　　　小花

　　　　　　　　　　2月20日

(Simplified characters)

小宁：

　　你好，好久没给你写信了。你一定觉得我这个笔友太懒了，是不是？其实不是我懒，而是前些时候，我老是生病，整天流鼻涕、咳嗽，甚至还发高烧，全身都疼，胃口也相当差。妈妈带我去看了医生，医生说我一天到晚坐在教室里上课，回家不是打电脑，就是看电视，生活习惯非常不好，再这么下去，身体肯定会越来越糟。听了医生的话以后，现在我每天早上都到附近的公园去跑步。早晨的公园人还真多呢，有骑车的，有遛狗的，有打太极拳的，还有人跟我一样，戴着耳机，边跑边听音乐。跑了两三个星期以后，我现在身体好多了。你平常都做些什么运动呢？

　　祝好！

　　　　　　　　　　　小花

　　　　　　　　　　2月20日

21. Which of the following statements can best describe Xiaohua's health?

    A) She has been sick for quite a while.

    B) She has a severe case of allergy.

    C) Her health has improved.

    D) She often has high fevers.

22. Which of the following statements is TRUE?

    A) Xiaohua doesn't like computers.

    B) Xiaohua enjoys watching television.

    C) Xiaohua's appetite was decent.

    D) Xiaohua jogs with her mother.

23. The doctor attributes her health problem to

    A) her life style

    B) her school work load

    C) her not drinking enough water

    D) her diet

24. Based on this letter, which of the following statements is FALSE?

    A) Xiaohua listens to music while jogging.

    B) There are people walking dogs in the morning.

    C) Xiaohua is interested in Tai-chi.

    D) The park is close to where she lives.

Read this article.

(Traditional characters)

中文與標點符號

中國以前的書籍都是沒有標點符號的，讀書人一般要拿著紅筆，一邊讀，一邊打圈圈來把文字隔開。這有個專門的詞語，叫作"斷句"。一直要到二十世紀初期，受到西洋語文的影響，出版的書籍纔有了標點符號。標點符號的使用，除了方便讀者閱讀之外，也能幫助正確地解讀文義，避免產生誤解。

歷史上有好幾個故事，說的都是標點符號標在不同處，文字就有不同的解讀。比如，有這麼一個故事，想要客人離去的主人寫下"下雨天留客天留我不留"，本意是說："下雨，天留客。天留，我不留！"可是臉皮厚的客人解讀成："下雨天，留客天。留我不？留！"主人看了也只好搖搖頭，無可奈何地笑了。

(Simplified characters)

> **中文与标点符号**
>
> 中国以前的书籍都是没有标点符号的,读书人一般要拿着红笔,一边读,一边打圈圈来把文字隔开。这有个专门的词语,叫作"断句"。一直要到二十世纪初期,受到西洋语文的影响,出版的书籍才有了标点符号。标点符号的使用,除了方便读者阅读之外,也能帮助正确地解读文义,避免产生误解。
>
> 历史上有好几个故事,说的都是标点符号标在不同处,文字就有不同的解读。比如,有这么一个故事,想要客人离去的主人写下"下雨天留客天留我不留",本意是说:"下雨,天留客。天留,我不留!"可是脸皮厚的客人解读成:"下雨天,留客天。留我不?留!"主人看了也只好摇摇头,无可奈何地笑了。

25. Based on this article, one of the unique features for the Chinese books published long ago is that

    A) there were only commas and periods

    B) there were only periods

    C) there were no punctuation marks

    D) the punctuations were printed in red

26. What is NOT mentioned as an advantage of using punctuation marks?

    A) To enable the readers to read

    B) To help correctly interpret the meaning of the text

    C) To help make the writing style better

    D) To avoid misunderstanding

27. Why did the host mentioned in this article shake his head in the end?

    A) He did not understand what his guest meant.

    B) He did not approve of what his guest intended to do.

    C) He was very upset with his guest.

    D) He understood what his guest meant, but there was nothing he could do.

Read this poster.

(Traditional characters)

熊貓展覽館
開放時間：週一至週五上午8點30分至下午5點30分，週六、日延長兩個小時
參觀方式：憑號碼牌入場，每梯次觀賞十分鐘
票價：全票60元 優待票減半（老人六十五歲以上，需出示身份證；學生需出示學生證），六歲以下兒童免費
交通：地鐵藍綫、黃綫均可，至動物園站下車

(Simplified characters)

熊猫展览馆
开放时间：周一至周五上午8点30分至下午5点30分，周六、日延长两个小时
参观方式：凭号码牌入场，每梯次观赏十分钟
票价：全票60元 优待票减半（老人六十五岁以上，需出示身份证；学生需出示学生证），六岁以下儿童免费
交通：地铁蓝线、黄线均可，至动物园站下车

28. How does the staff at the zoo decide whom to let in for the exhibit?

    A) First come, first served

    B) Seniors first

    C) Every visitor will be given a number.

    D) Students first

29. How long can the visitors stay in the special exhibit section of the zoo?

    A) Ten minutes

    B) Sixty minutes

    C) Half an hour

    D) As long as the visitors wish

30. Based on the poster, which of the following statements is FALSE?

    A) The zoo is very close to the subway station.

    B) A sixty-five-year-old man with an ID only needs to pay ¥30 for admission.

    C) Kids under six are admitted free of charge.

    D) Visitors can take the green line subway to the zoo.

31. Over the weekends, how long is the exhibit hall open?

   A) 2 hours

   B) 7 hours

   C) 9 hours

   D) 11 hours

Read this story.

(Traditional characters)

　　春秋時期，有個著名的琴師叫俞伯牙，他精通音律，琴藝高超。有一天晚上，月明風清，伯牙在荒山野地鼓琴，琴聲悠揚，飄揚於宇宙之間。他想象著高山，樂音從指尖流瀉而出，忽然聽到有人讚美道："好！好！巍巍峨峨，仿佛高聳入雲的泰山一般！"他想象著流水，那個人又說："好！好！仿佛滾滾無盡的流水一般！"伯牙一看，原來知曉他樂音意境的人是個路過的樵夫，叫鐘子期。他為鐘子期彈奏樂曲，無論他內心想表達什麼，鐘子期都能意會，從此二人成了非常要好的朋友。鐘子期死後，伯牙失去知音，傷心欲絕，覺得此生再無人可理解他琴音中的意境，彈琴已無意義，於是把琴摔壞，從此不再鼓琴。

(Simplified characters)

　　春秋时期，有个著名的琴师叫俞伯牙，他精通音律，琴艺高超。有一天晚上，月明风清，伯牙在荒山野地鼓琴，琴声悠扬，飘扬于宇宙之间。他想象着高山，乐音从指尖流泻而出，忽然听到有人赞美道："好！好！巍巍峨峨，仿佛高耸入云的泰山一般！"他想象着流水，那个人又说："好！好！仿佛滚滚无尽的流水一般！"伯牙一看，原来知晓他乐音意境的人是个路过的樵夫，叫钟子期。他为钟子期弹奏乐曲，无论他内心想表达什么，钟子期都能意会，从此二人成了非常要好的朋友。钟子期死后，伯牙失去知音，伤心欲绝，觉得此生再无人可理解他琴音中的意境，弹琴已无意义，于是把琴摔坏，从此不再鼓琴。

32. The musical instrument mentioned in this story is a

   A) piano

   B) lute

   C) drum

   D) Chinese flute

33. Based on the story, the musician liked to play music

    A) in the wilderness

    B) in a secluded studio

    C) with his best friend

    D) for the imperial court

34. We may conclude that the musician in the story drew inspiration from

    A) the moon and the stars

    B) the flowers and trees

    C) the mountains and the rivers

    D) the wind and the clouds

35. Why did the musician stop playing music after his friend passed away?

    A) Because his musical instrument was ruined.

    B) Because nobody could understand his music anymore.

    C) Because nobody could play with him well anymore.

    D) Because his friend told him that he would be heartbroken to play music.

END OF SECTION I

YOU MAY REVIEW WORK IF THERE IS TIME LEFT.

DO NOT GO ON TO SECTION II UNTIL YOU ARE TOLD TO DO SO.

Section II: Free Response

Part A: Writing (Story Narration and E-mail Response)

Note: In this part of the exam, the student may NOT move back and forth among questions.

Writing Part Directions

You will be asked to perform two writing tasks in Chinese. In each case, you will be asked to write for a specific purpose and to a specific person. You should write in as complete and as culturally appropriate a manner as possible, taking into account the purpose and the person described.

Presentational Writing: Story Narration (15%, 15 minutes)

The four pictures present a story. Imagine you are writing the story for a friend. Narrate a complete story as suggested by the pictures. Give your story a beginning, a middle, and an end.

Interpersonal Writing: E-mail Response (10%, 15 minutes)

Read this e-mail from a friend and then type a response.

(Traditional characters)

發件人：陳健
郵件主題：住宿問題

　　好消息！我前陣子申請了一個到中國去學習漢語和文化的項目，昨天剛收到錄取通知。學校告訴我，我可以選擇住在學校宿舍，是雙人間，或者是跟一個中國家庭居住，那個家庭有一個跟我年紀差不多的孩子。你以前到中國留過學，你覺得我應該怎麼選擇？應該從哪些方面考慮？謝謝。

(Simplified characters)

发件人：陈健
邮件主题：住宿问题

　　好消息！我前阵子申请了一个到中国去学习汉语和文化的项目，昨天刚收到录取通知。学校告诉我，我可以选择住在学校宿舍，是双人间，或者是跟一个中国家庭居住，那个家庭有一个跟我年纪差不多的孩子。你以前到中国留过学，你觉得我应该怎么选择？应该从哪些方面考虑？谢谢。

Part B: Speaking (Conversation and Cultural Presentation)

Note: In this part of the exam, you may NOT move back and forth among questions.

speaking

Speaking Part Directions: Conversation

You will participate in a simulated conversation. Each time it is your turn to speak, you will have 20 seconds to record. You should respond as fully and as appropriately as possible. There will be six times when it is your turn to speak.

Interpersonal Speaking: Conversation (10%, 4 minutes)

Xiaomei just came to the United States from China as an exchange student at your school. She would like to ask you some questions about studying and living in the United States.

Speaking Question 1 of 7

    1. Record your answer. (20 seconds)

Speaking Question 2 of 7

    2. Record your answer. (20 seconds)

Speaking Question 3 of 7

    3. Record your answer. (20 seconds)

Speaking Question 4 of 7

    4. Record your answer. (20 seconds)

Speaking Question 5 of 7

    5. Record your answer. (20 seconds)

Speaking Question 6 of 7

    6. Record your answer. (20 seconds)

Speaking Part Directions: Cultural Presentation

You will be asked to speak in Chinese on a specific topic. Imagine you are making an oral presentation to your Chinese class. First, you will read and hear the topic for your presentation. You will have 4 minutes to prepare your presentation. Then you will have 2 minutes to record your presentation. Your presentation should be as complete as possible.

Presentational Speaking: Cultural Presentation (15%, 7 minutes)

Speaking Question 7 of 7

7. Choose ONE of the Chinese festivals, such as the Spring Festival, Dragon Boat Festival, Mid-Autumn Festival, etc. In your presentation, describe the festival, how Chinese celebrate it, and explain its significance.

You have four minutes to prepare your presentation. (240 seconds)

You have two minutes to record your presentation. (120 seconds)

YOU HAVE FINISHED THIS PART OF THE EXAM.
END OF EXAM

AP Chinese Language and Culture Test 5

listening

Section I: Multiple Choice

Part A: Listening (Rejoinders and Listening Selections)

Listening Part Directions

You will answer two types of questions: rejoinders and questions based on listening selections.

For all tasks, you will have a specific amount of response time. When the response time has ended, you will automatically go on to the next question. You cannot return to previous questions.

Listening Part Directions: Rejoinders (10%, 10 minutes)

You will hear several short conversations or parts of conversations followed by four choices, designated A, B, C, and D. Choose the one that continues or completes the conversation in a logical and culturally appropriate manner. After you have decided which of the suggested answers is best, COMPLETELY fill in the corresponding circle on the answer sheet. You will have 5 seconds to answer each question.

YOU WILL NOW BEGIN THIS PART.

1. Mark your answer on your answer sheet.
2. Mark your answer on your answer sheet.
3. Mark your answer on your answer sheet.
4. Mark your answer on your answer sheet.
5. Mark your answer on your answer sheet.
6. Mark your answer on your answer sheet.
7. Mark your answer on your answer sheet.
8. Mark your answer on your answer sheet.
9. Mark your answer on your answer sheet.
10. Mark your answer on your answer sheet.
11. Mark your answer on your answer sheet.
12. Mark your answer on your answer sheet.
13. Mark your answer on your answer sheet.
14. Mark your answer on your answer sheet.
15. Mark your answer on your answer sheet.

83

Listening Part Directions: Listening Selections (15%, 10 minutes)

You will listen to several selections in Chinese. For each selection, you will be told whether it will be played once or twice. You may take notes as you listen. Your notes will not be graded. After listening to each selection, you will see questions in English. For each question, choose the response that is best according to the selection. You will have 12 seconds to answer each question.

YOU WILL NOW BEGIN THIS PART.

Selection 1: Announcement (Selection plays two times.)

16. The main purpose of the announcement is to

    A) tell the passengers that the restroom is temporarily closed

    B) ask the flight attendants to help the passengers

    C) tell the passengers to be seated

    D) thank the passengers for flying with the airlines

17. What are the flight attendants supposed to do after hearing the announcement?

    A) To be seated and fasten their seatbelts

    B) To make sure all passengers are seated

    C) To continue preparing the meal

    D) To make sure all children are with their parents

18. The announcement is made because

    A) too many passengers are lining up to use the restroom

    B) there are children running around

    C) the airplane is experiencing turbulence

    D) the safety lights are malfunctioning

Selection 2: Voice Message (Selection plays two times.)

19. Ziwei can't go to the group meeting because

    A) her mom is sick

    B) she has a doctor's appointment

    C) her grandfather was hospitalized

    D) she and her grandfather went to buy a car and came home too late

20. What does Ziwei prefer?

   A) To postpone the meeting until Monday

   B) To meet on Sunday instead of Saturday

   C) To ask the group to complete her task

   D) To discuss the work with the group over the phone

21. When will she be doing the group presentation?

   A) Saturday

   B) Sunday

   C) Monday

   D) In a week

Selection 3: Conversation (Selection plays one time.)

22. Meiyun is hesitant to go because

   A) she has too much school work

   B) her foot injury has not healed yet

   C) the boy is not planning to go

   D) she has not practiced since she was little

23. What holds the boy back from going?

   A) He does not think he is talented enough.

   B) He is too busy with other activities.

   C) His school work load will be too heavy.

   D) His parents want him to focus more on his academic performance.

24. Meiyun encourages the boy to go because

   A) she thinks he should continue with gymnastics

   B) she does not think he is that busy with school work

   C) she wants him to try out with her

   D) she wants him to cheer her on during the tryouts

25. What is the outcome of the conversation?

   A) Only the boy will try out for the team.

   B) Meiyun will further consider if she will go to try out.

   C) The boy decides not to try out.

   D) They will both try out.

Selection 4: Instructions (Selection plays one time.)

26. To qualify for the $50 rebate, the computer must be bought

    A) after June 28th, 2020

    B) between June 28th and Oct.11th, 2020

    C) on June 18th and Oct. 11th, 2020

    D) within 45 days starting from June 28th, 2020

27. The online rebate form must be filled out

    A) within 3 days after the purchase

    B) 5~10 days after the purchase

    C) after 45 days of the purchase

    D) within 45 days after the purchase

28. What document is NOT needed for the rebate?

    A) Purchase receipt

    B) Package delivery date

    C) Rebate form, and contact information

    D) Product number

29. How soon should customers expect to receive the $50 rebate credited to their account?

    A) Within 3 days

    B) Within 5 days

    C) Between 5 to 10 days

    D) longer than 10 days if outside of America

30. The rebate promotion is limited to people

    A) who live outside of the US

    B) who are over 18 years of age

    C) who live within the US

    D) who are American citizens

Selection 5: Report (Selection plays one time.)

31. Which city is the weather report for?

    A) Beijing

    B) Hangzhou

C) Xi'an

D) Shanghai

32. What does the weather report predict?

   A) Hailstorm

   B) Thunderstorm

   C) Heavy rain

   D) Strong winds

33. When will the predicted weather occur?

   A) 1:00 pm

   B) 3:00 pm

   C) Within 1 to 3 hours

   D) Between 1:00 pm and 3:00 pm

34. From where will the weather phenomenon come?

   A) East

   B) South

   C) West

   D) North

35. What does the report NOT suggest people do?

   A) To stay indoors

   B) To stay in open areas

   C) To watch the weather closely

   D) To call for help in case of emergency

Part B: Reading Selections

Note: In this part of the exam, you may move back and forth among all the questions.

Reading Part Directions: Reading Selections (25%, 60 minutes)

You will read several selections in Chinese. Each selection is accompanied by a number of questions in English. For each question, choose the response that is best according to the selection. After you have decided which of the suggested answers is best, COMPLETELY fill in the corresponding circle on the answer sheet. Chinese tests appear here in both traditional and simplified characters. You will have 60 minutes to answer all questions.

YOU WILL NOW BEGIN THIS PART.

Read this note.

(Traditional characters)

小馬：
　　我這個週末要去參加一個校外野營活動。活動結束後，星期二早上我直接坐車去學校，沒有時間回家取上學用的東西了。我想麻煩你去我家一趟，把幾樣東西幫我帶到學校：帽子、筆記本、化學課本和電腦。我的帽子在一進門的那個衣架上掛著，筆記本在桌子上，化學課本在書架上，電腦在我的書包裡。我父母都上夜班，所以你去我家時，他們可能都還沒回家呢。但是我已經告訴我媽媽你可能會去，所以她會把我們家的後門打開。謝謝你！學校見！

　　　　　　　　　　　王剛
　　　　　　　　　　　3月9日

(Simplified characters)

小马：
　　我这个周末要去参加一个校外野营活动。活动结束后，星期二早上我直接坐车去学校，没有时间回家取上学用的东西了。我想麻烦你去我家一趟，把几样东西帮我带到学校：帽子、笔记本、化学课本和电脑。我的帽子在一进门的那个衣架上挂着，笔记本在桌子上，化学课本在书架上，电脑在我的书包里。我父母都上夜班，所以你去我家时，他们可能都还没回家呢。但是我已经告诉我妈妈你可能会去，所以她会把我们家的后门打开。谢谢你！学校见！

　　　　　　　　　　　王刚
　　　　　　　　　　　3月9日

1. Wang Gang asked Xiao Ma to help bring some stuff to school because

    A) Xiao Ma lives near his house

    B) he forgot to take the things with him

    C) he has to go to school directly from the camping trip

    D) his parents are not home

2. Which item was NOT mentioned on the note?

    A) Computer

    B) Hat

    C) Chemistry textbook

    D) Calculator

3. Where did Wang Gang leave his hat?

    A) On a chair in the living room

    B) In his bedroom

    C) On a rack by the front door

    D) In his backpack

4. Wang Gang's parents were not at home because

   A) they both left home very early that morning

   B) they are on the way to pick up Wang Gang

   C) they are on vacation

   D) they work night shifts

5. How can Xiao Ma get into Wang Gang's house to pick up the stuff?

   A) From the side window

   B) The front door is usually unlocked.

   C) Xiao Ma has the key to Wang Gang's house.

   D) Wang Gang's parents will leave the backdoor open for Xiao Ma.

Read this e-mail.

(Traditional characters)

發件人：小紅

收件人：小包

郵件主題：學習中文的建議

郵件日期：5月6日

小包：

　　很高興聽到你選擇中文作爲你的高中外語課。你來信問我學習中文的體會，雖然我可以給你一些建議，但是我覺得現在還爲時過早，因爲你還沒有開始學習，過早地提出來，你可能并不理解，我以後會慢慢告訴你。但有一點非常重要，那就是學中文并不容易，如果你決定學了，就要堅持下去，千萬不要半途而廢。如果基礎沒打好，你就會越學越沒興趣，到了大學有可能得改學其他語言。這不僅浪費了你的時間、精力和金錢，更重要的是如果你的成績不理想，有可能會影響你的學習情緒，你會有挫折感。當然，如果你的成績很好，又有足夠的時間和興趣，且經濟條件允許的話，你可以選擇第三甚至第四外語。以上是我的一點建議，僅供你參考。

　　　　　　　　　　　　　　　　　　　　　　　　　　　　　　　姐姐

(Simplified characters)

发件人：小红

收件人：小包

邮件主题：学习中文的建议

邮件日期：5月6日

小包：

很高兴听到你选择中文作为你的高中外语课。你来信问我学习中文的体会，虽然我可以给你一些建议，但是我觉得现在还为时过早，因为你还没有开始学习，过早地提出来，你可能并不理解，我以后会慢慢告诉你。但有一点非常重要，那就是学中文并不容易，如果你决定学了，就要坚持下去，千万不要半途而废。如果基础没打好，你就会越学越没兴趣，到了大学有可能得改学其他语言。这不仅浪费了你的时间、精力和金钱，更重要的是如果你的成绩不理想，有可能会影响你的学习情绪，你会有挫折感。当然，如果你的成绩很好，又有足够的时间和兴趣，且经济条件允许的话，你可以选择第三甚至第四外语。以上是我的一点建议，仅供你参考。

姐姐

6. Why is the sister hesitant to give suggestions to her brother?

   A) It is too early for her to give suggestions.

   B) She doesn't know Chinese.

   C) She is concerned that her brother will not continue Chinese.

   D) She wants him to take another language besides Chinese.

7. What is the one suggestion that the sister gives to her brother?

   A) Do not waste time, money, and energy studying Chinese.

   B) Select another foreign language.

   C) Chinese is too hard to learn.

   D) Establish a good foundation to build upon.

8. When does the sister think her brother can study additional foreign languages?

   A) When her brother has the time and money

   B) When her brother is interested in other foreign languages

   C) When her brother's Chinese is good

   D) All of the above

9. What is the overall message of the passage?

   A) Complete all the tasks that you have started

   B) Do not take foreign languages

   C) Chinese is a hard language

   D) Accomplish things that you enjoy

Read this advertisement.

(Traditional characters)

飲食與減肥講座

減輕體重并非只是減少食物中的熱量攝取。本期講座會幫您瞭解有益於身心健康的科學減肥方法，讓您從日常飲食及鍛煉中找到減肥的真諦。如果您感興趣，請速報名參加此次講座。

講座地點：中醫大學禮堂

講座時間：9月20日下午1～3點

費用：中醫藥協會會員免費

　　　非中醫藥協會會員¥15

報名方法：請電洽（888）888-8888

主辦單位：中國中醫藥協會

(Simplified characters)

饮食与减肥讲座

减轻体重并非只是减少食物中的热量摄取。本期讲座会帮您了解有益于身心健康的科学减肥方法，让您从日常饮食及锻炼中找到减肥的真谛。如果您感兴趣，请速报名参加此次讲座。

讲座地点：中医大学礼堂

讲座时间：9月20日下午1～3点

费用：中医药协会会员免费

　　　非中医药协会会员¥15

报名方法：请电洽（888）888-8888

主办单位：中国中医药协会

10. What is the primary purpose of the seminar?

    A) To introduce certain foods and their nutrition facts

    B) To learn how to lose weight

C) To teach physical exercise techniques

D) To promote diet products

11. What is the fee to attend the seminar?

    A) Members of Chinese Medicine Association ¥15

    B) Non-members free

    C) All participants ¥15

    D) Free for members of Chinese Medicine Association

12. Where is the seminar held?

    A) At the Chinese Medicine Association

    B) At the Chinese Medicine University

    C) At the Chinese People's University

    D) None of the above

13. What methods for losing weight are suggested?

    A) To eat less and drink more water

    B) To eat healthy foods and exercise

    C) To buy diet products and eat less

    D) To sleep less and work out more

Read this public sign.

(Traditional characters)

如有火警，請走樓梯！

(Simplified characters)

如有火警，请走楼梯！

14. What is the message of this sign?

    A) Use the stairs in case of fire!

    B) Show where the fire exits are located!

    C) Do not smoke in the building!

    D) Show where the fire extinguisher is located!

15. Where would this sign most likely appear?

    A) At a building entrance

    B) By an elevator

    C) Near the fire extinguisher

    D) Outside of a building

Read this public sign.

(Traditional characters)　　　　　　　　(Simplified characters)

来也匆匆，去也沖沖　　　　　　　　来也匆匆，去也冲冲

16. Where would this sign most likely appear?

    A) In the library

    B) In the public restroom

    C) In the emergency room

    D) In the classroom

17. The purpose of the sign is to remind people

    A) to flush the toilet after using it

    B) not to waste time

    C) to move quickly from place to place

    D) not to stop here

Read this letter.

(Traditional characters)

表哥：

　　你好！我已經通過了高考，并且被省師範大學錄取了。我就要步入大學的校園，成爲一名大學生了！我現在又激動又緊張，能進入大學的校園，學習更多的知識，參加學校的社團組織，結識更多的朋友，這一切對我來說都好新鮮。

　　在開學之前，我會有一個很長的假期，我打算去一個農村小學做義工，當一名英語代課教師。我一直對英語很有興趣，高中期間我的英語成績也比別的科好，去那裡教孩子們英語，對我來說是個練習英語的好機會。這些天，我購買了好多英文故事書和英文歌曲唱片，同時我還在抓緊練習我的英語口語，希望能做好這個工作。

　　表哥，你已經在大學裡學習兩年了，一定有很多寶貴的大學生活經驗和我分享。另外，我們入學之後馬上就要選擇專業，還要選課，你能給我一些建議嗎？謝謝！

　　　　祝你學業順利！

　　　　　　　　　　　　　　　　　　　　　　　表妹　小英

　　　　　　　　　　　　　　　　　　　　　　　7月28日

(Simplified characters)

> 表哥：
>
> 　　你好！我已经通过了高考，并且被省师范大学录取了。我就要步入大学的校园，成为一名大学生了！我现在又激动又紧张，能进入大学的校园，学习更多的知识，参加学校的社团组织，结识更多的朋友，这一切对我来说都好新鲜。
>
> 　　在开学之前，我会有一个很长的假期，我打算去一个农村小学做义工，当一名英语代课教师。我一直对英语很有兴趣，高中期间我的英语成绩也比别的科好，去那里教孩子们英语，对我来说是个练习英语的好机会。这些天，我购买了好多英文故事书和英文歌曲唱片，同时我还在抓紧练习我的英语口语，希望能做好这个工作。
>
> 　　表哥，你已经在大学里学习两年了，一定有很多宝贵的大学生活经验和我分享。另外，我们入学之后马上就要选择专业，还要选课，你能给我一些建议吗？谢谢！
>
> 　　祝你学业顺利！
>
> 　　　　　　　　　　　　　　　　　　　　　　表妹　小英
> 　　　　　　　　　　　　　　　　　　　　　　7月28日

18. What is the most likely age of Xiaoying?

    A) 16

    B) 18

    C) 22

    D) 26

19. Why did Xiaoying write the letter?

    A) To ask her cousin to share his college experience

    B) To invite her cousin to travel with her

    C) To ask him for money

    D) To discuss her doubts about becoming an English teacher

20. What is Xiaoying going to do over the summer?

    A) To travel around China

    B) To take classes

    C) To teach English

    D) To work at a supermarket

21. In preparation for her summer activities, Xiaoying has

    A) purchased a camera for her travels

    B) purchased a laptop

    C) purchased English language textbooks

    D) purchased music albums of English songs

22. What type of college is Xiaoying going to?

    A) Technology institute

    B) Normal university

    C) Vocational school

    D) Foreign language school

Read this poster.

(Traditional characters)

華南大學計算機學院招聘信息

因2021級新生入學，學院辦公室工作量突增，故擬招聘一名勤工助學學生。

工作職責：

1. 協助學院辦公室老師處理日常工作
2. 負責維護學院網站

工作時間：

週一至週四上午8點至10點

週五上午9點至12點

薪酬：面談

招聘條件：

1. 本院2020級學生
2. 具備團隊精神，有責任心，工作認真嚴謹
3. 熟練掌握計算機基本操作

有意者請與學院辦公室嚴老師聯繫。

電話：（755）260-3506

計算機學院

2021年8月20日

(Simplified characters)

华南大学计算机学院招聘信息

因2021级新生入学，学院办公室工作量突增，故拟招聘一名勤工助学学生。

工作职责：

1. 协助学院办公室老师处理日常工作
2. 负责维护学院网站

工作时间：

周一至周四上午8点至10点

周五上午9点至12点

薪酬：面谈

招聘条件：

1. 本院2020级学生
2. 具备团队精神，有责任心，工作认真严谨
3. 熟练掌握计算机基本操作

有意者请与学院办公室严老师联系。

电话：（755）260-3506

计算机学院

2021年8月20日

23. The college is hiring a student for work-study because

   A) they have received new computers that need to be installed

   B) the school has obtained increased funding

   C) the work load will increase due to new incoming students

   D) there will be students that will graduate soon

24. How many hours per week does the job entail?

   A) 8

   B) 11

   C) 12

   D) 13

25. What is the pay for the job?

   A) Minimum wage

   B) Low pay because it is a part-time position

C) The pay will be discussed during the interview.

D) The poster does not say.

26. What is a requirement for the position?

    A) Anyone interested can apply.

    B) Applicants must be sophomores.

    C) Applicants must be athletic.

    D) Applicants must be computer science majors.

27. What does the work involve?

    A) Repairing the computers

    B) Promoting the computer science department

    C) Helping the faculty with daily tasks

    D) Developing software for the department

Read this article.

(Traditional characters)

> 指南針是中國古代的四大發明之一。在指南針發明以前，人們在茫茫的大海上航行，只能靠太陽和星星的位置辨認方向。是中國人發明了指南針，幫助人們解決了這個難題。
>
> 早在戰國時期，中國人就發現了磁石指示南北的特性，並根據這種特性製成了指示方向的儀器——司南。司南由一把光滑的磁勺和刻著方位的銅盤組成，勺把指示的方向是南方，勺頭指示的方向是北方。到了宋代，人們把經過人工磁化的指南針和方位盤結合起來，製成了羅盤。有了羅盤，無論在什麼情況下，人們都能準確地辨認方向。
>
> 指南針後來輾轉傳入了歐洲，並在航海大發現中發揮了不可替代的作用，例如：明朝初期鄭和帶領船隊七下西洋，十五世紀哥倫布發現新大陸，等等。但是非常有趣的是，最早解答"指南針為何能夠指南"問題的並不是中國人，而是英國的科學家。

(Simplified characters)

> 指南针是中国古代的四大发明之一。在指南针发明以前，人们在茫茫的大海上航行，只能靠太阳和星星的位置辨认方向。是中国人发明了指南针，帮助人们解决了这个难题。

早在战国时期，中国人就发现了磁石指示南北的特性，并根据这种特性制成了指示方向的仪器——司南。司南由一把光滑的磁勺和刻着方位的铜盘组成，勺把指示的方向是南方，勺头指示的方向是北方。到了宋代，人们把经过人工磁化的指南针和方位盘结合起来，制成了罗盘。有了罗盘，无论在什么情况下，人们都能准确地辨认方向。

指南针后来辗转传入了欧洲，并在航海大发现中发挥了不可替代的作用，例如：明朝初期郑和带领船队七下西洋，十五世纪哥伦布发现新大陆，等等。但是非常有趣的是，最早解答"指南针为何能够指南"问题的并不是中国人，而是英国的科学家。

28. What did people use to find their direction at sea before the compass was invented?

    A) The clouds

    B) The ocean waves

    C) Geographic features of the coastlines

    D) The position of the sun and the stars

29. What was the prototype of the compass?

    A) A non magnetic needle

    B) A nickel plate

    C) A magnetic spoon and a copper plate

    D) All of the above

30. During which dynasty was the copper plate invented?

    A) Ming Dynasty

    B) The Warring States Period

    C) Shang Dynasty

    D) Song Dynasty

31. Who was the first to discover how a compass works?

    A) A Chinese scientist

    B) Zheng He

    C) Christopher Columbus

    D) An English scientist

Read this story.

(Traditional characters)

　　太行和王屋兩座大山，方圓七百里。山的北面住著一位老人，叫愚公，年近九十。他家的房子正對著這兩座大山，由於大山的阻隔，出入十分困難。有一天他召集全家人商議說："我想和你們一起，盡一切力量去把山移走，開出一條大路，直通山的另一邊。"全家人紛紛表示贊同。

　　於是，愚公就率領著三個能挑擔子的子孫，鑿石頭、挖土塊，再用籮筐把石土運到離家很遠的地方，一年到頭他們纔能往返一次。愚公家搬山的事，驚動了鄰居。鄰居家的一位老奶奶，有個小孫女，纔剛七八歲，也蹦蹦跳跳跑去幫忙。

　　黃河邊上住著一個老頭兒，人稱智叟，是個很聰明的老人。他以嘲笑的語氣勸阻愚公說："你怎麼傻到這種地步呀！就憑你這把年紀，這點兒力氣，要拔掉山上的一棵樹都不容易辦到，又怎麼能搬掉這麼多的山石土塊呢？"愚公長歎了一口氣，說："我看你太頑固了，簡直不明事理。雖然我會死，可是我還有兒子呢！兒子又生孫子，孫子又生兒子，兒子又生兒子，兒子又生孫子，這樣子子孫孫都不會斷絕的呀！而這兩座山再也不會增高了，還怕挖不平嗎？"智叟聽了，無言以對。

　　山神聽到了愚公的這些話，就去稟告了天帝。天帝爲愚公移山的誠意所感動，就派了夸娥氏的兩個兒子去背走了那兩座大山。

(Simplified characters)

　　太行和王屋两座大山，方圆七百里。山的北面住着一位老人，叫愚公，年近九十。他家的房子正对着这两座大山，由于大山的阻隔，出入十分困难。有一天他召集全家人商议说："我想和你们一起，尽一切力量去把山移走，开出一条大路，直通山的另一边。"全家人纷纷表示赞同。

　　于是，愚公就率领着三个能挑担子的子孙，凿石头、挖土块，再用箩筐把石土运到离家很远的地方，一年到头他们才能往返一次。愚公家搬山的事，惊动了邻居。邻居家的一位老奶奶，有个小孙女，才刚七八岁，也蹦蹦跳跳跑去帮忙。

　　黄河边上住着一个老头儿，人称智叟，是个很聪明的老人。他以嘲笑的语气劝阻愚公说："你怎么傻到这种地步呀！就凭你这把年纪，这点儿力气，要拔掉山上的一棵树都不容易办到，又怎么能搬掉这么多的山石土块呢？"愚公长叹了一口气，说："我看你太顽固了，简直不明事理。虽然我会死，可是我还有儿子呢！儿子又生孙子，孙子又生儿子，儿子又生儿子，儿子又生孙子，这样子子孙孙都不会断绝的呀！而这两座山再也不会增高了，还怕挖不平吗？"智叟听了，无言以对。

> 山神听到了愚公的这些话，就去禀告了天帝。天帝为愚公移山的诚意所感动，就派了夸娥氏的两个儿子去背走了那两座大山。

32. Why does Yu Gong want to move the mountain?

    A) It blocked the path out of the village.

    B) It was blocking the river that provided water to the village.

    C) He wanted to prove his physical strength.

    D) He wanted to see beyond the mountain.

33. The older man was called 智叟 because

    A) he was arrogant

    B) he was wise

    C) he was an unhappy

    D) he was stubborn

34. What happened at the end of the story?

    A) The mountain gods sent someone to move the mountain.

    B) Yu Gong was able to move the mountain by himself.

    C) Everyone from the village helped Yu Gong move the mountain.

    D) Yu Gong could not move the mountain.

35. Yu Gong believed he could move the mountain because

    A) his neighbors would help him remove it

    B) he was praying for help from the gods

    C) the size of the mountain could only decrease if he and his descendant continued to carve out the mountain

    D) a miracle would happen if he kept carving out the mountain

END OF SECTION I
YOU MAY REVIEW WORK IF THERE IS TIME LEFT.
DO NOT GO ON TO SECTION II UNTIL YOU ARE TOLD TO DO SO.

Section II: Free Response

Part A: Writing (Story Narration and E-mail Response)

Note: In this part of the exam, the student may NOT move back and forth among questions.

Writing Part Directions

You will be asked to perform two writing tasks in Chinese. In each case, you will be asked to write for a specific purpose and to a specific person. You should write in as complete and as culturally appropriate a manner as possible, taking into account the purpose and the person described.

Presentational Writing: Story Narration (15%, 15 minutes)

The four pictures present a story. Imagine you are writing the story to a friend. Narrate a complete story as suggested by the pictures. Give your story a beginning, a middle, and an end.

Interpersonal Writing: E-mail Response (10%, 15 minutes)

Read this e-mail from a friend and then type a response.

(Traditional characters)

發件人：大偉
郵件主題：參加生日聚會
東東：
　　我昨天同時收到大中和小胖兒的生日聚會邀請，時間都是下個星期日的下午兩點。你知道大中是我在班上最要好的朋友，可是我和小胖兒從小一塊兒長大，又一起在球隊多年，我真的不忍心拒絕他們任何一個人的邀請。我感到非常爲難，你覺得我參加誰的比較好？我應該怎樣做纔不會傷害另一個人呢？請指教，謝謝！

(Simplified characters)

发件人：大伟
邮件主题：参加生日聚会
东东：
　　我昨天同时收到大中和小胖儿的生日聚会邀请，时间都是下个星期日的下午两点。你知道大中是我在班上最要好的朋友，可是我和小胖儿从小一块儿长大，又一起在球队多年，我真的不忍心拒绝他们任何一个人的邀请。我感到非常为难，你觉得我参加谁的比较好？我应该怎样做才不会伤害另一个人呢？请指教，谢谢！

Part B: Speaking (Conversation and Cultural Presentation)

Note: In this part of the exam, you may NOT move back and forth among questions.

speaking

Speaking Part Directions: Conversation

You will participate in a simulated conversation. Each time it is your turn to speak, you will have 20 seconds to record. You should respond as fully and as appropriately as possible. There will be six times when it is your turn to speak.

Interpersonal Speaking: Conversation (10%, 4 minutes)

You will have a conversation with Li Long, a Chinese student you met on the Great Wall, about your experiences in China.

Speaking Question 1 of 7

1. Record your answer. (20 seconds)

Speaking Question 2 of 7

2. Record your answer. (20 seconds)

Speaking Question 3 of 7

3. Record your answer. (20 seconds)

Speaking Question 4 of 7

4. Record your answer. (20 seconds)

Speaking Question 5 of 7

5. Record your answer. (20 seconds)

Speaking Question 6 of 7

6. Record your answer. (20 seconds)

Speaking Part Directions: Cultural Presentation

You will be asked to speak in Chinese on a specific topic. Imagine you are making an oral presentation to your Chinese class. First, you will read and hear the topic for your presentation. You will have 4 minutes to prepare your presentation. Then you will have 2 minutes to record your presentation. Your presentation should be as complete as possible.

Presentational Speaking: Cultural Presentation (15%, 7 minutes)

Speaking Question 7 of 7

7. Choose ONE contemporary Chinese celebrity (athlete, musician, actor, politician, etc.) and describe the reason for his or her popularity, his or her achievements, and any influence he or she has had on Chinese culture at large or on your life.

You have four minutes to prepare your presentation. (240 seconds)
You have two minutes to record your presentation. (120 seconds)

YOU HAVE FINISHED THIS PART OF THE EXAM.
END OF EXAM

AP Chinese Language and Culture Test 6

listening

Section I: Multiple Choice

Part A: Listening (Rejoinders and Listening Selections)

Listening Part Directions

You will answer two types of questions: rejoinders and questions based on listening selections.

For all tasks, you will have a specific amount of response time. When the response time has ended, you will automatically go on to the next question. You cannot return to previous questions.

Listening Part Directions: Rejoinders (10%, 10 minutes)

You will hear several short conversations or parts of conversations followed by four choices, designated A, B, C, and D. Choose the one that continues or completes the conversation in a logical and culturally appropriate manner. After you have decided which of the suggested answers is best, COMPLETELY fill in the corresponding circle on the answer sheet. You will have 5 seconds to answer each question.

YOU WILL NOW BEGIN THIS PART.

---

1. Mark your answer on your answer sheet.
2. Mark your answer on your answer sheet.
3. Mark your answer on your answer sheet.
4. Mark your answer on your answer sheet.
5. Mark your answer on your answer sheet.
6. Mark your answer on your answer sheet.
7. Mark your answer on your answer sheet.
8. Mark your answer on your answer sheet.
9. Mark your answer on your answer sheet.
10. Mark your answer on your answer sheet.
11. Mark your answer on your answer sheet.
12. Mark your answer on your answer sheet.
13. Mark your answer on your answer sheet.
14. Mark your answer on your answer sheet.
15. Mark your answer on your answer sheet.

Listening Part Directions: Listening Selections (15%, 10 minutes)

You will listen to several selections in Chinese. For each selection, you will be told whether it will be played once or twice. You may take notes as you listen. Your notes will not be graded. After listening to each selection, you will see questions in English. For each question, choose the response that is best according to the selection. You will have 12 seconds to answer each question.

YOU WILL NOW BEGIN THIS PART.

Selection 1: Announcement (Selection plays two times.)

16. This announcement is most likely broadcast

    A) at the train station

    B) right after the departure of the train

    C) right before approaching the final destination

    D) at the subway station

17. This announcement is to inform the passengers

    A) to be aware of thieves

    B) where to transfer to the connecting trains

    C) where to go to claim baggage

    D) where to go to file a complaint about the service

Selection 2: Conversation (Selection plays one time.)

18. The dance party Mingming is attending is

    A) the Homecoming party

    B) the senior prom

    C) Xiaoli's birthday party

    D) a party the man is hosting

19. Mingming is concerned about

    A) too much homework to do

    B) what attire to wear

    C) a coffee stain on her dress

    D) not having enough money to shop for clothes

20. The party is going to be held
    A) on Friday
    B) on Saturday
    C) tomorrow
    D) the day after tomorrow

21. The dress that Mingming wore to a friend's party last time was
    A) white with little blue flowers
    B) blue with little white flowers
    C) blue with white stripes
    D) white with little blue polka dots

22. What is Mingming most likely to wear to the dance party?
    A) Her sister's dress
    B) One of her own dresses
    C) Her friend's dress
    D) A brand new dress

Selection 3: Instructions (Selection plays one time.)

23. Who cannot apply for a library card?
    A) People who work in the city but do not reside there
    B) People who go to school in the city but do not reside there
    C) People who do not have a driver's license
    D) People who do not have a passport

24. Which type of identification is NOT mentioned in the instructions?
    A) Student ID
    B) Birth certificate
    C) Passport
    D) Driver's license

25. Besides IDs, what else does one need to apply for a library card?
    A) One two-inch color photo
    B) Two one-inch color photos
    C) One two-inch black-and-white photo
    D) Two one-inch black-and-white photos

26. Which of the following statements is FALSE?

   A) Everyone has to apply in person.

   B) Students have to apply in person.

   C) No mail application is accepted.

   D) You can check out books on the same day you apply for a library card.

Selection 4: Voice Message (Selection plays two times.)

27. The woman left this message

   A) to warn her father that they may lose the game this weekend

   B) to ask her father to cancel her violin lesson

   C) to ask her father for a ride home

   D) to arrange for a ride after the game

28. We may best describe the team's attitude as

   A) enthusiastic

   B) pessimistic

   C) cheerful

   D) realistic

29. Which of the following statements is TRUE?

   A) The coach doesn't have any hope for a good result this weekend.

   B) The coach would like them to practice an extra hour every day until the game.

   C) Not everyone can stay.

   D) The team thinks the opponents of the upcoming game are weak.

30. What sport does the speaker engage herself in?

   A) Volleyball

   B) Basketball

   C) Badminton

   D) Golf

Selection 5: Report (Selection plays one time.)

31. The survey was conducted by

   A) a certain class

   B) the school

   C) the student union

   D) the PTA

32. The result of the survey is

   A) unreliable because there were not enough data

   B) reliable because over 80% of the questionnaires were turned in

   C) unreliable because the data were not analyzed

   D) to help the school decide whether to penalize the students for being late

33. Which of the following vehicles is NOT mentioned in the report?

   A) School bus

   B) One's own car

   C) Train

   D) Public bus

34. What kind of students tends to be late for school?

   A) Those who walk

   B) Those who rely on their parents to drive them

   C) Those who ride their bicycles

   D) Those who car pool with other families

35. What is the percentage of the students surveyed who don't need parents to drive them to school or take them home at all?

   A) 15%

   B) 25%

   C) 45%

   D) 60%

Part B: Reading Selections

Note: In this part of the exam, you may move back and forth among all the questions.

Reading Part Directions: Reading Selections (25%, 60 minutes)

You will read several selections in Chinese. Each selection is accompanied by a number of questions in English. For each question, choose the response that is best according to the selection. After you have decided which of the suggested answers is best, COMPLETELY fill in the corresponding circle on the answer sheet. Chinese tests appear here in both traditional and simplified characters. You will have 60 minutes to answer all questions.

YOU WILL NOW BEGIN THIS PART.

Read this e-mail.

(Traditional characters)

發件人：星星高中校長辦公室
收件人：全校家長
郵件主題：開學前注意事項
發件日期：8月1日
附件：1. 免費午餐申請表
　　　2. 緊急聯絡表

各位家長：

　　學校定於9月1日開學，開學之前，有些重要事項希望家長注意。附件中有兩份表格：一份是免費午餐申請表，如果您的孩子符合學校提供免費午餐的條件，您可以填表申請；另一份是緊急聯絡表，請您在表格上填寫三個親朋好友的名字、住址和聯絡方式，除了電郵和手機號碼之外，最重要的是他們的電話號碼及您的簽名。兩份表格必須在開學後兩個星期內交給校長秘書王小姐。如果您不用申請免費午餐，則只需提交緊急聯絡表。謝謝您的支持與合作！

　　祝您暑期愉快！

　　　　　　　　　　　　　　　　　　　　　　　　星星高中校長辦公室

(Simplified characters)

发件人：星星高中校长办公室
收件人：全校家长
邮件主题：开学前注意事项
发件日期：8月1日
附件：1. 免费午餐申请表
　　　2. 紧急联络表

各位家长：

　　学校定于9月1日开学，开学之前，有些重要事项希望家长注意。附件中有两份表格：一份是免费午餐申请表，如果您的孩子符合学校提供免费午餐的条件，您可以填表申请；另一份是紧急联络表，请您在表格上填写三个亲朋好友的名字、住址和联络方式，除了电邮和手机号码之外，最重要的是他们的电话号码及您的签名。两份表格必须在开学后两个星期内交给校长秘书王小姐。如果您不用申请免费午餐，则只需提交紧急联络表。谢谢您的支持与合作！

　　祝您暑期愉快！

　　　　　　　　　　　　　　　　　　　　　　　　星星高中校长办公室

1. How long do the parents have to fill out and turn in the forms after the e-mail is sent?

    A) One month

    B) Two weeks

    C) One month and two weeks

    D) Two months

2. Where can the parents get the forms?

    A) From Miss Wang of the principal's office

    B) From the students, as the forms have been sent home with the students

    C) From the principal

    D) From the e-mail attachment

3. One of the two forms is

    A) for lunch card purchase

    B) for free lunch application

    C) for picnic signup

    D) for homework buddy signup

4. Of the two forms, the parents are informed that

    A) both have to be turned in

    B) only one must be turned in

    C) neither one has to be turned in

    D) neither one requires a parent's signature

5. Which of the following statements is FALSE?

    A) The emergency card requires parents' contact information.

    B) The emergency card asks for the emergency contacts' telephone numbers.

    C) The emergency card asks for the emergency contacts' e-mail addresses.

    D) The emergency card requires the emergency contacts' cell phone numbers.

Read this public sign.

(Traditional characters)

如厠後請沖水，
給自己養成好習慣，
爲別人留下好環境。

(Simplified characters)

如厕后请冲水，
给自己养成好习惯，
为别人留下好环境。

6. Where would this sign most likely appear?

   A) In the classroom

   B) In front of a drinking fountain

   C) In the restroom

   D) On the deck of a swimming pool

7. The purpose of this sign is to

   A) keep the swimming pool clean

   B) have a nice environment for the students to study

   C) be sure that students do not waste water

   D) assure that the toilet is properly flushed after use

Read this public sign.

(Traditional characters)

施工重地
行人止步

(Simplified characters)

施工重地
行人止步

8. Where would this sign most likely appear?

   A) Inside a library

   B) On a construction site

   C) In front of a factory

   D) On a crosswalk

9. What does the sign mean?

   A) No trespassing.

   B) No smoking.

   C) Be aware of pedestrians.

   D) No parking.

Read this note.

(Traditional characters)

小梅姐姐：

　　剛纔媽媽說阿姨明天要從舊金山開車來看我們，小表姐也會一道來。阿姨對去年我們一起去吃的那家烤鴨店還念念不忘，媽媽說既然她那麼喜歡，那明天晚上就再到那兒去給阿姨和小表姐接風吧。可是那家店客人很多，總是大排長龍，不預先訂位，恐怕到時候得等上一兩個小時。媽媽急著去開會，要我打電話去訂，可是他們現在沒人接電話。我得上課去了，只好麻煩你了。媽媽說爸爸公司明天晚上有個飯局，就只有我們和阿姨她們。桌子要訂六點半的，座位不要太靠近廚房或廁所。辛苦你了，晚上見。

小蘭
11月15日上午10點

(Simplified characters)

小梅姐姐：

　　刚才妈妈说阿姨明天要从旧金山开车来看我们，小表姐也会一道来。阿姨对去年我们一起去吃的那家烤鸭店还念念不忘，妈妈说既然她那么喜欢，那明天晚上就再到那儿去给阿姨和小表姐接风吧。可是那家店客人很多，总是大排长龙，不预先订位，恐怕到时候得等上一两个小时。妈妈急着去开会，要我打电话去订，可是他们现在没人接电话。我得上课去了，只好麻烦你了。妈妈说爸爸公司明天晚上有个饭局，就只有我们和阿姨她们。桌子要订六点半的，座位不要太靠近厨房或厕所。辛苦你了，晚上见。

小兰
11月15日上午10点

10. Who is coming to visit?

   A) Father's sister and her daughter

   B) Father's brother and his daughter

   C) Mother's sister and her daughter

   D) Mother's brother and his daughter

11. What kind of food are the family and their guests having tomorrow evening?

   A) Roast duck

   B) Hot pot

   C) Steak

   D) Salmon

12. From the note, we can infer that

   A) the family and their guests see each other very often

B) the family and their guests do not live far from each other

C) the guests came to see them last year

D) the guest's daughter is older than Xiaolan but younger than Xiaomei

13. Xiaolan would like Xiaomei to make reservations because

    A) Xiaomei is elder and knows how to handle it better

    B) Xiaolan has to go to a meeting right now

    C) without reservations, they may have to sit by the restroom

    D) Xiaolan does not have the time to make them now

14. Their mother would be happy if the reservation is

    A) for six people at six o'clock

    B) for six people at six-thirty and the table is far from the kitchen door

    C) for five people at six-thirty and the table is right in the center of the dining area

    D) for five people at six-thirty and as long as they don't have to wait, it doesn't matter where they would be sitting

15. Which of the following statements is TRUE?

    A) The family lives in San Francisco.

    B) Father works at a company.

    C) Mother does not have a job.

    D) Mother is not informed of father's schedule.

Read this advertisement.

(Traditional characters)   (Simplified characters)

自助餐	自助餐
新春期間（正月初一至初六）	新春期间（正月初一至初六）
特價優惠顧客	特价优惠顾客
成人一律八五折	成人一律八五折
兒童半價（五歲至十二歲，身高一米二以下）	儿童半价（五岁至十二岁，身高一米二以下）
五歲以下兒童免費	五岁以下儿童免费

16. What is this advertisement for?

    A) For a New Year special offer

B) For a Chinese New Year special offer

C) For a winter vacation special offer

D) For a summer vacation special offer

17. What type of food does this restaurant serve?

    A) Buffet

    B) Fast food

    C) A-la-carte

    D) Barbeque

18. How much discount does the promotion offer for adults?

    A) 85% off the regular price

    B) 50% off the regular price

    C) 25% off the regular price

    D) 15% off the regular price

Read this advertisement.

(Traditional characters)

(Simplified characters)

中年女性，應聘做全職家教、保姆及清潔工作	中年女性，应聘做全职家教、保姆及清洁工作
本人曾在國內從事中學教育工作多年，在美國有做數理家教、幼兒保姆及清潔的相關工作經驗。認真負責，極具愛心及耐心，有駕照，美國合法居留身份，能用英語進行日常會話。如有需要，亦可提供雇主電話以供參考。有意者請於每晚十點後打電話至（415）886-2773找顧女士。	本人曾在国内从事中学教育工作多年，在美国有做数理家教、幼儿保姆及清洁的相关工作经验。认真负责，极具爱心及耐心，有驾照，美国合法居留身份，能用英语进行日常会话。如有需要，亦可提供雇主电话以供参考。有意者请于每晚十点后打电话至（415）886-2773找顾女士。

19. What kind of work did the woman NOT express an interest in doing?

    A) Being a nanny

    B) Gardening

    C) Tutoring

    D) House cleaning

20. Which of the following statements is FALSE?

    A) The woman has taught at secondary schools in America.

    B) The woman has a driver's license.

    C) The woman is only interested in a full time job.

    D) The woman speaks adequate English.

21. Which of the following qualities did the woman NOT list in the advertisement?

    A) Responsible

    B) Patient

    C) Hardworking

    D) Honest

Read this letter.

(Traditional characters)

> 李老師：
>
> 　　學期即將結束，我要代表我們"我愛中文"社團向您道謝。這一年來，您每週四下午都來指導我們活動，對許多同學來說，一週中最有意思的就是我們社團活動的那兩個小時。您不但給我們提供了課外練習中文的機會，也傳授了很多中國傳統文化習俗的知識，還帶領我們吟唱中國古詩、製作剪紙、編中國結。逢年過節，我們在佈置得極有節日氣氛的教室裡，品嚐餃子、元宵、粽子等，真讓人回味無窮。通過這樣的活動，我們無形中更熱愛漢語，也深深體會到中國文化的博大精深。李老師，我們衷心感謝您對我們長期的教導。
>
> 　　敬祝教安！
>
> 　　　　　　　　　　　　　　　　　　　　學生 陳亦文敬上
> 　　　　　　　　　　　　　　　　　　　　5月30日

(Simplified characters)

> 李老师：
>
> 　　学期即将结束，我要代表我们"我爱中文"社团向您道谢。这一年来，您每周四下午都来指导我们活动，对许多同学来说，一周中最有意思的就是我们社团活动的那两个小时。您不但给我们提供了课外练习中文的机会，也传授了很多中国传统文化习俗的知识，还带领我们吟唱中国古诗、制作剪纸、编中国结。逢年过节，我们在布置得极有节日气氛的教室里，品尝饺子、元宵、粽子等，真让人回味无穷。

通过这样的活动，我们无形中更热爱汉语，也深深体会到中国文化的博大精深。李老师，我们衷心感谢您对我们长期的教导。

敬祝教安！

学生 陈亦文敬上

5月30日

22. The student wrote this letter to Teacher Li

   A) to express her gratitude for teaching her Chinese language this past year

   B) to express her gratitude for sponsoring the Chinese club

   C) to ask her to be the sponsor for the Chinese club next year

   D) to ask her to come to an "I Love Chinese Language Club" end-of-the-year celebration

23. From the food mentioned in the letter, what holidays we may infer have been observed in the past year?

   A) Chinese New Year, the Dragon Boat Festival, and the Mid-Autumn Festival

   B) Chinese New Year, the Lantern Festival, and the Mid-Autumn Festival

   C) Chinese New Year, the Lantern Festival, and the Dragon Boat Festival

   D) The Lantern Festival, the Dragon Boat Festival, and the Mid-Autumn Festival

24. Which of the following activities is NOT mentioned in the letter?

   A) Chinese poetry chanting

   B) Chinese calligraphy

   C) Chinese paper cutting

   D) Chinese knot making

Read this article.

(Traditional characters)

公園該不該收門票

我最近參加了一場討論會，主題是"公園該不該收門票"。贊成收門票的學生認爲，有了門票收入，公園有專人管理，可以保持一定的整潔和安全，再說花木也會有人按時修剪、照顧，只要門票不要定得太高，一般老百姓都負擔得起。不贊成收門票的學生認爲，公園是公共場所，應該是免費的，再說爲了收門票，就要建圍墻、修大門，難免會影響市容。討論非常熱烈，但最後并沒有結論。不過，散場時有人做了一項調查，結果是贊成收門票的只有10%，不贊成的占了70%，有20%的學生沒有意見。

(Simplified characters)

公园该不该收门票

我最近参加了一场讨论会，主题是"公园该不该收门票"。赞成收门票的学生认为，有了门票收入，公园有专人管理，可以保持一定的整洁和安全，再说花木也会有人按时修剪、照顾，只要门票不要定得太高，一般老百姓都负担得起。不赞成收门票的学生认为，公园是公共场所，应该是免费的，再说为了收门票，就要建围墙、修大门，难免会影响市容。讨论非常热烈，但最后并没有结论。不过，散场时有人做了一项调查，结果是赞成收门票的只有10%，不赞成的占了70%，有20%的学生没有意见。

25. What was the forum about?

    A) How to keep the park clean

    B) Whether admission to the park should be free

    C) Where to build a fence in the park

    D) How to afford to hire gardeners to take care of the park regularly

26. Who attended this forum?

    A) Students

    B) The general public

    C) Students and teachers

    D) Students and parents

27. Some people believe that having revenues could enable the authority to

    A) build a fence and a secure main gate

    B) plant more trees and flowers in the park

    C) keep the park cleaner and safer

    D) promote the image of the city

28. What is the writer's attitude toward the issue being discussed in the forum?

    A) He agreed with the majority of the participants.

    B) He agreed with the minority of the participants.

    C) He did not agree with anyone.

    D) He did not express his personal view.

Read this poster.

(Traditional characters)

擁抱陽光　走向自然
歡迎踴躍參加野營活動
舉辦單位：學生會
地點：市郊快樂谷
活動日期：4月23日至25日（三天兩夜）
費用：¥75（需要申請補助者，可到課外活動小組辦公室辦理）
人數：60
報名地點：活動中心二樓206室學生會
報名時間：即日起，額滿為止

(Simplified characters)

拥抱阳光　走向自然
欢迎踊跃参加野营活动
举办单位：学生会
地点：市郊快乐谷
活动日期：4月23日至25日（三天两夜）
费用：¥75（需要申请补助者，可到课外活动小组办公室办理）
人数：60
报名地点：活动中心二楼206室学生会
报名时间：即日起，额满为止

29. This activity is for

    A) fundraising

    B) community service

    C) camping

    D) enrichment

30. When can the interested students apply for this activity?

    A) Immediately

    B) April 23rd

    C) April 25th

    D) No information is provided.

31. The role that the office for the extracurricular activities plays in this activity is to

    A) provide logistical support

    B) plan and sponsor the activity

    C) offer financial assistance to those who need it

    D) assure safety of the activity

Read this story.

(Traditional characters)

　　宋朝有個叫陳堯咨的人，擅長射箭，在當時舉世無雙，因此他對自己的射箭本領很是自負。有一天，陳堯咨在自家的菜園子裡練習射箭，有一個賣油的老頭兒正巧挑著擔子經過。他停了下來，放下擔子，斜著眼睛看陳堯咨射箭，久久都不離開。陳堯咨的射箭本領果然名不虛傳，射出的箭十有八九都射中靶心。賣油的老頭兒，仍是斜眼瞅著，只稍微點了一下頭。

　　陳堯咨見老頭兒似乎不把他射箭的本事放在眼裡，心裡有點兒惱火，就放下弓箭走過去問老頭兒說："你也懂得射箭嗎？難道你認為我的射技不夠精湛嗎？"老頭兒回答說："我覺得這也沒什麼特別了不起的，只不過你的手法嫻熟罷了。"陳堯咨非常惱怒，質問道："你怎麼敢如此輕視我的絕技！"老頭兒不慌不忙地說："我怎麼敢呢！我不過是從我多年倒油的經驗中懂得這個道理的。"

　　說完以後，就把一個葫蘆放在地上，又用一枚圓形方孔的銅錢蓋在葫蘆嘴上，然後用一個油勺從油桶裡舀了一滿勺的油，往蓋著銅錢的葫蘆嘴裡倒。只見那油慢慢地流進了葫蘆嘴。等油倒完了，銅錢竟然連一滴油都沒有沾上。賣油的老頭兒笑了笑，說道："我這也沒有什麼了不起的，純粹是手熟而已。"

　　陳堯咨聽了之後，笑著把賣油的老頭兒打發走了。

(Simplified characters)

　　宋朝有个叫陈尧咨的人，擅长射箭，在当时举世无双，因此他对自己的射箭本领很是自负。有一天，陈尧咨在自家的菜园子里练习射箭，有一个卖油的老头儿正巧挑着担子经过。他停了下来，放下担子，斜着眼睛看陈尧咨射箭，久久都不离开。陈尧咨的射箭本领果然名不虚传，射出的箭十有八九都射中靶心。卖油的老头儿，仍是斜眼瞅着，只稍微点了一下头。

　　陈尧咨见老头儿似乎不把他射箭的本事放在眼里，心里有点儿恼火，就放下弓箭走过去问老头儿说："你也懂得射箭吗？难道你认为我的射技不够精湛吗？"老头儿回答说："我觉得这也没什么特别了不起的，只不过你的手法娴熟罢了。"陈尧咨非常恼怒，质问道："你怎么敢如此轻视我的绝技！"老头儿不慌不忙地说："我怎么敢呢！我不过是从我多年倒油的经验中懂得这个道理的。"

　　说完以后，就把一个葫芦放在地上，又用一枚圆形方孔的铜钱盖在葫芦嘴上，然后用一个油勺从油桶里舀了一满勺的油，往盖着铜钱的葫芦嘴里倒。只见那油慢慢地流进了葫芦嘴。等油倒完了，铜钱竟然连一滴油都没有沾上。卖油的老头儿笑了笑，说道："我这也没有什么了不起的，纯粹是手熟而已。"

　　陈尧咨听了之后，笑着把卖油的老头儿打发走了。

32. What adjective best describes the archer's attitude toward his own archery skills?

   A) Modest

   B) Proud

   C) Insecure

   D) Ambitious

33. Which of the following statements is TRUE?

   A) The archer performed his skills for a large audience.

   B) The old man was a great archery master himself.

   C) The archer challenged the old man to prove his skills.

   D) The old man did not think the archer's skills were a big deal.

34. How did the archer react to the old man watching him perform archery?

   A) He did not pay attention to the old guy.

   B) He thought the old man showed contempt toward his skills.

   C) He wished he had not been disturbed by the old guy.

   D) He was afraid that the old man was better than he in archery.

35. The moral of the story is that

   A) in order to excel in anything, we need to practice over and over again

   B) one should always respect other people

   C) even among the oil vendors, there are great masters

   D) one should not show off one's own skills

END OF SECTION I.

YOU MAY REVIEW WORK IF THERE IS TIME LEFT.

DO NOT GO ON TO SECTION II UNTIL YOU ARE TOLD TO DO SO.

Section II: Free Response

Part A: Writing (Story Narration and E-mail Response)

Note: In this part of the exam, the student may NOT move back and forth among questions.

Writing Part Directions

You will be asked to perform two writing tasks in Chinese. In each case, you will be asked to write for a specific purpose and to a specific person. You should write in as complete and as culturally appropriate a manner as possible, taking into account the purpose and the person described.

Presentational Writing: Story Narration (15%, 15 minutes)

The four pictures present a story. Imagine you are writing the story to a friend. Narrate a complete story as suggested by the pictures. Give your story a beginning, a middle, and an end.

Interpersonal Writing: E-mail Response (10%, 15 minutes)

Read this e-mail from a friend and then type a response.

(Traditional characters)

發件人：林文
郵件主題：打工看孩子

　　我們家隔壁搬來了一戶人家，有兩個男孩兒，一個四歲，一個六歲。他們的父母晚上常常不在家，讓我一個星期去三個晚上幫他們照看小孩兒，七點到十一點。我很想掙這個錢，可又擔心會影響學習。請你告訴我你的經驗以及對一邊學習一邊打工的看法。謝謝。

(Simplified characters)

发件人：林文
邮件主题：打工看孩子

　　我们家隔壁搬来了一户人家，有两个男孩儿，一个四岁，一个六岁。他们的父母晚上常常不在家，让我一个星期去三个晚上帮他们照看小孩儿，七点到十一点。我很想挣这个钱，可又担心会影响学习。请你告诉我你的经验以及对一边学习一边打工的看法。谢谢。

speaking

Part B: Speaking (Conversation and Cultural Presentation)

Note: In this part of the exam, you may NOT move back and forth among questions.

Speaking Part Directions: Conversation

You will participate in a simulated conversation. Each time it is your turn to speak, you will have 20 seconds to record. You should respond as fully and as appropriately as possible. There will be six times when it is your turn to speak.

Interpersonal Speaking: Conversation (10%, 4 minutes)

You will have a conversation with Chen Chong, the community service director, about your applying for volunteering to teach English to the new immigrant Chinese students at the local elementary schools.

Speaking Question 1 of 7

1. Record your answer. (20 seconds)

Speaking Question 2 of 7

2. Record your answer. (20 seconds)

Speaking Question 3 of 7

3. Record your answer. (20 seconds)

Speaking Question 4 of 7

4. Record your answer. (20 seconds)

Speaking Question 5 of 7

5. Record your answer. (20 seconds)

Speaking Question 6 of 7

6. Record your answer. (20 seconds)

Speaking Part Directions: Cultural Presentation

You will be asked to speak in Chinese on a specific topic. Imagine you are making an oral presentation to your Chinese class. First, you will read and hear the topic for your presentation. You will have 4 minutes to prepare your presentation. Then you will have 2 minutes to record your presentation. Your presentation should be as complete as possible.

Presentational Speaking: Cultural Presentation (15%, 7 minutes)

Speaking Question 7 of 7

7. Choose ONE "成语故事"（成语故事）, such as "守株待兔"（守株待兔）"画龙点睛"（畫龍點睛）"自相矛盾"（自相矛盾）"亡羊补牢"（亡羊補牢）"拔苗助长"（拔苗助長）"南辕北辙"（南轅北轍）"望梅止渴"（望梅止渴）"买椟还珠"（買櫝還珠）"夜郎自大"（夜郎自大）"滥竽充数"（濫竽充數）, etc.. In your presentation, describe the original story of the expression, what the expression means, and give an example to explain how the expression is used, and explain its significance.

You have four minutes to prepare your presentation. (240 seconds)

You have two minutes to record your presentation. (120 seconds)

YOU HAVE FINISHED THIS PART OF THE EXAM.

END OF EXAM

AP Chinese Language and Culture Test 7

listening

Section I: Multiple Choice

Part A: Listening (Rejoinders and Listening Selections)

Listening Part Directions

You will answer two types of questions: rejoinders and questions based on listening selections.

For all tasks, you will have a specific amount of response time. When the response time has ended, you will automatically go on to the nest question. You cannot return to previous questions.

Listening Part Directions: Rejoinders (10%, 10 minutes)

You will hear several short conversations or parts of conversations followed by four choices, designated A, B, C, and D. Choose the one that continues or completes the conversation in a logical and culturally appropriate manner. After you have decided which of the suggested answers is best, COMPLETELY fill in the corresponding circle on the answer sheet. You will have 5 seconds to answer each question.

YOU WILL NOW BEGIN THIS PART.

1. Mark your answer on your answer sheet.
2. Mark your answer on your answer sheet.
3. Mark your answer on your answer sheet.
4. Mark your answer on your answer sheet.
5. Mark your answer on your answer sheet.
6. Mark your answer on your answer sheet.
7. Mark your answer on your answer sheet.
8. Mark your answer on your answer sheet.
9. Mark your answer on your answer sheet.
10. Mark your answer on your answer sheet.
11. Mark your answer on your answer sheet.
12. Mark your answer on your answer sheet.
13. Mark your answer on your answer sheet.
14. Mark your answer on your answer sheet.
15. Mark your answer on your answer sheet.

Listening Part Directions: Listening Selections (15%, 10 minutes)

You will listen to several selections in Chinese. For each selection, you will be told whether it will be played once or twice. You may take notes as you listen. Your notes will not be graded. After listening to each selection, you will see questions in English. For each question, choose the response that is best according to the selection. You will have 12 seconds to answer each question.

YOU WILL NOW BEGIN THIS PART.

Selection 1: Announcement (Selection plays two times.)

16. Where was the sports bag found?

    A) In the classroom

    B) On the sport field

    C) In the school dining hall

    D) In the auditorium

17. Which of the following items was NOT in the bag?

    A) Cash

    B) Calculator

    C) Cellphone

    D) Sports shoes

18. Where can the student get the lost items back?

    A) The school office

    B) Lost and Found

    C) The principal's office

    D) The teachers' office

Selection 2: Voice Message (Selection plays two times.)

19. Li Shuaishuai's mother called the teacher because

    A) she had a few questions to ask

    B) she wanted to know the teacher's phone number

    C) she could attend the meeting

    D) her husband would give the speech instead

20. The topic of the meeting is

    A) how to improve the quality of education

    B) the Chinese culture

    C) the Chinese immigrant experience

    D) the experience of educating children

21. Which of the following statements is NOT TRUE?

    A) The mom does not know how much time she has for her presentation.

    B) The mom wants to know if the presentation should be in Chinese or English.

    C) The mom wonders if the students will like her presentation.

    D) The mom is not sure if she needs a written copy of her speech for students.

Selection 3: Conversation (Selection plays one time.)

22. The girl's classmate called her house because he wants to

    A) tell the girl that he is going to the party

    B) tell her that he will give her a ride to the party

    C) know if her parents would allow her to go with him

    D) know if she has the right dress to wear

23. The girl's younger brother wants to go to the party because

    A) he likes dancing

    B) he wants to go to school to have fun with his friends

    C) he is scared of being home alone

    D) he is bored by himself at home

24. Why was the girl's younger brother questioning the reason for having a party?

    A) There were no sports events.

    B) It was not a holiday or a weekend.

    C) It was not graduation day.

    D) It was not someone's birthday.

25. The girl's parents cannot send her to the party because

    A) they were at their friend's house

    B) they both work at night

    C) they were on vacation in China

    D) they were on a business trip in Shanghai

Selection 4: Instructions (Selection plays one time.)

26. Where should students go for registration?

    A) The auditorium

    B) The administration building

    C) The library

    D) The cafeteria

27. How do students pay for their tuition?

    A) By credit card

    B) To pay upfront at registration

    C) By campus card

    D) By personal check

28. When should students purchase their textbooks?

    A) Before registration

    B) After registration

    C) On the first day of class

    D) The first week of school

29. What is in the packet that students receive upon registration?

    A) A calendar

    B) A yearbook

    C) Physical exam form

    D) School planner

30. Which meeting do the students NOT have to attend?

    A) Opening ceremony

    B) Class meeting

    C) Freshman orientation meeting

    D) Course introductions

Selection 5: Report (Selection plays one time.)

31. What percentage of the students turned in their survey?

    A) 85%

    B) 90%

    C) 87%

    D) 76%

32. What is the percentage of students who understand the importance of environmental protection?

   A) 67%

   B) 76%

   C) 85%

   D) 87%

33. 18% of the students

   A) think they should do more to protect the environment

   B) did not participate in the survey

   C) are motivated to protect the environment

   D) do not care about the environment

34. How many students in total participated in this survey?

   A) 120

   B) 210

   C) 2,000

   D) 200

35. The majority of the students think

   A) they should correct people's bad behavior in public

   B) they only need to watch their own behavior

   C) they would help pick up waste that other people throw away

   D) it is other people's job to keep the environment clean

Part B: Reading Selections

Note: In this part of the exam, you may move back and forth among all the questions.

> **Reading Part Directions: Reading Selections (25%, 60 minutes)**
>
> You will read several selections in Chinese. Each selection is accompanied by a number of questions in English. For each question, choose the response that is best according to the selection. After you have decided which of the suggested answers is best, COMPLETELY fill in the corresponding circle on the answer sheet. Chinese tests appear here in both traditional and simplified characters. You will have 60 minutes to answer all questions.
>
> YOU WILL NOW BEGIN THIS PART.

Read this e-mail.

(Traditional characters)

發件人：楊東
收件人：小明
郵件主題：全國民族音樂大賽門票

小明：

　　你好！我已經幫你買到了在北京舉辦的全國民族音樂大賽首場比賽的門票。門票特別難買，因爲這個比賽每隔一年纔舉辦一次。比賽在中國國家大劇院舉行，看演出那天你可以早點兒去，先參觀一下大劇院。比賽包括民間歌曲、民間歌舞音樂、民間器樂、民間說唱音樂和民間戲曲音樂五個部分，大賽持續七天。多位國家著名的藝術家會同臺獻藝。由於各大媒體的積極宣傳報道，所有門票早已售完。

　　知道你們全家都能來北京，我父母別提多高興了！他們已經把客房準備好了。我家現在住的房子是兩年前纔搬進來的，你們還沒來過呢。這兒的環境非常好，離市中心也不算太遠，生活非常方便。從我們家出門走兩分鐘，就有地鐵站。地鐵四通八達，幾乎可到達任何你要去的地方。從早晨4點到晚上12點，每15分鐘就有一班地鐵，比自己開車或坐出租車都方便。盼望你們的到來，并請代我向你父母和姐姐問好。

　　　　　　　　　　　　　　　　　　　　　　　　　　　　楊東

(Simplified characters)

发件人：杨东
收件人：小明
邮件主题：全国民族音乐大赛门票

小明：

　　你好！我已经帮你买到了在北京举办的全国民族音乐大赛首场比赛的门票。门票特别难买，因为这个比赛每隔一年才举办一次。比赛在中国国家大剧院举行，看演出那天你可以早点儿去，先参观一下大剧院。比赛包括民间歌曲、民间歌舞音乐、民间器乐、民间说唱音乐和民间戏曲音乐五个部分，大赛持续七天。多位国家著名的艺术家会同台献艺。由于各大媒体的积极宣传报道，所有门票早已售完。

　　知道你们全家都能来北京，我父母别提多高兴了！他们已经把客房准备好了。我家现在住的房子是两年前才搬进来的，你们还没来过呢。这儿的环境非常好，离市中心也不算太远，生活非常方便。从我们家出门走两分钟，就有地铁站。地铁四通八达，几乎可到达任何你要去的地方。从早晨4点到晚上12点，每15分钟就有一班地铁，比自己开车或坐出租车都方便。盼望你们的到来，并请代我向你父母和姐姐问好。

杨东

1. The tickets that Yang Dong bought for Xiaoming are for

    A) the opening performance

    B) the folk instrumental music competition

    C) the final performance

    D) the folk opera music competition

2. The best way to get to the National Center for the Performing Arts is

    A) by walking

    B) by car

    C) by taxi

    D) by subway

3. Where does Yang Dong's family live in Beijing?

    A) In the suburbs

    B) In the center of the city

    C) Near the center of the city

    D) Right next to Chinese National Center for the Performing Arts

4. How frequently does the Bart run?

    A) Every 15 minutes, from 4:00 pm to 12:00 am

    B) Every 15 minutes, from 4:00 am to 12:00 am

    C) Every 15 minutes, from 4:00 am to 12:00 pm

    D) Every 5 minutes, from 4:00 am to 12:00 am

5. Which of the following statements is FALSE according to this e-mail?

    A) Yang Dong's family has lived in this place for a long time.

    B) Xiaoming's family will come to Beijing.

    C) Yang Dong's house is in a good area.

    D) Xiaoming is going to Yang Dong's house for the first time.

Read this advertisement.

(Traditional characters)

萬達計算機學校招生通告

萬達計算機學校擁有一流的教學環境和實習基地。萬達師資優秀，教風嚴謹，設備先進，并提供校內住宿及用餐。學校還將給合格的畢業生頒發國家計算機技師證書，并由學校推薦、協助就業。

一、教學內容：
    1. 電腦基礎知識
    2. CAD繪圖及三維動畫
    3. 多媒體應用技術
    4. 數據庫管理
    5. C語言程序設計
    6. 電腦維修

二、學制：全日制班4個月，夜校班10個月，隔日制班8個月

三、招收條件：面向全國招收初中及以上文化水平的各界人士，年齡不限

四、收費標準：學費、教材費、上機實習費，共計13,500元；住宿費另算

五、報名時間及方式：即日起至7月15日，可登錄www.wanda.com網站，或電（688）456-7788報名

六、開學時間：8月28日

另：即日起報名的前40名學生，可享有500元的折扣。

(Simplified characters)

万达计算机学校招生通告

万达计算机学校拥有一流的教学环境和实习基地。万达师资优秀，教风严谨，设备先进，并提供校内住宿及用餐。学校还将给合格的毕业生颁发国家计算机技师证书，并由学校推荐、协助就业。

一、教学内容：
    1. 电脑基础知识
    2. CAD绘图及三维动画
    3. 多媒体应用技术
    4. 数据库管理
    5. C语言程序设计
    6. 电脑维修

> 二、学制：全日制班4个月，夜校班10个月，隔日制班8个月
>
> 三、招收条件：面向全国招收初中及以上文化水平的各界人士，年龄不限
>
> 四、收费标准：学费、教材费、上机实习费，共计13,500元；住宿费另算
>
> 五、报名时间及方式：即日起至7月15日，可登录www.wanda.com网站，或电（688）456-7788报名
>
> 六、开学时间：8月28日
>
> 另：即日起报名的前40名学生，可享有500元的折扣。

6. Which of the following courses does the school NOT teach?

    A) Introduction to computers

    B) Computer network

    C) Database management

    D) 3D animation

7. Which of the following expenses is NOT included in enrollment fee?

    A) Tuition

    B) Textbook

    C) Computer practice

    D) Room and board

8. Which of the following information is NOT mentioned in this advertisement?

    A) Full-time classes are 4 months long.

    B) Part-time classes are 8 months long.

    C) Evening classes are 10 months long.

    D) Summer classes are 8 weeks long.

9. According to the advertisement, which of the following statements is FALSE?

    A) There is a discount of ¥500 for students who enroll before August 28th, 2020.

    B) The school will recommend jobs for qualified students.

    C) The school will provide boarding.

    D) The enrollment fee is ¥13,500.

10. This program is open to anyone

    A) who has at least a high school diploma

    B) who has any kind of educational background

C) who has basic computer knowledge

D) who has at least a middle school education

Read this public sign.

(Traditional characters)　　　　　　　　(Simplified characters)

愛護公物，人人有責　　　　　　　　爱护公物，人人有责

11. What does the sign mean?

    A) Please keep away from this area.

    B) This is a public property.

    C) You will be fined for damaging this property.

    D) Everyone has the responsibility to take care of public property.

12. Where is this sign most likely seen?

    A) Near a private property

    B) At a residential area

    C) At a public park

    D) Inside a library

Read this public sign.

(Traditional characters)　　　　　　　　(Simplified characters)

溫馨提示：
步行健體、益腦、利心，
您不妨走走樓梯！

温馨提示：
步行健体、益脑、利心，
您不妨走走楼梯！

13. Where do you see this kind of sign?

    A) At a drug store

    B) At the gym

    C) Near an elevator

    D) In an airport

14. The purpose of the sign is to

    A) suggest this medicine is good for the heart

    B) warn people who have health problems not to use the stairs

C) warn that the stairs are not safe here

D) remind people of the benefit of taking the stairs

Read this article.

(Traditional characters)

中國武術

中國武術有著悠久的歷史，它不僅是中華文化的國粹，也在全世界享有盛名。武術一詞在歷史上有很多不同的名稱：戰國時期稱之爲"技擊"，漢代出現了"武藝"一詞，并延用到明末，清代初期纔出現了"武術"一詞，民國時稱"國術"，20世紀中期沿用清初的"武術"一詞至今。

首先，武術是指用武的技術。它是以踢、打、摔、拿、擊、刺等技擊動作爲主要內容，通過徒手或借助於器械的身體運動表現攻防格鬥的能力。其次，武術也是體育項目，它明顯區別於致人傷殘的實用技擊技術。

武術特指中國武術，也有廣義和狹義之分。從廣義上講，中國武術和中國功夫是一個意思。功夫是各種搏鬥技巧的統稱，像跆拳道、散打和摔跤等都可以叫作功夫。從狹義上講，中國武術只是指中國傳統的武術套路，包括太極、少林功等，而不包含摔跤和目前流行的散打。所以，確切地說，中國武術是中國功夫的一種。

(Simplified characters)

中国武术

中国武术有着悠久的历史，它不仅是中华文化的国粹，也在全世界享有盛名。武术一词在历史上有很多不同的名称：战国时期称之为"技击"，汉代出现了"武艺"一词，并延用到明末，清代初期才出现了"武术"一词，民国时称"国术"，20世纪中期沿用清初的"武术"一词至今。

首先，武术是指用武的技术。它是以踢、打、摔、拿、击、刺等技击动作为主要内容，通过徒手或借助于器械的身体运动表现攻防格斗的能力。其次，武术也是体育项目，它明显区别于致人伤残的实用技击技术。

武术特指中国武术，也有广义和狭义之分。从广义上讲，中国武术和中国功夫是一个意思。功夫是各种搏斗技巧的统称，像跆拳道、散打和摔跤等都可以叫作功夫。从狭义上讲，中国武术只是指中国传统的武术套路，包括太极、少林功等，而不包含摔跤和目前流行的散打。所以，确切地说，中国武术是中国功夫的一种。

15. The term "武术"（武術）began to be used during

    A) The Warring States Period

    B) The Han Dynasty

    C) The Ming Dynasty

    D) The Qing Dynasty

16. How many fighting styles do Martial Arts include?

    A) 3

    B) 4

    C) 5

    D) 6

17. Which sport does Chinese Martial Arts NOT include?

    A) Boxing

    B) Tai Chi

    C) Taekwondo

    D) Shao Lin Kungfu

18. Which of the following statements is TRUE?

    A) Martial Arts are only studied by men.

    B) Martial Arts were originally a synonym for Shao Lin Kungfu.

    C) Martial Arts are one type of Kungfu.

    D) Martial Arts are not considered a sport in China.

Read this announcement on a poster.

(Traditional characters)

喜報

新星高中：

　　貴校學子在2021年高考中取得優異成績，并將在九月正式進入西南科技大學學習。特發喜報，感謝貴校向我校不斷輸送優秀學子。

　　西南科技大學是有著悠久歷史的理工科名校。我們希望與貴校繼續加強交流互動，不斷探索高校與高中的銜接貫通培養體系，助力優秀學子成長、成才，共同爲國家輸送更多優秀人才。預祝貴校2022年高考再創佳績！

　　2021年貴校本科錄取名單：

　　1. 牛　進—計算機科學與技術專業

2. 柳　青—通信工程專業

3. 王心月—土木工程專業

4. 張遠航—電氣工程專業

(Simplified characters)

喜报

新星高中：

贵校学子在2021年高考中取得优异成绩，并将在九月正式进入西南科技大学学习。特发喜报，感谢贵校向我校不断输送优秀学子。

西南科技大学是有着悠久历史的理工科名校。我们希望与贵校继续加强交流互动，不断探索高校与高中的衔接贯通培养体系，助力优秀学子成长、成才，共同为国家输送更多优秀人才。预祝贵校2022年高考再创佳绩！

2021年贵校本科录取名单：

1. 牛　进—计算机科学与技术专业

2. 柳　青—通信工程专业

3. 王心月—土木工程专业

4. 张远航—电气工程专业

19. What is this notice for?

    A) Students' college entrance exam result

    B) Letter of appreciation from a college to a high school

    C) To announce the arrival of the new students

    D) A list of high scoring students

20. What kind of th college is it?

    A) A liberal arts college

    B) A college of architecture

    C) A college of engineering

    D) A college of science and technology

21. What is Xinyue Wang going to study in college?

    A) Environmental engineering

    B) Civil Engineering

    C) Environmental Sustainability

    D) Environmental science

Read this story.

(Traditional characters)

> 相傳在宋國，有一個農夫種了幾畝地，每天到地裡去幹活兒。遇到好年景，也不過勉強吃飽穿暖，一遇災荒，可就要忍饑挨餓了。他想過好的生活，但膽子小，人又懶，總想碰上送上門來的意外之財。
>
> 奇跡終於發生了。有一天早上，他正在田裡耕地，看到周圍有人在打獵。突然，他看到一隻受驚的兔子箭一般地飛奔過來，不偏不倚，一頭撞在他田邊的大樹上，蹬了蹬腿就死了。農夫趕緊把兔子撿起來，拎回家，當天晚上他就美美地飽餐了一頓。從此，他就不再種地，一天到晚等在那棵神奇的樹下，等著奇跡再次出現。等啊等，幾天過去了，沒有兔子撞過來，可是他還是不死心，一直等到地裡的草長得比莊稼都高了，還是什麼也沒等到。因爲地沒耕，全荒了，最後什麼收成也沒有。
>
> "守株待兔"的成語就是從這個故事來的。人們常用它來比喻不想努力而希望獲得成功的僥倖心理。

(Simplified characters)

> 相传在宋国，有一个农夫种了几亩地，每天到地里去干活儿。遇到好年景，也不过勉强吃饱穿暖，一遇灾荒，可就要忍饥挨饿了。他想过好的生活，但胆子小，人又懒，总想碰上送上門来的意外之财。
>
> 奇迹终于发生了。有一天早上，他正在田里耕地，看到周围有人在打猎。突然，他看到一只受惊的兔子箭一般地飞奔过来，不偏不倚，一头撞在他田边的大树上，蹬了蹬腿就死了。农夫赶紧把兔子捡起来，拎回家，当天晚上他就美美地饱餐了一顿。从此，他就不再种地，一天到晚等在那棵神奇的树下，等着奇迹再次出现。等啊等，几天过去了，没有兔子撞过来，可是他还是不死心，一直等到地里的草长得比庄稼都高了，还是什么也没等到。因为地没耕，全荒了，最后什么收成也没有。
>
> "守株待兔"的成语就是从这个故事来的。人们常用它来比喻不想努力而希望获得成功的侥幸心理。

22. Which statement is TRUE about the farmer?

   A) He was lazy and often dreamed of having unexpected blessings.

   B) He was a farmer during Qing Dynasty.

   C) He worked hard and brought his family a comfortable life.

   D) He was known for being a brave man.

23. What happened the day he was working in the fields?

    A) He saw a dead bird in front of him.

    B) He saw a dead person under a tree.

    C) A terrified rabbit fled over and hit a tree.

    D) A gunshot startled him.

24. What did the farmer do with the hunted game?

    A) He took it home and tried to rescue it.

    B) He cooked and ate it.

    C) He shared the game with his neighbors.

    D) He kept it in the backyard.

25. What is NOT TRUE about the farmer after that incident?

    A) He waited under the tree everyday hoping for a miracle.

    B) He was not going to farm anymore.

    C) His wife was disappointed in him.

    D) The grains were covered with weeds.

26. What does this proverb tell people?

    A) It is better to be a hunter than a farmer.

    B) Dreams do not come true without hard work.

    C) A man needs to be brave in the face of danger.

    D) Always share your fortune with your friends.

Read this letter.

(Traditional characters)

親愛的媽媽：

　　您好！昨天我和妹妹給爸爸慶祝他的五十歲生日。您外出學習不在家，我和妹妹心裡有些發慌，不知道用什麼方法給爸爸過生日最酷，給他送什麼樣的禮物最好。幾天前，我們倆商量爭論了很久，最後，我們想出了一個頂好頂妙的辦法，那就是給爸爸獻上我們各自剛剛在學校得到的優秀學生獎狀。

　　昨天，我跟妹妹把獎狀包好，高高興興地給了爸爸。爸爸拿過獎狀，仔細地看著，笑得合不攏嘴，然後把我倆拉到他的懷裡，高興地說："好孩子，你們最懂得爸爸的心，你們的優異成績就是給爸爸最好的禮物！"聽了爸爸的話我們也很開心，覺得爸爸是那麼的親切。後面的事就別提了！我和妹妹給爸爸包的餃子，因爲放的時間太長了，全都粘到一起了，結果煮成了一鍋片兒湯。您猜爸爸怎麽説？"沒問題，等媽媽回來時，再請我一頓吧！"媽媽，您可千萬別忘了請爸爸吃生日餐，反正我們已經替您答應了。

祝您學習順利！早日回家！

女兒 麗麗敬上
8月6日

(Simplified characters)

亲爱的妈妈：

您好！昨天我和妹妹给爸爸庆祝他的五十岁生日。您外出学习不在家，我和妹妹心里有些发慌，不知道用什么方法给爸爸过生日最酷，给他送什么样的礼物最好。几天前，我们俩商量争论了很久，最后，我们想出了一个顶好顶妙的办法，那就是给爸爸献上我们各自刚刚在学校得到的优秀学生奖状。

昨天，我跟妹妹把奖状包好，高高兴兴地给了爸爸。爸爸拿过奖状，仔细地看着，笑得合不拢嘴，然后把我俩拉到他的怀里，高兴地说："好孩子，你们最懂得爸爸的心，你们的优异成绩就是给爸爸最好的礼物！"听了爸爸的话我们也很开心，觉得爸爸是那么的亲切。后面的事就别提了！我和妹妹给爸爸包的饺子，因为放的时间太长了，全都粘到一起了，结果煮成了一锅片儿汤。您猜爸爸怎么说？"没问题，等妈妈回来时，再请我一顿吧！"妈妈，您可千万别忘了请爸爸吃生日餐，反正我们已经替您答应了。

祝您学习顺利！早日回家！

女儿 丽丽敬上
8月6日

27. Why did Lili write the letter?

   A) She did not know how to celebrate her father's birthday.

   B) She and her sister gave their dad a wonderful birthday gift.

   C) To tell her mother to come home early

   D) To tell her mom that she got good grades this semester

28. What Lili and her younger sister gave to their father was

   A) school report cards

   B) their graduation photos

C) gifts they bought

D) an award for academic excellence

29. Lili asked her mom to take her father out to dinner because

A) the meal Lili and her sister made was too simple

B) her mom missed the birthday celebration

C) Lili messed up the birthday meal

D) Lili does not have her enough money

30. Why did Lili feel uncertain about what to do for her father's birthday?

A) Her father is a picky person.

B) Her father doesn't care for her academic performance.

C) She does not have experience in organizing a party.

D) She is unsure who will come to the celebration.

Read this note.

(Traditional characters)

> 欣怡：
>
> 　　這個週末，遠東師範大學畢業生要自發組織一個畢業生舊物大集，就是把用不著的書本和一些生活用品集中在一起，互換或廉價甩賣。每年畢業生要離開母校時都會有類似的集市，但今年規模最大。聽說那些外地的學生很多東西帶不回家，就賣得非常便宜。你要是有興趣，咱們可以一起去，反正不遠，騎車去就行。我手上有他們的廣告，上面說"無論您是初中生、高中生，還是大學生，只要有一些閒置物品，希望通過這樣一個平臺以物換物或低價轉讓，都可以報名參加"。怎麼樣，想不想去湊湊熱鬧？咱們可以連買帶賣，一舉兩得。快點兒告訴我，我都等不及了，想去的話，我們得把要賣的東西找一找。我有些樣子過時的衣服，還有一些舊電器可以拿去試試。等你的信兒！
>
> 　　　　　　　　　　　　　　　　　　　　　　　　　玉娟
> 　　　　　　　　　　　　　　　　　　　　　　　　　6月28日下午4點半

(Simplified characters)

> 欣怡：
>
> 　　这个周末，远东师范大学毕业生要自发组织一个毕业生旧物大集，就是把用不着的书本和一些生活用品集中在一起，互换或廉价甩卖。每年毕业生要离开母校时

都会有类似的集市，但今年规模最大。听说那些外地的学生很多东西带不回家，就卖得非常便宜。你要是有兴趣，咱们可以一起去，反正不远，骑车去就行。我手上有他们的广告，上面说"无论您是初中生、高中生，还是大学生，只要有一些闲置物品，希望通过这样一个平台以物换物或低价转让，都可以报名参加"。怎么样，想不想去凑凑热闹？咱们可以连买带卖，一举两得。快点儿告诉我，我都等不及了，想去的话，我们得把要卖的东西找一找。我有些样子过时的衣服，还有一些旧电器可以拿去试试。等你的信儿！

玉娟

6月28日下午4点半

31. Which of the following statements is TRUE?

A) You can only sell the items on this market.

B) This is not the first time a market like this has been organized.

C) To register for the event, you must be a student at the university.

D) The event is organized by a teachers' university.

32. Which of the following statements is FALSE?

A) Yujuan has some out-of-fashion clothes to sell.

B) Yujuan is planning to buy and sell things.

C) Yujuan will drive to the event.

D) Yujuan will bring her used electronics to the market.

Read this article.

(Traditional characters)

讀書報告

我最近讀了一本由蔡穎卿寫的關於家庭教育的書，書名叫《媽媽是最初的老師》。這是一本我所看到的最好的親子教育書。書中講述一個母親在臺北、曼谷、新加坡三種不同的教育環境中養育兩個女兒的故事。

"孩子小的時候，幫他們扎根；孩子長大了，給他們翅膀。"這是身兼數職而永遠以家庭為中心的書中女主人公最喜歡的一句名言。二十年來，她努力在不斷變動的環境裡讓家安定下來，住在旅館時設法自己做飯，堅持讓孩子每天都能跟家人共享晚餐，因為她認為幸福蘊藏在隨手可得的日常生活裡。媽媽對女兒的親情和養育女兒的心路歷程都真切地表述在書中："你們像是快樂的日曆，每撕一頁，既不舍隨之而逝的喜怒哀樂，又期待即將到來的驚喜成長，媽媽珍惜女兒們的每一個腳印，仔細端詳並深深愛憐。"

我被深深地感動了，想到了自己的媽媽，媽媽的形象無比高大起來。的確，在我的心中，媽媽不僅僅是最初的老師，也是最好的老師，是世界上最親最偉大的人。

(Simplified characters)

读书报告

我最近读了一本由蔡颖卿写的关于家庭教育的书，书名叫《妈妈是最初的老师》。这是一本我所看到的最好的亲子教育书。书中讲述一个母亲在台北、曼谷、新加坡三种不同的教育环境中养育两个女儿的故事。

"孩子小的时候，帮他们扎根；孩子长大了，给他们翅膀。"这是身兼数职而永远以家庭为中心的书中女主人公最喜欢的一句名言。二十年来，她努力在不断变动的环境里让家安定下来，住在旅馆时设法自己做饭，坚持让孩子每天都能跟家人共享晚餐，因为她认为幸福蕴藏在随手可得的日常生活里。妈妈对女儿的亲情和养育女儿的心路历程都真切地表述在书中："你们像是快乐的日历，每撕一页，既不舍随之而逝的喜怒哀乐，又期待即将到来的惊喜成长，妈妈珍惜女儿们的每一个脚印，仔细端详并深深爱怜。"

我被深深地感动了，想到了自己的妈妈，妈妈的形象无比高大起来。的确，在我的心中，妈妈不仅仅是最初的老师，也是最好的老师，是世界上最亲最伟大的人。

33. What did the woman do to strengthen the bond between her and her daughters?

   A) She gave them everything they asked for.

   B) She bought books for them.

   C) She cooked and had family dinners with them whenever they could.

   D) She encouraged her daughters to work part time.

34. The woman believes that a mother should

   A) make sure her children eat well

   B) force her children to have dinner with the family

   C) foster her children well when they are young

   D) accept that children grow up and move on eventually

35. What is the writer's attitude towards the issue discussed in the book?

   A) A mother should be highly regarded.

   B) All mothers are similar to the character in the book.

   C) She recalled her mom was a tall woman.

   D) Each mother has her own nurturing style.

END OF SECTION I
YOU MAY REVIEW WORK IF THERE IS TIME LEFT.
DO NOT GO ON TO SECTION II UNTIL YOU ARE TOLD TO DO SO.

Section II: Free Response
Part A: Writing (Story Narration and E-mail Response)

Note: In this part of the exam, the student may NOT move back and forth among questions.

Writing Part Directions

You will be asked to perform two writing tasks in Chinese. In each case, you will be asked to write for a specific purpose and to a specific person. You should write in as complete and as culturally appropriate a manner as possible, taking into account the purpose and the person described.

Presentational Writing: Story Narration (15%, 15 minutes)

The four pictures present a story. Imagine you are writing the story to a friend. Narrate a complete story as suggested by the pictures. Give your story a beginning, a middle, and an end.

Interpersonal Writing: E-mail Response (10%, 15 minutes)

Read the e-mail from someone and then type a response inside the box below.

(Traditional characters)

发件人：高健
郵件主題：關於女朋友

表哥：

　　你好！有件事想告訴你，但是請你暫時替我保密，我有女朋友了。她人長得漂亮，也很聰明，學習又好，我們很談得來。我最近夜裡常常睡不好覺，總是想著她，白天上課老打瞌睡。老師總盯著我，我一睡覺，他就提問我，同學們也常開我玩笑。我還沒敢告訴我父母，因為我知道他們肯定不會同意我在高中交女朋友。我現在心裡很矛盾，既不想讓我父母生氣，又不想結束這個關係。您是過來人，在這方面有什麼高招可以指導一下？盼速回信！

(Simplified characters)

发件人：高健
邮件主题：关于女朋友

表哥：

　　你好！有件事想告诉你，但是请你暂时替我保密，我有女朋友了。她人长得漂亮，也很聪明，学习又好，我们很谈得来。我最近夜里常常睡不好觉，总是想着她，白天上课老打瞌睡。老师总盯着我，我一睡觉，他就提问我，同学们也常开我玩笑。我还没敢告诉我父母，因为我知道他们肯定不会同意我在高中交女朋友。我现在心里很矛盾，既不想让我父母生气，又不想结束这个关系。您是过来人，在这方面有什么高招可以指导一下？盼速回信！

Part B: Speaking (Conversation and Cultural Presentation)

Note: In this part of the exam, you may NOT move back and forth among questions.

speaking

Speaking Part Directions: Conversation

You will participate in a simulated conversation. Each time it is your turn to speak, you will have 20 seconds to record. You should respond as fully and as appropriately as possible. There will be six times when it is your turn to speak.

Interpersonal Speaking: Conversation (10%, 4 minutes)

You will have a conversation with Xiaoliang, a Chinese student you met for the first time at a summer program in China, about American schools.

Speaking Question 1 of 7

1. Record your answer. (20 seconds)

Speaking Question 2 of 7

2. Record your answer. (20 seconds)

Speaking Question 3 of 7

3. Record your answer. (20 seconds)

Speaking Question 4 of 7

4. Record your answer. (20 seconds)

Speaking Question 5 of 7

5. Record your answer. (20 seconds)

Speaking Question 6 of 7

6. Record your answer. (20 seconds)

Speaking Part Directions: Cultural Presentation

You will be asked to speak in Chinese on a specific topic. Imagine you are making an oral presentation to your Chinese class. First, you will read and hear the topic for your presentation. You will have 4 minutes to prepare your presentation. Then you will have 2 minutes to record your presentation. Your presentation should be as complete as possible.

Presentational Speaking: Cultural Presentation (15%, 7 minutes)

Speaking Question 7 of 7

7. Please describe the culinary diversity in China in terms of the various food styles and geographic regions. Choose ONE specific culinary style, and talk about its popular dishes, commonly used ingredients, and unique cooking techniques, and explain its significance.

You have four minutes to prepare your presentation. (240 seconds)

You have two minutes to record your presentation. (120 seconds)

YOU HAVE FINISHED THIS PART OF THE EXAM.
END OF EXAM

AP Chinese Language and Culture Test 8

listening

Section I: Multiple Choice

Part A: Listening (Rejoinders and Listening Selections)

Listening Part Directions

You will answer two types of questions: rejoinders and questions based on listening selections.

For all tasks, you will have a specific amount of response time. When the response time has ended, you will automatically go on to the nest question. You cannot return to previous questions.

Listening Part Directions: Rejoinders (10%, 10 minutes)

You will hear several short conversations or parts of conversations followed by four choices, designated A, B, C, and D. Choose the one that continues or completes the conversation in a logical and culturally appropriate manner. After you have decided which of the suggested answers is best, COMPLETELY fill in the corresponding circle on the answer sheet. You will have 5 seconds to answer each question.

YOU WILL NOW BEGIN THIS PART.

1. Mark your answer on your answer sheet.
2. Mark your answer on your answer sheet.
3. Mark your answer on your answer sheet.
4. Mark your answer on your answer sheet.
5. Mark your answer on your answer sheet.
6. Mark your answer on your answer sheet.
7. Mark your answer on your answer sheet.
8. Mark your answer on your answer sheet.
9. Mark your answer on your answer sheet.
10. Mark your answer on your answer sheet.
11. Mark your answer on your answer sheet.
12. Mark your answer on your answer sheet.
13. Mark your answer on your answer sheet.
14. Mark your answer on your answer sheet.
15. Mark your answer on your answer sheet.

Listening Part Directions: Listening Selections (15%, 10 minutes)

You will listen to several selections in Chinese. For each selection, you will be told whether it will be played once or twice. You may take notes as you listen. Your notes will not be graded. After listening to each selection, you will see questions in English. For each question, choose the response that is best according to the selection. You will have 12 seconds to answer each question.

YOU WILL NOW BEGIN THIS PART.

Selection 1: Announcement (Selection plays two times.)

16. How long will the exhibit be on?

    A) One day

    B) Two days

    C) Three days

    D) Two weeks

17. Where will the exhibit be?

    A) In the museum

    B) In the auditorium

    C) In the library

    D) In a large classroom

18. Which of the following statements is TRUE?

    A) The teacher assigned the students topics to work on at the beginning of the semester.

    B) The projects that the students worked on were group projects.

    C) The students chose topics related to their own culture to work on.

    D) The students worked on the exhibit for two weeks.

19. Which of the following methods did the students NOT employ?

    A) Writing articles

    B) Designing the display board

    C) Interviewing people

    D) Creating a powerpoint presentation

20. Which group of people can go to the exhibit tomorrow afternoon?

    A) Parents

    B) 9th graders

149

C) 10th graders

D) 12th graders

Selection 2: Conversation (Selection plays one time.)

21. The girl was in a bad mood, because

    A) her parents may get a divorce

    B) her mother left home

    C) her father is drunk all the time

    D) her mother is angry at her

22. The boy's parents are

    A) divorced

    B) separated

    C) back together again

    D) undergoing a divorce

23. Which of the following statements is FALSE?

    A) The boy's mother is even nicer to him now than before.

    B) The boy's father is an alcoholic.

    C) The girl wishes that she were not dragged into her parents' dispute.

    D) The boy tries to give the girl some advice.

24. Which of the following statements is TRUE?

    A) The girl always maintains a neutral stance toward her parents' quarreling.

    B) The girl would like her parents to vent their frustration and anger to her rather than to each other.

    C) The girl thinks her parents' problems are all her fault.

    D) The girl believes that if she tries hard she may be able to help her parents solve their problems.

Selection 3: Instructions (Selection plays one time.)

25. The woman asked her mother to take care of her fish because

    A) she will be traveling to Asia

    B) she will be doing research in Asia

    C) she will be going to Chicago to participate in a sports game

    D) she will be on an exchange program to Europe

26. The fish requires to be fed

   A) on demand

   B) three or four times a day

   C) three or four pellets a day

   D) three or four pellets each time

27. The fish tank needs to be cleaned with

   A) hot water

   B) tab water of room temperature

   C) specially treated water

   D) distilled water

28. Which of the following statements is TRUE?

   A) The woman thinks her fish is very happy.

   B) The woman thinks her mother is very happy.

   C) The woman thinks taking care of the fish is no trouble at all.

   D) The woman wants the fish to keep her mother company.

Selection 4: Voice Message (Selection plays two times.)

29. What did the girl suspect?

   A) Her friend turned off the cell phone.

   B) Her friend was in the English class when she called.

   C) Her friend was talking on the cell phone when she called.

   D) Her friend's cell phone was misplaced.

30. Which of the following statements is TRUE?

   A) The girl and her friend have to work on an English project together.

   B) The girl's mother made a dental appointment for her at four o'clock today.

   C) The girl would like her friend to go to her house at five o'clock today.

   D) The girl's friend does not like Chinese food at all.

31. The girl needs to see the dentist because

   A) she woke up with a toothache this morning

   B) her routine check-up is due

   C) her braces were a little too tight

   D) her braces were a little too loose

Selection 5: Report (Selection plays one time.)

32. How many students were in charge of the survey?

    A) Two students

    B) Three students

    C) Two groups of three students each

    D) Three groups of two students each

33. What is the percentage of the students who update their daily activities?

    A) 75%

    B) 60%

    C) 90%

    D) 10%

34. According the survey, which of the following statements is FALSE?

    A) Over half of the students would click "like" on their friends' postings.

    B) Cell phones are allowed in class.

    C) Every student has at least two social media accounts.

    D) Less than 10% of the students don't respond to their friends' postings on social media.

35. Which of the following statements is TRUE?

    A) The students feel guilty for checking social media in class.

    B) The students all have had experience posting or checking friends' postings on social media in class.

    C) The students feel that as long as the teacher is unaware of what they are doing it's alright to go on social media platforms in class.

    D) The students don't think that being active on social media platforms interferes with their concentration in class.

Part B: Reading Selections

Note: In this part of the exam, you may move back and forth among all the questions.

Reading Part Directions: Reading Selections (25%, 60 minutes)

You will read several selections in Chinese. Each selection is accompanied by a number of questions in English. For each question, choose the response that is best according to the selection. After you have decided which of the suggested answers is best, COMPLETELY fill in the corresponding circle on the answer sheet. Chinese tests appear here in both traditional and simplified characters. You will have 60 minutes to answer all questions.

YOU WILL NOW BEGIN THIS PART.

Read this e-mail.

(Traditional characters)

發件人：曼如

收件人：思敏

郵件主題：學校餐廳

發件日期：9月18日

　　告訴你一個天大的好消息，上個學期我不是告訴過你我們學校餐廳賣的東西難吃得要命嗎？經過我們再三的抗議，甚至集體拒吃，學校這個學期終於換了餐廳的老闆。這個新老闆的理念非常新穎，懂得怎麼經營。餐廳每天更換菜單，可供選擇的菜式增加了不少，不像以前那樣，不是千篇一律的三明治，就是漢堡包和熱狗等垃圾食品，真讓人倒胃口。另外，餐廳的蔬菜、水果，以至雞蛋、牛奶、肉類等，無一不是新鮮的有機食品，而且美味可口。雖然價錢比以前稍微貴了一點兒，但是無論是從營養、健康還是口味的角度來看，我們對新餐廳都十分滿意。你們學校的餐廳沒有我們的酷吧？光聽我描述就饞得流口水了吧？你哪天有空兒，非得來嚐嚐不可。

(Simplified characters)

发件人：曼如

收件人：思敏

邮件主题：学校餐厅

发件日期：9月18日

　　告诉你一个天大的好消息，上个学期我不是告诉过你我们学校餐厅卖的东西难吃得要命吗？经过我们再三的抗议，甚至集体拒吃，学校这个学期终于换了餐厅的老板。这个新老板的理念非常新颖，懂得怎么经营。餐厅每天更换菜单，可供选择的菜式增加了不少，不像以前那样，不是千篇一律的三明治，就是汉堡包和热狗等垃圾食品，真让人倒胃口。另外，餐厅的蔬菜、水果，以至鸡蛋、牛奶、肉类等，无一不是新鲜的有机食品，而且美味可口。虽然价钱比以前稍微贵了一点儿，但是无论是从营养、健康还是口味的角度来看，我们对新餐厅都十分满意。你们学校的餐厅没有我们的酷吧？光听我描述就馋得流口水了吧？你哪天有空儿，非得来尝尝不可。

1. What made the school change the cafeteria management?

   A) The school realized that the food was not tasty at all.

   B) The students went through a series of protests against the previous management.

C) The students advocated the benefits of serving organic food.

D) The school felt the food was too expensive before.

2. What appeals to the students about the new cafeteria?

A) It offers a lot of fast food.

B) The decoration is new.

C) It's cheaper than before.

D) It offers more varied, fresher food.

3. The students' general attitude toward the new cafeteria is

A) satisfied

B) critical

C) lukewarm

D) happy, but with suggestions for further improvement

4. What does the speaker invite the e-mail recipient to do?

A) To come to talk to the manager about her recipes for the food she serves

B) To go out to a restaurant to get a break from cafeteria food

C) To come to try the food at the new cafeteria

D) To join the efforts to improve nutrition at the cafeteria

Read this public sign.

(Traditional characters)

珍惜糧食，遠離浪費！

(Simplified characters)

珍惜粮食，远离浪费！

5. Where would this sign most likely appear?

A) By a water fountain

B) At a cafeteria

C) Next to a light switch

D) Next to a copy machine

6. Which of the following statements is TRUE?

A) The purpose of this sign is to encourage people to think before they act.

B) The purpose of this sign is to encourage people to save paper.

C) The purpose of this sign is to encourage people not to be wasteful of food.

D) The purpose of this sign is to instruct people not to eat too much.

Read this public sign.

(Traditional characters)

請將塑料、鋁罐等廢棄物品
放至回收桶內

(Simplified characters)

请将塑料、铝罐等废弃物品
放至回收桶内

7. What is the purpose of this sign?

   A) To discourage littering of bottles and cans

   B) To request that plastic and cans be placed in recycling bins

   C) To encourage recycling of electronic waste

   D) To request that plastic and cans be placed in green garbage bins

Read this note.

(Traditional characters)

小南：

　　剛纔旅行社的林小姐打電話來，說是代你辦理簽證出現了一些問題。首先是你的護照有效期不到三個月了，你得趕緊去延期。其次是你交的照片格式不對，得補交一式兩張的兩寸免冠正面照片。他們還說要是你沒有時間親自去辦理護照延期，他們可以代辦。不過，由於現在離你預定到中國的日期只有兩個月了，時間非常緊迫，簽證恐怕得加急，否則來不及，而加急必須額外再付150元。他們希望你儘快決定，並且通知他們你打算如何處理。

　　　　　　　　　　　　　　　　　　　　　　　　　　　　東梅
　　　　　　　　　　　　　　　　　　　　　　　　　　　　4月2日上午10點

(Simplified characters)

小南：

　　刚才旅行社的林小姐打电话来，说是代你办理签证出现了一些问题。首先是你的护照有效期不到三个月了，你得赶紧去延期。其次是你交的照片格式不对，得补交一式两张的两寸免冠正面照片。他们还说要是你没有时间亲自去办理护照延期，他们可以代办。不过，由于现在离你预定到中国的日期只有两个月了，时间非常紧迫，签证恐怕得加急，否则来不及，而加急必须额外再付150元。他们希望你尽快决定，并且通知他们你打算如何处理。

　　　　　　　　　　　　　　　　　　　　　　　　　　　　东梅
　　　　　　　　　　　　　　　　　　　　　　　　　　　　4月2日上午10点

8. What has Dongmei just done?

    A) Spoken with a Ms. Lin from the Chinese Consulate

    B) Spoken with a Ms. Lin from a travel agency

    C) Spoken with a Ms. Lin from the passport photo shop

    D) Spoken with a Ms. Lin from the airlines

9. What is the purpose of this note?

    A) To transmit information about documents needed for Xiaonan's upcoming trip to China

    B) To transmit information about preparations to receive a delegation from China

    C) To transmit questions about what types of items are appropriate to take to China

    D) To transmit information about how to apply for a passport

10. What is wrong with Xiaonan's current documents?

    A) He has submitted a good photograph, but not a proper passport.

    B) He has not submitted a passport or photos that reflect his current age.

    C) He has submitted both a passport and photos, but both have problems.

    D) He has submitted a passport and photos, but didn't include the extra ¥150.

11. Why does Ms. Lin suggest paying an extra ¥150?

    A) To expedite processing his passport application so that he can receive it in time to apply for his visa

    B) To expedite the preparation of new photos in time to submit them for his new visa application

    C) To prepare new photos of the correct dimensions so that they can be submitted in time to process the visa

    D) To expedite processing his visa application so that he can receive it before his departure date

Read this advertisement.

(Traditional characters)

二手豪華車廉售

德國銀色寶馬，內部淺灰色系，八成新，五門七座家庭用車，配有電子防盜裝備、倒車雷達、車載DVD導航，36,000千米，要價25,000美元，急售，有議價空間。晚上6點前請電二手車經紀李麥克（415）563-9111。

(Simplified characters)

> **二手豪华车廉售**
>
> 德国银色宝马，内部浅灰色系，八成新，五门七座家庭用车，配有电子防盗装备、倒车雷达、车载DVD导航，36,000千米，要价25,000美元，急售，有议价空间。晚上6点前请电二手车经纪李麦克（415）563-9111。

12. What kind of vehicle is advertised for sale?

    A) A car with a driving recorder

    B) A new car with five doors and seven seats

    C) A used car with odometer reading of 36,000 kilometers

    D) A used car with manual transmission

13. Is the seller anxious to sell?

    A) Yes, and the posted price is negotiable.

    B) Yes, and parking spaces in his area have become limited.

    C) No, because he can only discuss it in the daytime, when most people are at work.

    D) No, because he has engaged the services of an agent.

14. From what country does this item originate?

    A) France

    B) Italy

    C) Germany

    D) None of the above

15. Who is Li Maike?

    A) A friend of the owner

    B) The owner of a used car dealership

    C) An agent at a used car dealership

    D) A salesman for a European car dealership

16. What color is the car?

    A) Silver interior, gray exterior

    B) Gray interior, silver exterior

    C) Maroon interior, brown exterior

    D) Brown interior, gray exterior

Read this letter.

(Traditional characters)

婷婷表姐：

你好！我上個週末從中國回來了。由於時差的問題，前兩天一直日夜顛倒，白天發睏，晚上精神抖擻，我媽說我的身體以及我的心都還留在中國呢。我特別感激你鼓勵我報名參加這次"尋根之旅"的活動，短短的四週帶給我的不止是歡樂和喜悅，也給我留下了美好難忘的回憶。

我們除了學習漢語和中華文化知識、練習武術、參觀名勝古跡之外，還動手學習中國民族工藝製作，如剪紙、中國結、泥塑、風箏等，也有很多機會跟來自世界各地的華裔青少年和中國當地的青少年學生交流。我還學到了一句諺語"有緣千里來相會"，有一位書法家用毛筆給我寫了這一句話。我把那幅字掛在書房裡了，非常醒目。你下次到我們家來時，就可以欣賞到他揮灑自如的筆法了。

請代我問舅舅、舅媽好！祝你健康快樂！

表妹 薇薇上
8月20日

(Simplified characters)

婷婷表姐：

你好！我上个周末从中国回来了。由于时差的问题，前两天一直日夜颠倒，白天发困，晚上精神抖擞，我妈说我的身体以及我的心都还留在中国呢。我特别感激你鼓励我报名参加这次"寻根之旅"的活动，短短的四周带给我的不止是欢乐和喜悦，也给我留下了美好难忘的回忆。

我们除了学习汉语和中华文化知识、练习武术、参观名胜古迹之外，还动手学习中国民族工艺制作，如剪纸、中国结、泥塑、风筝等，也有很多机会跟来自世界各地的华裔青少年和中国当地的青少年学生交流。我还学到了一句谚语"有缘千里来相会"，有一位书法家用毛笔给我写了这一句话。我把那幅字挂在书房里了，非常醒目。你下次到我们家来时，就可以欣赏到他挥洒自如的笔法了。

请代我问舅舅、舅妈好！祝你健康快乐！

表妹 薇薇上
8月20日

17. What is the relationship between the letter writer and her addressee?

    A) Aunt and niece

    B) Sisters

    C) friends

    D) Cousins

18. Why does Weiwei express gratitude to Tingting?

    A) Tingting has given her advice about where to go and what to do while in the program, "Travel in Search of Roots".

    B) Tingting encouraged her to join "Travel in Search of Roots", which she greatly enjoyed.

    C) Tingting introduced her to the head of "Travel in Search of Roots", who is a noted teacher of traditional arts and crafts.

    D) Tingting told her to join "Travel in Search of Roots", and paid all of her expenses.

19. What sorts of people did she meet while in China?

    A) Young overseas Chinese from many countries, as well as young people in China

    B) Students and faculty of the schools they visited while traveling in various places in China

    C) Diverse people of many backgrounds interested in Chinese culture and language

    D) Musicians, artists, dancers, and practitioners of traditional Chinese medicine

20. In the letter, Weiwei did NOT mention that she had lessons of

    A) clay sculpture making

    B) Chinese culture

    C) calligraphy

    D) martial arts

21. Why does Weiwei treasure the piece of calligraphy she received while in China?

    A) It is written in a script that is extremely difficult to write, and thus rare.

    B) It is beautiful in appearance and expresses a meaning that she appreciates.

    C) It was written by a famous calligrapher whom she enjoyed meeting and conversing with.

    D) She loves its meaning: "Even 1,000 miles from home, we encounter people from our hometown."

Read this article.

(Traditional characters)

文學作品裡的風箏

中國是風箏的故鄉，秋天是放風箏最好的季節。中國自古以來就有許多與風箏有關的故事。清代的著名文學家李漁，寫了一個劇本，叫《風箏誤》，故事的發展就是由風箏斷綫引出一連串誤會和巧合，情節曲折起伏，引人入勝。

中國著名的古典小說《紅樓夢》裡面也有放風箏的情節。小說的主角之一林黛玉從小體弱多病，放風箏時，大家先是把形形色色、製作精美的風箏放到空中，有美人的、鳳凰的、大雁的、蝙蝠的、螃蟹的，五顏六色，在空中飄揚飛舞、爭奇鬥豔，等樂了一陣子以後，再把繫風箏的綫剪斷，說是把晦氣送走，也讓林黛玉的病根隨著斷了綫的風箏飄搖而去。

(Simplified characters)

文学作品里的风筝

中国是风筝的故乡，秋天是放风筝最好的季节。中国自古以来就有许多与风筝有关的故事。清代的著名文学家李渔，写了一个剧本，叫《风筝误》，故事的发展就是由风筝断线引出一连串误会和巧合，情节曲折起伏，引人入胜。

中国著名的古典小说《红楼梦》里面也有放风筝的情节。小说的主角之一林黛玉从小体弱多病，放风筝时，大家先是把形形色色、制作精美的风筝放到空中，有美人的、凤凰的、大雁的、蝙蝠的、螃蟹的，五颜六色，在空中飘扬飞舞、争奇斗艳，等乐了一阵子以后，再把系风筝的线剪断，说是把晦气送走，也让林黛玉的病根随着断了线的风筝飘摇而去。

22. What did Li Yu write about a kite?

   A) A play about a kite that could be flown and even ridden by young children

   B) A tale about a young girl who learned to fly kites even though she was physically weak

   C) A novel about a kite contest between several members of a large, extended family

   D) A play about a kite that breaks away and leads to all sorts of accidental meetings and coincidences

23. Which of the following kite designs are NOT included in the novel *Dream of Red Mansions*?

   A) Bats

   B) Frogs

C) Wild geese

D) Crabs

24. Why do the characters in *Dream of Red Mansions* cut the strings to the kites they have been flying?

    A) They are frustrated that their kites are not as beautiful as some of the others.

    B) The kites are all entangled in the air, and the only way to separate them is to cut the strings and let go.

    C) They hope that by letting the kite go, the sick girl's illnesses will fly away with it.

    D) They are so exhausted by the kite contest that they want to cut off the possibility of any further involvement.

Read this poster.

(Traditional characters)

美化環境日

時間：4月25日上午9時至下午3時

地點：下列三處，請依照個人興趣選擇參加

　　1. 本校花圃

　　2. 圓石海灘

　　3. 市立公園

活動內容：種植花草，撿拾垃圾，以期美化環境

注意事項：

　　1. 請穿著輕便衣物

　　2. 請帶防曬油及園藝用手套

　　3. 請自備午餐（學校供應開水及各式冷飲，請自帶水瓶或水杯）

　　4. 若家有小型園藝工具，亦請攜帶

　人數不限，多多益善。請自行準時前往。到達時請向各活動負責老師報到，實際參與時數可抵社區服務時數。

(Simplified characters)

美化环境日

时间：4月25日上午9时至下午3时

地点：下列三处，请依照个人兴趣选择参加

> 1. 本校花圃
> 2. 圆石海滩
> 3. 市立公园
>
> 活动内容：种植花草，捡拾垃圾，以期美化环境
>
> 注意事项：
> 1. 请穿着轻便衣物
> 2. 请带防晒油及园艺用手套
> 3. 请自备午餐（学校供应开水及各式冷饮，请自带水瓶或水杯）
> 4. 若家有小型园艺工具，亦请携带
>
> 人数不限，多多益善。请自行准时前往。到达时请向各活动负责老师报到，实际参与时数可抵社区服务时数。

25. What is the occasion for the above announcement on the poster?

    A) Mother Earth Day (traditionally celebrated in China at the end of April)

    B) A day for beautifying the environment

    C) A day for enhancing one's own health and beauty by beautifying the physical environment

    D) Save the Earth Day

26. Which most accurately describes the intended audience for this poster?

    A) The students of a school or college

    B) The neighbors of a municipal park

    C) The residents of a resort town near the ocean

    D) Homeowners with their own small gardens

27. What should the participants bring?

    A) Light, informal clothing

    B) Gardening tools if available

    C) Gloves and sunscreen

    D) All of the above

28. Which is NOT the locations where the work will be performed?

    A) The school's garden

    B) The school sports grounds

    C) A municipal park

    D) The Yuanshi Beach

29. What will the sponsors provide to the participants?

   A) Lunch

   B) Hot drinks

   C) Soda

   D) None of the above

30. What type of transportation is advised for the participants to take to go to the three locations?

   A) Buses

   B) Bicycles

   C) Cars

   D) Not specified

Read this story.

(Traditional characters)

> 孔融是東漢末年（約公元二世紀）一個很博學的人，是孔子的二十世孫。他從小就很聰明，特別擅長辭令。十歲時，孔融隨他父親到了都城洛陽。當地的行政長官李元禮由於頗負盛名，日常拜訪他的人不是親戚，就是當時享有才名的人，絡繹不絕。如果來訪的人是無名之輩，守門的人一般不通報。孔融很想見見這位大學者。
>
> 　一天，他走到李元禮的府門前，對守門人說：＂我是李先生的親戚，請給我通報一下。＂李元禮接見了孔融，非常好奇地問他：＂你和我有什麼親戚關係呢？＂孔融回答道：＂我是孔子的後代，老子李聃是你的祖先。孔子曾經向老子請教過關於禮節的問題，他們是師生關係，所以我和你說來也是世交。＂
>
> 　當時有很多賓客在座，大家都對年僅十歲的孔融的這番話感到驚奇。這時有一個叫陳韙的人來拜訪李元禮，在座的賓客就將孔融剛纔的表現告訴了他。誰知陳韙完全不以為然，隨口就說道：＂小時了了，大未必佳。＂意思是小時候雖然很聰明，可長大了卻未必能夠成材。聰明的孔融立即反駁道：＂我想陳先生小的時候，一定是很聰明的。＂也就是暗指陳韙是個庸才。陳韙被孔融一句話難住了，半天都說不出話來。

(Simplified characters)

> 孔融是东汉末年（约公元二世纪）一个很博学的人，是孔子的二十世孙。他从小就很聪明，特别擅长辞令。十岁时，孔融随他父亲到了都城洛阳。当地的行政长官李元礼由于颇负盛名，日常拜访他的人不是亲戚，就是当时享有才名的人，络绎不

> 绝。如果来访的人是无名之辈，守门的人一般不通报。孔融很想见见这位大学者。
>
> 　　一天，他走到李元礼的府门前，对守门人说："我是李先生的亲戚，请给我通报一下。"李元礼接见了孔融，非常好奇地问他："你和我有什么亲戚关系呢？"孔融回答道："我是孔子的后代，老子李聃是你的祖先。孔子曾经向老子请教过关于礼节的问题，他们是师生关系，所以我和你说来也是世交。"
>
> 　　当时有很多宾客在座，大家都对年仅十岁的孔融的这番话感到惊奇。这时有一个叫陈韪的人来拜访李元礼，在座的宾客就将孔融刚才的表现告诉了他。谁知陈韪完全不以为然，随口就说道："小时了了，大未必佳。"意思是小时候虽然很聪明，可长大了却未必能够成材。聪明的孔融立即反驳道："我想陈先生小的时候，一定是很聪明的。"也就是暗指陈韪是个庸才。陈韪被孔融一句话难住了，半天都说不出话来。

31. What was Kong Rong famous for?

    A) Erudition and wit

    B) As a 30th generation descendant of Confucius

    C) Filial obedience to his father

    D) None of the above

32. What did Kong Rong say to the gatekeeper to gain admittance to Li Yuanli's house?

    A) He pretended to be the descendant of Confucius.

    B) He pretended to be the son of Li's student.

    C) He pretended to be the son of an important official in the government of the time.

    D) He pretended to be a relative of Li's.

33. To what sorts of people did Li Yuanli limit his friendships?

    A) People who were famous for their talent or intelligence

    B) People who came from rich, well-established families

    C) People with whom he could discuss important matters of state

    D) People who were skilled in politics and governmental affairs

34. What is the capital of the Eastern Han Dynasty?

    A) Xi'an

    B) Luoyang

    C) Beijing

    D) Nanjing

35. Why does Chen Wei become embarrassed by Kong Rong's retort?

A) Kong implies that Chen had gained admittance to Li's house for the wrong reasons.

B) Kong implies that Chen is not particularly smart or talented.

C) Kong implies that Chen has grown too old to be useful to Li.

D) Kong implies that Chen no longer respects Li in his old age.

END OF SECTION I

YOU MAY REVIEW WORK IF THERE IS TIME LEFT.

DO NOT GO ON TO SECTION II UNTIL YOU ARE TOLD TO DO SO.

Section II: Free Response

Part A: Writing (Story Narration and E-mail Response)

Note: In this part of the exam, the student may NOT move back and forth among questions.

Writing Part Directions

You will be asked to perform two writing tasks in Chinese. In each case, you will be asked to write for a specific purpose and to a specific person. You should write in as complete and as culturally appropriate a manner as possible, taking into account the purpose and the person described.

Presentational Writing: Story Narration (15%, 15 minutes)

The four pictures present a story. Imagine you are writing the story to a friend. Narrate a complete story as suggested by the pictures. Give your story a beginning, a middle, and an end.

Interpersonal Writing: E-mail Response (10%, 15 minutes)

Read this e-mail from a friend and then type a response.

(Traditional characters)

發件人：王容
收件人：李紅
郵件主題：手寫漢字與電腦打字

　　從上個學期開始，老師要我們多練習電腦打字，無論是做作業還是考試，都用電腦，手寫漢字的機會就越來越少了。我一方面覺得電腦打字比寫漢字更快更方便，另一方面又擔心以前好不容易學會寫的漢字會不會漸漸地就都忘了，而且電腦打字容易出錯。你對電腦打字和手寫漢字有什麼看法？你覺得電腦打字要注意些什麼纔不容易出錯？另外，漢字的書寫要怎麼樣纔不會忘得一乾二淨呢？謝謝。

(Simplified characters)

发件人：王容
收件人：李红
邮件主题：手写汉字与电脑打字

　　从上个学期开始，老师要我们多练习电脑打字，无论是做作业还是考试，都用电脑，手写汉字的机会就越来越少了。我一方面觉得电脑打字比写汉字更快更方便，另一方面又担心以前好不容易学会写的汉字会不会渐渐地就都忘了，而且电脑打字容易出错。你对电脑打字和手写汉字有什么看法？你觉得电脑打字要注意些什么才不容易出错？另外，汉字的书写要怎么样才不会忘得一干二净呢？谢谢。

Part B: Speaking (Conversation and Cultural Presentation)

Note: In this part of the exam, you may NOT move back and forth among questions.

speaking

Speaking Part Directions: Conversation

You will participate in a simulated conversation. Each time it is your turn to speak, you will have 20 seconds to record. You should respond as fully and as appropriately as possible. There will be six times when it is your turn to speak.

Interpersonal Speaking: Conversation (10%, 4 minutes)

You will have a conversation with Jiang Ning, a passenger sitting next to you on the bus, about your experience in learning Chinese.

Speaking Question 1 of 7

1. Record your answer. (20 seconds)

Speaking Question 2 of 7

2. Record your answer. (20 seconds)

Speaking Question 3 of 7

3. Record your answer. (20 seconds)

Speaking Question 4 of 7

4. Record your answer. (20 seconds)

Speaking Question 5 of 7

5. Record your answer. (20 seconds)

Speaking Question 6 of 7

6. Record your answer. (20 seconds)

Speaking Part Directions: Cultural Presentation

You will be asked to speak in Chinese on a specific topic. Imagine you are making an oral presentation to your Chinese class. First, you will read and hear the topic for your presentation. You will have 4 minutes to prepare your presentation. Then you will have 2 minutes to record your presentation. You presentation should be as complete as possible.

Presentational Speaking: Cultural Presentation (15%, 7 minutes)

Speaking Question 7 of 7

7. Choose ONE of your favorite Chinese writers, ancient or contemporary. In your presentation, describe this writer's background, name one of his/her most famous works and introduce its form and content, and explain the writer's significance in the history of Chinese literature.

You have four minutes to prepare your presentation. (240 seconds)
You have two minutes to record your presentation. (120 seconds)

YOU HAVE FINISHED THIS PART OF THE EXAM.
END OF EXAM

AP Chinese Language and Culture Test 9

listening

Section I: Multiple Choice

Part A: Listening (Rejoinders and Listening Selections)

Listening Part Directions

You will answer two types of questions: rejoinders and questions based on listening selections.

For all tasks, you will have a specific amount of response time. When the response time has ended, you will automatically go on to the next question. You cannot return to previous questions.

Listening Part Directions: Rejoinders (10%, 10 minutes)

You will hear several short conversations or parts of conversations followed by four choices, designated A, B, C, and D. Choose the one that continues or completes the conversation in a logical and culturally appropriate manner. After you have decided which of the suggested answers is best, COMPLETELY fill in the corresponding circle on the answer sheet. You will have 5 seconds to answer each question.

YOU WILL NOW BEGIN THIS PART.

1. Mark your answer on your answer sheet.
2. Mark your answer on your answer sheet.
3. Mark your answer on your answer sheet.
4. Mark your answer on your answer sheet.
5. Mark your answer on your answer sheet.
6. Mark your answer on your answer sheet.
7. Mark your answer on your answer sheet.
8. Mark your answer on your answer sheet.
9. Mark your answer on your answer sheet.
10. Mark your answer on your answer sheet.
11. Mark your answer on your answer sheet.
12. Mark your answer on your answer sheet.
13. Mark your answer on your answer sheet.
14. Mark your answer on your answer sheet.
15. Mark your answer on your answer sheet.

Listening Part Directions: Listening Selections (15%, 10 minutes)

You will listen to several selections in Chinese. For each selection, you will be told whether it will be played once or twice. You may take notes as you listen. Your notes will not be graded. After listening to each selection, you will see questions in English. For each question, choose the response that is best according to the selection. You will have 12 seconds to answer each question.

YOU WILL NOW BEGIN THIS PART.

Selection 1: Transportation Announcement (Selection plays two times.)

16. Where would the announcement be heard?

　　A) On a train

　　B) At an airport

　　C) In a bus terminal

　　D) At a ferry boat dock

17. The announcement is specifically addressed to people who are

　　A) traveling in groups

　　B) checking luggage

　　C) boarding a flight

　　D) seeing off passengers

Selection 2: Voice Message (Selection plays two times.)

18. What happened to Xiao'an?

　　A) She didn't go to school.

　　B) She didn't pick up the phone.

　　C) She didn't do her homework.

　　D) She left her book at school.

19. What was the reason for the absence of some students?

　　A) They had a cold.

　　B) They got up late.

　　C) There was a snowstorm.

　　D) There was a rainstorm.

20. The deadline for the grammar homework has been extended to

    A) next Monday

    B) next Tuesday

    C) next Wednesday

    D) any day next week

Selection 3: School Conversation (Selection plays one time.)

21. What will be the penalty if the man does not get a good grade on the test?

    A) His mom will not let him play video games next month.

    B) His mom will not give him allowance next month.

    C) He will need to review vocabulary and grammar.

    D) His mom will ask him to do lots of house chores.

22. What is likely to be the subject of the upcoming test?

    A) A history test

    B) A biology test

    C) A language test

    D) A mathematics test

23. What will the woman do?

    A) She will give the man a mock test.

    B) She will lend the man her class notes.

    C) She will study in the library with the man.

    D) She will help the man prepare for the test.

Selection 4: Radio Report (Selection plays one time.)

24. What is the topic of the radio report?

    A) Ticket policy for the train

    B) Fee policy on the highway

    C) Road construction during holidays

    D) Promotion of carpool on the highway

25. Which holiday is the news related to?

    A) Chinese New Year

    B) Labor Day Weekend

C) Mid-Autumn Festival

D) Dragon Boat Festival

26. According to the radio, what types of vehicles will benefit from the arrangement?

    A) Commercial buses, vans, and trucks

    B) Cars with 7 or less than 7 seats

    C) Cars with 5 or less than 5 seats

    D) All types of cars and motorcycles

Selection 5: Instructions (Selection plays one time.)

27. The instructions are given

    A) in a hardware store

    B) in a bookstore

    C) in a shoe store

    D) in a department store

28. The instructions provide information about

    A) the closing time of the store

    B) the opening time of the store

    C) location of the emergency exits

    D) special discounts of products

29. What may be the actions that the audience need to take?

    A) To exit from the emergency exits immediately

    B) To pay for the merchandise immediately

    C) To visit the sections that are on sale

    D) To watch weather news on their phone

Selection 6: Conversation (Selection plays one time.)

30. What is likely to be the two speakers' occupation?

    A) They are high school students.

    B) They are college students.

    C) They are teachers.

    D) They are librarians.

31. What is the theme of this conversation?

    A) The place to go for universities

    B) The place to go for jobs

    C) The place to go for vacation

    D) The place to go for food

32. According to the conversation, what is special about New York city?

    A) It is the cultural and economic center of America.

    B) It has two Chinatowns and many good restaurants.

    C) It has the tallest building in the world.

    D) It is home to the best university in the United States.

33. Where does the man plan to go for college?

    A) A college that is close to home

    B) A college that is far away from home

    C) A college in New York city

    D) A college in China

Part B: Reading Selections

Note: In this part of the exam, you may move back and forth among all the questions.

Reading Part Directions: Reading Selections (25%, 60 minutes)

You will read several selections in Chinese. Each selection is accompanied by a number of questions in English. For each question, choose the response that is best according to the selection. After you have decided which of the suggested answers is best, COMPLETELY fill in the corresponding circle on the answer sheet. Chinese tests appear here in both traditional and simplified characters. You will have 60 minutes to answer all questions.

YOU WILL NOW BEGIN THIS PART.

Read this note.

(Traditional characters)

張老師：

　　您好！我叫王育英，是國際貿易專業的大一新生。我剛參加完中文分級考試，新生訓練的輔導老師讓我來請教您，我應該註冊哪一個中文班。我高中學了四年中文，計劃上大學以後直接上中級班或者高級班的中文課。

下個星期就開學了，我希望這幾天就能決定應該上哪一個班的中文課。現在是上午10點，真不巧，您剛好不在辦公室。我會給您發電郵，下午我再來找您。

　　　　　　　　　　　　　　　　　　　　　　　　　　　育英
　　　　　　　　　　　　　　　　　　　　　　　　　　　8月25日

(Simplified characters)

张老师：

您好！我叫王育英，是国际贸易专业的大一新生。我刚参加完中文分级考试，新生训练的辅导老师让我来请教您，我应该注册哪一个中文班。我高中学了四年中文，计划上大学以后直接上中级班或者高级班的中文课。

下个星期就开学了，我希望这几天就能决定应该上哪一个班的中文课。现在是上午10点，真不巧，您刚好不在办公室。我会给您发电邮，下午我再来找您。

　　　　　　　　　　　　　　　　　　　　　　　　　　　育英
　　　　　　　　　　　　　　　　　　　　　　　　　　　8月25日

1. What is Yuying's purpose for visiting Teacher Zhang?

    A) To discuss which Chinese course she should take

    B) To ask for information about Chinese minor

    C) To take a Chinese placement exam

    D) To have a Chinese oral interview

2. When does Yuying need to decide on the course she should take?

    A) In a few weeks

    B) Yesterday

    C) Tomorrow

    D) In a few days

3. Where did Yuying get the contact information about Teacher Zhang?

    A) From new student orientation

    B) From the university website

    C) From her high school teacher

    D) From her good friend

Read this e-mail.

(Traditional characters)

收件箱

發件人：李哲明

收件人：高永亮

郵件主題：夏令營的生活

發件日期：7月9日

阿亮：

　　很高興收到你的電郵。我到中文夏令營已經一個星期了。我每天早上6點起床後就和我的同學去操場跑步，然後回到宿舍洗澡，接著去食堂吃早飯。吃完飯，我就回宿舍拿書，然後去教室。我們有口語課、閱讀課、寫作課、聽力課等。我最喜歡口語課，因為我們上課的時候常常表演或者做遊戲，大家都覺得很有趣。

　　中午我們去食堂吃午飯。剛下課的時候人特別多，有時候要排隊。午飯是自助餐，有很多選擇，我覺得很健康。吃完午飯我們一般都回宿舍休息一下，要不然下午會太累。

　　下午的課比較輕鬆，有書法課、太極拳課，或者是由助教組織的小組對話練習。下午上課到5點。吃完晚飯以後我會做作業、複習或者準備考試。10點宿舍就熄燈了。熄燈後大家還是喜歡玩兒手機，快12點纔睡覺。我覺得這樣不好，早睡早起纔是最健康的。

　　我覺得夏令營的生活是很有意思的體驗。你可以考慮明年也來參加這個夏令營。先寫到這兒，下次再聊。

大明

(Simplified characters)

收件箱

发件人：李哲明

收件人：高永亮

邮件主题：夏令营的生活

发件日期：7月9日

阿亮：

　　很高兴收到你的电邮。我到中文夏令营已经一个星期了。我每天早上6点起床后就和我的同学去操场跑步，然后回到宿舍洗澡，接着去食堂吃早饭。吃完饭，我就回宿舍拿书,然后去教室。我们有口语课、阅读课、写作课、听力课等。我最喜欢口语课,因为我们上课的时候常常表演或者做游戏,大家都觉得很有趣。

中午我们去食堂吃午饭。刚下课的时候人特别多,有时候要排队。午饭是自助餐,有很多选择,我觉得很健康。吃完午饭我们一般都回宿舍休息一下,要不然下午会太累。

下午的课比较轻松,有书法课、太极拳课,或者是由助教组织的小组对话练习。下午上课到5点。吃完晚饭以后我会做作业、复习或者准备考试。10点宿舍就熄灯了。熄灯后大家还是喜欢玩儿手机,快12点才睡觉。我觉得这样不好,早睡早起才是最健康的。

我觉得夏令营的生活是很有意思的体验。你可以考虑明年也来参加这个夏令营。先写到这儿,下次再聊。

大明

4. What do we know about the summer camp based on Daming's e-mail?

   A) The camp has a vigorous schedule.

   B) The camp is activity-based.

   C) The camp is focused on sports.

   D) The camp attendees live at home.

5. Where does Daming go after he wakes up?

   A) The shower room

   B) The cafeteria

   C) The classroom

   D) The sports field

6. What does Daming do after lunch?

   A) Jogging

   B) Taking a nap

   C) Working on homework

   D) Studying for classes

7. Why does Daming attend the summer camp?

   A) He wants to develop his language skills.

   B) He wants to get physical training.

C) He wants to experience the dorm life.

D) He wants to make more friends.

Read this e-mail.

(Traditional characters)

收件箱
發件人：高宜文
收件人：王麗平
郵件主題：逛購物中心
發件日期：2月18日

麗平：

我很期待這個星期六帶你去逛我家旁邊的新銀購物中心。很可惜，你要1點纔能到，這樣我們就只有下午可以逛了。新銀分爲六個區，有一百多家店，一個下午怎麼夠呢？既然我們都喜歡逛運動服和戶外用品店，我建議週六我們就逛"年輕活力區"。那裡有很多運動服和運動鞋的專賣店，還有幾家泳裝店。剛好夏天快到了，我們可以去看看有什麼好看的新泳裝。那一區還有一家又大又漂亮的登山釣魚用品店，他們的魚池裡面有特別多的魚。我們逛累了，可以坐在池邊喝可樂、看魚。其他的店只好你下次來我們再去了。你看這樣安排行嗎？

宜文

(Simplified characters)

收件箱
发件人：高宜文
收件人：王丽平
邮件主题：逛购物中心
发件日期：2月18日

丽平：

我很期待这个星期六带你去逛我家旁边的新银购物中心。很可惜，你要1点才能到，这样我们就只有下午可以逛了。新银分为六个区，有一百多家店，一个下午怎么够呢？既然我们都喜欢逛运动服和户外用品店，我建议周六我们就逛"年轻活力区"。那里有很多运动服和运动鞋的专卖店，还有几家泳装店。刚好夏天快到了，我们可以去看看有什么好看的新泳装。那一区还有一家又大又漂亮的登山钓鱼用品店，他们的鱼池里面有特别多的鱼。我们逛累了，可以坐在池边喝可乐、看鱼。其他的店只好你下次来我们再去了。你看这样安排行吗？

宜文

8. Which section of the shopping mall do Liping and Yiwen plan to visit?

   A) Women's Wear

   B) Home Goods

   C) Deals of the Day

   D) Active Lifestyle

9. What are Liping and Yiwen likely to buy this Saturday?

   A) New skirts

   B) New swimsuits

   C) New fishing poles

   D) New hiking boots

10. Where will Liping and Yiwen drink coke?

    A) Next to the fish pond

    B) In the ice cream shop

    C) Next to the shoe store

    D) In the food court

Read this pen-pal letter.

(Traditional characters)

安妮：

很高興收到你的來信！你說你外婆認識的一些中國人看起來比實際年齡年輕，所以她對中國老人的休閒健身方式感興趣。那我就為你介紹一下吧！

中國老人的確很注重健康，休閒方式也很多。跑步、爬山、游泳、跳廣場舞，也有遛狗散步的，還有在家練書法、養花的。我早上去公園，經常能看到很多老人在鍛煉。我發現他們的活動有一些特點。比如，他們比較喜歡很多人在一起活動，可以一邊運動一邊聊天兒，比較有意思。雖然有的人做，有的人看，可能互相不認識，可是大家都很高興。

你問我建議你外婆做什麼中式健身活動，我聽說美國現在很多地方都有太極拳課，她可以找一個太極拳館去試試。練太極拳可以很好地鍛鍊身體。我媽媽以前常常生病，後來，她認真練了兩年太極拳，身體就變得好多了。我媽媽喜歡練太極拳，因為動作慢慢的，很優美，很舒展，她不喜歡滿頭大汗的運動。我建議你外婆去試試。

　　祝健康平安！

麗心

(Simplified characters)

安妮：

　　很高兴收到你的来信！你说你外婆认识的一些中国人看起来比实际年龄年轻，所以她对中国老人的休闲健身方式感兴趣。那我就为你介绍一下吧！

　　中国老人的确很注重健康，休闲方式也很多。跑步、爬山、游泳、跳广场舞，也有遛狗散步的，还有在家练书法、养花的。我早上去公园，经常能看到很多老人在锻炼。我发现他们的活动有一些特点。比如，他们比较喜欢很多人在一起活动，可以一边运动一边聊天儿，比较有意思。虽然有的人做，有的人看，可能互相不认识，可是大家都很高兴。

　　你问我建议你外婆做什么中式健身活动，我听说美国现在很多地方都有太极拳课，她可以找一个太极拳馆去试试。练太极拳可以很好地锻炼身体。我妈妈以前常常生病，后来，她认真练了两年太极拳，身体就变得好多了。我妈妈喜欢练太极拳，因为动作慢慢的，很优美，很舒展，她不喜欢满头大汗的运动。我建议你外婆去试试。

　　祝健康平安！

丽心

11. Lixin is writing this letter to her pen-pal to

　　A) reply to her questions about Chinese senior activities

　　B) answer her questions about Chinese diet

　　C) promote the benefit of a healthy lifestyle

　　D) suggest places to visit in Beijing

12. Why is Annie's grandma interested in Chinese workout activities?

　　A) Because she knows some Chinese seniors who are really active.

　　B) Because she knows some Chinese who are very healthy.

　　C) Because she knows some Chinese who look younger than their age.

D) Because she has some friends who have benefited from Chinese workout activities.

13. According to the e-mail, what is NOT TRUE about senior people in China?

    A) They pay attention to their health.

    B) They like to do workout activities in groups.

    C) They like to hang out in the park.

    D) They are mostly vegetarians.

14. What workout activity does Lixin recommend?

    A) Taekwondo

    B) Tai Chi

    C) Qigong

    D) Akido

15. What type of exercises does Lixin's mom dislike?

    A) Exercises that make people sweat

    B) Exercises that are slow in motion

    C) Exercises that need a partner

    D) Exercises that need a ball

Read this poster announcement.

(Traditional characters)

東南醫藥大學動物醫學專業
免費養寵知識講座
跟您分享
- 辦理狗證
- 文明遛狗
- 科學餵養
- 疾病防治
回答您
- 養寵物的問題
地點：動物醫學樓108教室
時間：9月2日（星期一）下午4點到6點
歡迎參加！

(Simplified characters)

东南医药大学动物医学专业
免费养宠知识讲座
跟您分享
- 办理狗证
- 文明遛狗
- 科学喂养
- 疾病防治
回答您
- 养宠物的问题
地点：动物医学楼108教室
时间：9月2日（星期一）下午4点到6点
欢迎参加！

16. Who is the organizer of the event?

   A) A veterinary clinic

   B) A medical university

   C) An association of pets

   D) A community center

17. What will NOT be included in the workshop?

   A) Where to adopt pets

   B) How to get pet ID tags

   C) How to raise pets

   D) How to vaccinate pets

18. How long is the workshop?

   A) Two hours

   B) One hour

   C) One and a half hours

   D) Two and a half hours

Read this advertisement.

(Traditional characters)

廣南圖書館徵義工

活動：環境保護教育活動

　　　歡迎 15～25 歲的高中生和大學生加入我們的義工團隊

服務對象：6～10 歲的小學生

地點：廣南圖書館手工藝教室

日期：6 月 1 日～30 日（每週六或者週日）

時間：上午 10:00～下午 5:00（義工可以自由選擇服務的時間）

工作內容：

　1. 協助管理小朋友參觀團

　2. 協助帶領小朋友做手工藝

　3. 協助組織教育講座，維持秩序

報名截止：5月15日

申請資料：姓名、出生年月日、電話、地址、全身正面照片

報名方式：請將申請資料寄至 kidseducation@library.gov 廣南圖書館，李真真女士

(Simplified characters)

广南图书馆征义工

活动：环境保护教育活动

　　欢迎15～25岁的高中生和大学生加入我们的义工团队

服务对象：6～10岁的小学生

地点：广南图书馆手工艺教室

日期：6月1日～30日（每周六或者周日）

时间：上午10:00～下午5:00（义工可以自由选择服务的时间）

工作内容：

　1. 协助管理小朋友参观团

　2. 协助带领小朋友做手工艺

　3. 协助组织教育讲座，维持秩序

报名截止：5月15日

申请资料：姓名、出生年月日、电话、地址、全身正面照片

报名方式：请将申请资料寄至 kidseducation@library.gov 广南图书馆，李真真女士

19. This advertisement is seeking

　A) story tellers for the library's kid program

　B) art teachers for handicraft lessons

　C) volunteers to assist an environmental education program

　D) students to perform in an environmental protection skit

20. Which of the following statements is TURE?

　A) Applications must be submitted to the front desk.

　B) The person who receives application is a staff member in a school.

　C) The work time will be 10:00 am to 5:00 pm from Monday to Friday.

　D) Applicants must be high school or college students.

Read this public sign.

(Traditional characters)   (Simplified characters)

上下扶梯
緊握扶手

上下扶梯
紧握扶手

21. Where would the sign most likely appear?

   A) Next to an escalator

   B) Next to a crosswalk

   C) In a classroom

   D) In an elevator

22. What is the purpose of the sign?

   A) To remind everyone to slow down

   B) To remind everyone of the detour ahead

   C) To remind everyone of the road work ahead

   D) To remind everyone how to stay safe

Read this event brochure.

(Traditional characters)

愛華超市爲回饋顧客推出中秋美食節

10月15日至30日，在北德州愛華超市分店舉辦的中秋美食節將帶給顧客一場不用出國的中國美食之旅。活動包括品嚐中國各地小吃、聽中國文化講座、學做中國菜、學寫中國字、學畫中國畫等。每天中午還有精彩的中國民族舞蹈表演。

入場費每人5美元（不限大人小孩兒）。只要5美元，您就可以享用現場所有美食并參加所有的活動。由於場地大小限制，一天只允許200人入場。有意參加者請在10月15日以前報名，并交付5美元費用。名額有限，欲報從速！

詳情請查詢本超市網站:http://txmarket.com

(Simplified characters)

爱华超市为回馈顾客推出中秋美食节

10月15日至30日，在北德州爱华超市分店举办的中秋美食节将带给顾客一场不用出国的中国美食之旅。活动包括品尝中国各地小吃、听中国文化讲座、学做中国菜、学写中国字、学画中国画等。每天中午还有精彩的中国民族舞蹈表演。

入场费每人5美元（不限大人小孩儿）。只要5美元，您就可以享用现场所有美食并参加所有的活动。由于场地大小限制，一天只允许200人入场。有意参加者请在10月15日以前报名，并交付5美元费用。名额有限，欲报从速！

详情请查询本超市网站:http://txmarket.com

23. What type of event does the brochure announce?

    A) A film festival

    B) An art festival

    C) A beer festival

    D) A food festival

24. Which of the following statements about the program is TRUE?

    A) There is a limit on the number of participants each day.

    B) Children will pay half of the entrance fee.

    C) There is an extra fee for attending cooking classes.

    D) The festival is organized by an immigrant's association.

25. The program will include each of the following activities EXCEPT

    A) food tasting

    B) wine tasting

    C) dance performance

    D) cultural presentations

Read this journalistic article.

(Traditional characters)

紙幣會消失嗎

你多久沒使用紙幣了？你最近一次到取款機取現金是什麼時候？在美國生活需要用到紙幣的地方非常少，大多數的時候都可以用電子貨幣來付錢。用電子貨幣付錢比用紙幣方便、安全、快速。使用信用卡、電子支付這些電子貨幣最大的好處是所有的消費行爲都有記錄，可以防止一些非法的交易行爲，比如買賣毒品、非法打工、地下經濟交易等。

消費稅也可以通過信用卡、電子支付這類公司來收取，可以避免現金交易時不交稅的情況。甚至官員、領導也不能貪污受賄，即使他們通過一些方式得到了錢也不敢花，因爲電子貨幣的使用全部都有記錄。

但是，電子貨幣也有一些缺點，比如，信用卡系統有時會出故障，刷卡機讀不出來；刷卡和手機電子支付需要網絡和電，有些山區和鄉村的網絡可能不穩定。電子貨幣雖然方便，但只要還有需要用到紙幣的場合和情境，紙幣就不會被淘汰。

(Simplified characters)

纸币会消失吗

你多久没使用纸币了？你最近一次到取款机取现金是什么时候？在美国生活需要用到纸币的地方非常少，大多数的时候都可以用电子货币来付钱。用电子货币付钱比用纸币方便、安全、快速。使用信用卡、电子支付这些电子货币最大的好处是所有的消费行为都有记录，可以防止一些非法的交易行为，比如买卖毒品、非法打工、地下经济交易等。

消费税也可以通过信用卡、电子支付这类公司来收取，可以避免现金交易时不交税的情况。甚至官员、领导也不能贪污受贿，即使他们通过一些方式得到了钱也不敢花，因为电子货币的使用全部都有记录。

但是，电子货币也有一些缺点，比如，信用卡系统有时会出故障，刷卡机读不出来；刷卡和手机电子支付需要网络和电，有些山区和乡村的网络可能不稳定。电子货币虽然方便，但只要还有需要用到纸币的场合和情境，纸币就不会被淘汰。

26. What is the theme of this article?

    A) Electronic money is better than paper money.

    B) Paper money is better than electronic money.

    C) Automated Teller Machines (ATM) are replacing banks.

    D) The best way to prevent identity theft is to use credit cards.

27. According to the article, how is electronic money different from paper money?

    A) They are more eco-friendly.

    B) They can be used everywhere.

    C) They are more convenient to use.

    D) They can be shared by the whole family.

28. The article mentioned the following benefits when using electronic money EXCEPT

    A) preventing illegal working

    B) preventing underground trading

    C) tracking spending activities

    D) earning certain benefits for discounts

29. The article mentioned the following possible problems when using electronic money EXCEPT

   A) occasional system malfunctions

   B) unstable internet connection

   C) account overdraft

   D) devices out of power

30. According to the author, what will happen in a world using only electronic money?

   A) There will be no crime of bribery anymore.

   B) There will be more cases of tax evasion.

   C) No need to carry a wallet anymore.

   D) Everyone will have a smart phone.

Read this short story.

(Traditional characters)

意文很喜歡海，一看到一望無際的大海就心情舒暢。今年暑假她又到小姨在佛羅里達的家去玩兒，天天跟著表姐到海邊，一會兒游泳，一會兒划船，玩兒得很開心。今年她還學會了浮潛，只要帶著浮潛面罩和呼吸管，隨時都可以下水去看看海裡的世界，而且穿著救生衣浮在海上，一點兒都不累。海裡有些地方什麼都沒有，只有沙，有些地方有各式各樣的魚和水草，還有彩色的珊瑚礁，讓她大開眼界。

意文從小就愛漂亮，她雖然喜歡到海邊去曬太陽，但是她天天都擦厚厚的防曬霜。甚至只要不在水裡，比如在船上或者在海邊，她就會穿上長袖襯衫遮陽。她可一點兒都不想曬傷。

在小姨家玩兒了一個星期後，她的臉又紅又腫，她以為是因為花了太多時間曬太陽、泡海水，所以就決定只在海邊散步吹風，不下水了。而且塗上更厚的防曬霜，還戴上大帽子。沒想到過了幾天，皮膚還是紅腫，而且摸起來厚厚的，有點兒像雞皮，雖然不疼也不癢。小姨越看越擔心，就決定帶意文到急診室去。

護士把意文叫進去後，先幫她量體溫和血壓，接著問了她的症狀，然後就把她帶到一個大房間裡坐下。她跟小姨等了快一個小時纔有一位醫生來看她。醫生檢查完她的臉和手，跟她說這是過敏，還問她吃了什麼、臉上塗了什麼；最後醫生說她可能是對防曬霜過敏。意文覺得很奇怪，因為這個牌子的防曬霜，她用了很多年了，從來不過敏。醫生說過敏的原因很多，有些東西你用了二十年都沒事兒，也會突然就過敏了。

意文按照醫生的處方買了藥膏來擦，也不再擦防曬霜，兩天后皮膚就恢復了。

原來她是對防曬霜過敏啊！在她找到新的、不過敏的防曬霜之前，她到海邊去玩兒就只能夠通過穿長袖衣服和長褲、戴大帽子來防曬了。

(Simplified characters)

意文很喜欢海，一看到一望无际的大海就心情舒畅。今年暑假她又到小姨在佛罗里达的家去玩儿，天天跟着表姐到海边，一会儿游泳，一会儿划船，玩儿得很开心。今年她还学会了浮潜，只要带着浮潜面罩和呼吸管，随时都可以下水去看看海里的世界，而且穿着救生衣浮在海上，一点儿都不累。海里有些地方什么都没有，只有沙，有些地方有各式各样的鱼和水草，还有彩色的珊瑚礁，让她大开眼界。

意文从小就爱漂亮，她虽然喜欢到海边去晒太阳，但是她天天都擦厚厚的防晒霜。甚至只要不在水里，比如在船上或者在海边，她就会穿上长袖衬衫遮阳。她可一点儿都不想晒伤。

在小姨家玩儿了一个星期后，她的脸又红又肿，她以为是因为花了太多时间晒太阳、泡海水，所以就决定只在海边散步吹风，不下水了。而且涂上更厚的防晒霜，还戴上大帽子。没想到过了几天，皮肤还是红肿，而且摸起来厚厚的，有点儿像鸡皮，虽然不疼也不痒。小姨越看越担心，就决定带意文到急诊室去。

护士把意文叫进去后，先帮她量体温和血压，接着问了她的症状，然后就把她带到一个大房间里坐下。她跟小姨等了快一个小时才有一位医生来看她。医生检查完她的脸和手，跟她说这是过敏，还问她吃了什么、脸上涂了什么；最后医生说她可能是对防晒霜过敏。意文觉得很奇怪，因为这个牌子的防晒霜，她用了很多年了，从来不过敏。医生说过敏的原因很多，有些东西你用了二十年都没事儿，也会突然就过敏了。

意文按照医生的处方买了药膏来擦，也不再擦防晒霜，两天后皮肤就恢复了。原来她是对防晒霜过敏啊！在她找到新的、不过敏的防晒霜之前，她到海边去玩儿就只能够通过穿长袖衣服和长裤、戴大帽子来防晒了。

31. Yiwen did many activities this past summer EXCEPT

　　A) swimming

　　B) kayaking

　　C) snorkeling

　　D) fishing

32. Why didn't Yiwen get tired when snorkeling?

　　A) Because she wore a life jacket.

B) Because she was not moving her legs.

C) Because her cousin carried her in the water.

D) Because she is a good swimmer.

33. Which of the following procedures did the medical professionals in the article NOT perform?

    A) Taking temperature

    B) Taking blood pressure

    C) Asking for symptoms

    D) Drawing blood

34. Why does Yiwen's skin turn red?

    A) She has red makeup on her cheeks.

    B) She wears a red hat.

    C) She has skin allergy.

    D) She drinks too much carrot juice.

35. Why does Yiwen always wear sunscreen when going to the beach?

    A) Because her doctor advised her to do so.

    B) Because she wants to protect her skin from the sun.

    C) Because she is allergic to sunshine.

    D) Because her mother asks her to do so.

36. According to the doctor, what is the reason that caused the allergy?

    A) The illness is genetic.

    B) The illness is contagious.

    C) There are many possible reasons.

    D) The sunscreen has poor quality.

37. What is Yiwen unlikely to wear when she visits the beach next summer?

    A) A long-sleeved shirt

    B) A pair of long pants

    C) A big hat

    D) A swimsuit

END OF SECTION I

YOU MAY REVIEW WORK IF THERE IS TIME LEFT.

DO NOT GO ON TO SECTION II UNTIL YOU ARE TOLD TO DO SO.

Section II: Free Response

Part A: Writing (Story Narration and E-mail Response)

Note: In this part of the exam, the student may NOT move back and forth among questions.

> **Writing Part Directions**
>
> You will be asked to perform two writing tasks in Chinese. In each case, you will be asked to write for a specific purpose and to a specific person. You should write in as complete and as culturally appropriate a manner as possible, taking into account the purpose and the person described.

> **Presentational Writing: Story Narration (15%, 15 minutes)**
>
> The four pictures present a story. Imagine you are writing the story for a friend. Narrate a complete story as suggested by the pictures. Give your story a beginning, a middle, and an end.

Interpersonal Writing: E-mail Response (10%, 15 minutes)

Read this e-mail from a friend and then type a response.

(Traditional characters)

收件箱
發件人：林安娜
收件人：王宜靜
郵件主題：送爺爺什麼生日禮物
發件日期：10月8日
宜靜：
　　謝謝你請我下個週末去你家參加王爺爺的生日會。每次去你家，你爺爺都做很多又新鮮又美味的廣東菜請我吃，還耐心地教我下棋。我很感謝他。今年他七十歲了，我想要給他選一個特別的禮物。你覺得我送什麼禮物比較合適？爲什麼？除了禮物以外，我還應該帶些什麼？我打算後天去買禮物，希望很快收到你的回信！謝謝！
　　　　　　　　　　　　　　　　　　　　　　　　　　　　　　安娜

(Simplified characters)

收件箱
发件人：林安娜
收件人：王宜静
邮件主题：送爷爷什么生日礼物
发件日期：10月8日
宜静：
　　谢谢你请我下个周末去你家参加王爷爷的生日会。每次去你家，你爷爷都做很多又新鲜又美味的广东菜请我吃，还耐心地教我下棋。我很感谢他。今年他七十岁了，我想要给他选一个特别的礼物。你觉得我送什么礼物比较合适？为什么？除了礼物以外，我还应该带些什么？我打算后天去买礼物，希望很快收到你的回信！谢谢！
　　　　　　　　　　　　　　　　　　　　　　　　　　　　　　安娜

Part B: Speaking (Conversation and Cultural Presentation)

Note: In this part of the exam, you may NOT move back and forth among questions.

speaking

> **Speaking Part Directions: Conversation**
>
> You will participate in a simulated conversation. Each time it is your turn to speak, you will have 20 seconds to record. You should respond as fully and as appropriately as possible. There will be six times when it is your turn to speak.

> **Interpersonal Speaking: Conversation (10%, 4 minutes)**
>
> Faculty adviser Tianzhen is interviewing you for a volunteer position in a Student Internet Committee at your school. The goal of the committee is to promote correct use of the internet.

Speaking Question 1 of 7

1. Record your answer. (20 seconds)

Speaking Question 2 of 7

2. Record your answer. (20 seconds)

Speaking Question 3 of 7

3. Record your answer. (20 seconds)

Speaking Question 4 of 7

4. Record your answer. (20 seconds)

Speaking Question 5 of 7

5. Record your answer. (20 seconds)

Speaking Question 6 of 7

6. Record your answer. (20 seconds)

Speaking Part Directions: Cultural Presentation

You will be asked to speak in Chinese on a specific topic. Imagine you are making an oral presentation to your Chinese class. First, you will read and hear the topic for your presentation. You will have 4 minutes to prepare your presentation. Then you will have 2 minutes to record your presentation. Your presentation should be as complete as possible.

Presentational Speaking: Cultural Presentation (15%, 7 minutes)

Speaking Question 7 of 7

7. Choose ONE Chinese art form (calligraphy, painting, paper cutting, jade jewelry, porcelain pottery, Beijing Opera, etc.). In your presentation, describe this art form and explain its significance.

You have four minutes to prepare your presentation. (240 seconds)
You have two minutes to record your presentation. (120 seconds)

YOU HAVE FINISHED THIS PART OF THE EXAM.
END OF EXAM

AP Chinese Language and Culture Test 10

listening

Section I: Multiple Choice

Part A: Listening (Rejoinders and Listening Selections)

Listening Part Directions

You will answer two types of questions: rejoinders and questions based on listening selections.

For all tasks, you will have a specific amount of response time. When the response time has ended, you will automatically go on to the nest question. You cannot return to previous questions.

Listening Part Directions: Rejoinders (10%, 10 minutes)

You will hear several short conversations or parts of conversations followed by four choices, designated A, B, C, and D. Choose the one that continues or completes the conversation in a logical and culturally appropriate manner. After you have decided which of the suggested answers is best, COMPLETELY fill in the corresponding circle on the answer sheet. You will have 5 seconds to answer each question.

YOU WILL NOW BEGIN THIS PART.

1. Mark your answer on your answer sheet.
2. Mark your answer on your answer sheet.
3. Mark your answer on your answer sheet.
4. Mark your answer on your answer sheet.
5. Mark your answer on your answer sheet.
6. Mark your answer on your answer sheet.
7. Mark your answer on your answer sheet.
8. Mark your answer on your answer sheet.
9. Mark your answer on your answer sheet.
10. Mark your answer on your answer sheet.
11. Mark your answer on your answer sheet.
12. Mark your answer on your answer sheet.
13. Mark your answer on your answer sheet.
14. Mark your answer on your answer sheet.
15. Mark your answer on your answer sheet.

Listening Part Directions: Listening Selections (15%, 10 minutes)

You will listen to several selections in Chinese. For each selection, you will be told whether it will be played once or twice. You may take notes as you listen. Your notes will not be graded. After listening to each selection, you will see questions in English. For each question, choose the response that is best according to the selection. You will have 12 seconds to answer each question.

YOU WILL NOW BEGIN THIS PART.

Selection 1: Transportation Announcement (Selection plays two times.)

16. Where would the announcement be heard?

    A) On a subway train

    B) On a domestic flight

    C) On a school bus

    D) On a ferry boat

17. Part of the announcement specifically addresses people who are

    A) going to the library

    B) going to a martial art gym

    C) getting on the train on the left side

    D) transiting to another subway line

Selection 2: Voice Message (Selection plays two times.)

18. According to the message, where is Grandma now?

    A) In a hospital

    B) At a park

    C) In her apartment

    D) In a meeting

19. What is the speaker's plan after school?

    A) To go home

    B) To ride a bicycle

    C) To visit Grandma

    D) To visit neighbors

20. What happened to Grandma?

    A) She fell from stairs.

    B) She fell off from a bike.

    C) She fell off from a chair.

    D) She fell on a bus.

Selection 3: School Conversation (Selection plays one time.)

21. What is the overall topic of this conversation?

    A) Peking opera

    B) Beijing drama

    C) Nanjing opera

    D) Chinese Kungfu

22. The speakers talked about some aspects of the performance EXCEPT

    A) the stage designs

    B) the martial arts

    C) the costumes

    D) the music

23. What are the speakers likely to do in the near future?

    A) To go to see a movie

    B) To perform in a show

    C) To attend a singing class

    D) To go to a live performance

Selection 4: Radio Report (Selection plays one time.)

24. What is the topic of the radio report?

    A) The opening of a new supermarket

    B) The closing of a shopping mall

    C) Air pollution index for today

    D) A new policy for stores

25. The regulation will be in effect starting on

    A) June 1st of this year

    B) June 1st of next year

    C) June 21st of this year

    D) July 1st of next year

26. What action should the audience take?

   A) Stocking up on non-perishable food

   B) Stocking up on coins and paper money

   C) Preparing candles and a generator

   D) Preparing reusable shopping bags

Selection 5: Instructions (Selection plays one time.)

27. The instructions are given on a

   A) airplane

   B) bus

   C) train

   D) boat

28. The instructions provide information about

   A) the next stop for the train

   B) the embarking of the boat

   C) the departure of the airplane

   D) the descent of the airplane

29. The instructions end with

   A) an announcement of the arrival time

   B) a request to turn off electronic devices

   C) an invitation to become a member

   D) a report of the local weather

Selection 6: Conversation (Selection plays one time.)

30. Where did the conversation most likely take place?

   A) In a pharmacy

   B) In a restaurant

   C) In a department store

   D) In a grocery store

31. The first speaker thinks the red skirt is good for

   A) her birthday

   B) Mother's Day

C) Thanksgiving

D) New Year

32. Which one is NOT the reason why the mother refuses to buy the skirt?

   A) Her daughter has too many skirts.

   B) Her daughter has bought too many new clothes recently.

   C) She has bought a birthday gift for her daughter.

   D) She does not have enough cash with her.

33. Is the daughter able to purchase the red skirt?

   A) Yes, she can use her allowance.

   B) Yes, she has a gift card.

   C) No, it is not on sale.

   D) No, someone already bought it.

Part B: Reading Selections

Note: In this part of the exam, you may move back and forth among all the questions.

> **Reading Part Directions: Reading Selections (25%, 60 minutes)**
>
> You will read several selections in Chinese. Each selection is accompanied by a number of questions in English. For each question, choose the response that is best according to the selection. After you have decided which of the suggested answers is best, COMPLETELY fill in the corresponding circle on the answer sheet. Chinese tests appear here in both traditional and simplified characters. You will have 60 minutes to answer all questions.
> YOU WILL NOW BEGIN THIS PART.

Read this note.

(Traditional characters)

> 云云：
>
> 　　你到哪兒去了？這麼晚了還沒回宿舍。今天中午和晚上我來找你，都沒見到你。你借給我的企業管理課的筆記，我都看完了，太謝謝你了。剛好你的室友在，我就把筆記給了她，讓她轉交給你。你別忘了我們金融課的幾個同學約好了明天中午在學生餐廳一邊吃午飯一邊預習金融投資的課本。明天12點餐廳見，別不小心走錯地方。我們先吃飯、預習，再一起走到教室去上課。
>
> 　　　　　　　　　　　　　　　　　　　　　　　　　　　　　　小紅

(Simplified characters)

> 云云：
>
> 　　你到哪儿去了？这么晚了还没回宿舍。今天中午和晚上我来找你，都没见到你。你借给我的企业管理课的笔记，我都看完了，太谢谢你了。刚好你的室友在，我就把笔记给了她，让她转交给你。你别忘了我们金融课的几个同学约好了明天中午在学生餐厅一边吃午饭一边预习金融投资的课本。明天12点餐厅见，别不小心走错地方。我们先吃饭、预习，再一起走到教室去上课。
>
> 　　　　　　　　　　　　　　　　　　　　　　　　　　　　　　　　小红

1. What is likely to be the major of Yunyun and Xiaohong?

   A) Engineering

   B) History

   C) Psychology

   D) Business

2. What is the plan for Yunyun and Xiaohong tomorrow?

   A) To preview the textbook before going to the class

   B) To go to the class before reviewing the textbook

   C) To preview the textbook while eating dinner

   D) To go to the class before having lunch

3. What did Xiaohong borrow from Yunyun?

   A) Her notes about a novel

   B) Her notes for a class

   C) Her textbook of a class

   D) Her travel diary

Read this e-mail.

(Traditional characters)

> 收件箱
>
> 發件人：李建中
>
> 收件人：李明潔
>
> 郵件主題：我的一天
>
> 發件日期：11月9日

小潔：

很高興收到你的電郵。你的老師讓你們採訪爺爺或奶奶的一天？這個題目真好！老師是讓你們多關心老人吧？那爺爺就給你介紹介紹我一天的生活吧！

我每天一早起床就先出去買早餐，最常吃的是肉包和饅頭夾蛋，接著去便利商店買報紙。回家看完報紙就看看電視上的球賽；沒有球賽的時候，就在網絡上打麻將。你爺爺我很聰明，打麻將百戰百勝，連電腦都輸給我，哈哈！我中午一般會煮一碗湯麵。雖然吃得簡單，但是我很注重營養，湯麵裡會放很多肉和青菜。

午飯後我去睡一個小時的午覺。下午會出門找鄰居或者朋友喝喝茶聊聊天兒，每三天去市場買一次菜，偶爾也去看醫生。晚上，我一般會準備兩菜一湯的晚餐，一邊吃著豐盛的晚餐，一邊看精彩的電視劇。我最近學會了在網上找電視劇，所以現在我可以看的電視劇就更多了。9點我就準備睡覺了。雖然一個人住，但是我把自己照顧得很好，你跟你爸就別擔心我了。先寫到這兒，下次再聊。

爺爺

(Simplified characters)

收件箱
发件人：李建中
收件人：李明洁
邮件主题：我的一天
发件日期：11月9日

小洁：

很高兴收到你的电邮。你的老师让你们采访爷爷或奶奶的一天？这个题目真好！老师是让你们多关心老人吧？那爷爷就给你介绍介绍我一天的生活吧！

我每天一早起床就先出去买早餐，最常吃的是肉包和馒头夹蛋，接着去便利商店买报纸。回家看完报纸就看看电视上的球赛；没有球赛的时候，就在网络上打麻将。你爷爷我很聪明，打麻将百战百胜，连电脑都输给我，哈哈！我中午一般会煮一碗汤面。虽然吃得简单，但是我很注重营养，汤面里会放很多肉和青菜。

午饭后我去睡一个小时的午觉。下午会出门找邻居或者朋友喝喝茶聊聊天儿，每三天去市场买一次菜，偶尔也去看医生。晚上，我一般会准备两菜一汤的晚餐，一边吃着丰盛的晚餐，一边看精彩的电视剧。我最近学会了在网上找电视剧，所以现在我可以看的电视剧就更多了。9点我就准备睡觉了。虽然一个人住，但是我把自己照顾得很好，你跟你爸就别担心我了。先写到这儿，下次再聊。

爷爷

4. What game is Grandpa very good at?

   A) Mahjong

   B) Chinese Go

   C) Ping Pong

   D) Chess

5. What does Grandpa do in the morning?

   A) Chatting with friends

   B) Cooking breakfast

   C) Watching TV drama series

   D) Reading newspaper

6. What does Grandpa do in the afternoon occasionally?

   A) Going to the doctors

   B) Having tea with friends

   C) Chatting with neighbors

   D) Taking a nap

7. Who is Grandpa Li?

   A) A man living by himself

   B) A man living in a nursing home

   C) A man who has a full-time job

   D) A man who likes to exercise

Read this e-mail.

(Traditional characters)

收件箱

發件人：李育英

收件人：王美文

郵件主題：參觀學生活動中心

發件日期：8月28日

美文：

　　對不起，本來說好今天傍晚5點要帶你參觀學生活動中心，可是我的家教學生臨時有事，家教課往後推遲了一個小時，所以我6點纔會到。你還是可以5點到，先到處看一看。

從大門一進去就能看到右邊的咖啡館，再往前走會看到很多桌椅，有學生在那裡做作業、吃飯。那裡有五家各式各樣的餐飲店，你先隨便看看，想想晚餐吃哪一家。我一下課就去那邊找你，我們先吃飯，然後我再帶你參觀書店、電腦室、社團活動室和沙發休息區。之後，我們再到活動中心外面的湖邊散步，你看這樣好嗎？

育英

(Simplified characters)

收件箱
发件人：李育英
收件人：王美文
邮件主题：参观学生活动中心
发件日期：8月28日

美文：

对不起，本来说好今天傍晚5点要带你参观学生活动中心，可是我的家教学生临时有事，家教课往后推迟了一个小时，所以我6点才会到。你还是可以5点到，先到处看一看。

从大门一进去就能看到右边的咖啡馆，再往前走会看到很多桌椅，有学生在那里做作业、吃饭。那里有五家各式各样的餐饮店，你先随便看看，想想晚餐吃哪一家。我一下课就去那边找你，我们先吃饭，然后我再带你参观书店、电脑室、社团活动室和沙发休息区。之后，我们再到活动中心外面的湖边散步，你看这样好吗？

育英

8. Which of the following is located next to the entrance?

A) A coffee shop

B) A cafeteria

C) A lounge

D) A study area

9. Where is the student activity center?

    A) Next to the gym

    B) Next to a small lake

    C) Next to a dorm

    D) Next to the sports field

10. Which of the following does the student activity center have?

    A) A bank

    B) A computer room

    C) A small clinic

    D) A library

Read this pen-pal letter.

(Traditional characters)

傑克：

真不好意思，剛到家的時候我太累了，就只給你發了短信。現在纔有精神給你寫信。

非常感謝你的招待，在舊金山遊玩的一個月我真的太開心了，一點兒也不想回家。星期一從舊金山坐了12個小時的飛機回到北京，我在飛機上睡不著，回到家實在累壞了。到的時候雖然是白天，但我還是睡著了。醒來的時候天已經黑了。

中國和加州有15個小時的時差，所以雖然是半夜，我還是很清醒，看了一個晚上的電視，吃了一堆零食，天亮的時候我又累了。第二天第三天，甚至是第四天也一樣：半夜很清醒，白天什麼都不想做，給家人的禮物都還在我的行李箱裡呢！

我媽問我怎麼四天了還在睡，還說我這不是時差，是懶惰，是因爲快開學了，不想回學校。到第五天我終於把時差倒過來了，也把行李整理好了。希望你寒假來北京玩兒的時候不會有時差問題。

祝你新學期一切順利！

學文

(Simplified characters)

杰克：

真不好意思，刚到家的时候我太累了，就只给你发了短信。现在才有精神给你写信。

非常感谢你的招待，在旧金山游玩的一个月我真的太开心了，一点儿也不想回家。星期一从旧金山坐了12个小时的飞机回到北京，我在飞机上睡不着，回到家实在累坏了。到的时候虽然是白天，但我还是睡着了。醒来的时候天已经黑了。

中国和加州有15个小时的时差，所以虽然是半夜，我还是很清醒，看了一个晚上的电视，吃了一堆零食，天亮的时候我又累了。第二天第三天，甚至是第四天也一样：半夜很清醒，白天什么都不想做，给家人的礼物都还在我的行李箱里呢！

我妈问我怎么四天了还在睡，还说我这不是时差，是懒惰，是因为快开学了，不想回学校。到第五天我终于把时差倒过来了，也把行李整理好了。希望你寒假来北京玩儿的时候不会有时差问题。

祝你新学期一切顺利！

学文

11. Xuewen is writing the letter to his pen-pal in order to

    A) express his gratitude and chat about his daily life

    B) discuss his plan to visit San Francisco

    C) give him information about international flight

    D) share his school experience in Beijing

12. What did Xuewen experience after returning home?

    A) Stress of getting back to school

    B) Lots of house chores to do

    C) Serious jet lag due to travel

    D) Exhaustion due to over-exercise

13. How does Xuewen keep in touch with Jack?

    A) Text messaging and writing letters

    B) Making audio and video calls on the internet

    C) Playing online video games together

    D) Following each other's social media posts

14. What does Xuewen do when he cannot fall asleep at night?

    A) Unpacking his luggage

    B) Preparing for school

    C) Watching television

    D) Writing letters

15. What does Jack plan to do this winter?

    A) To visit Beijing

    B) To study abroad

    C) To go to Nanjing

    D) To rest at home

Read this poster announcement.

(Traditional characters)

向陽區圖書館免費電影欣賞
　　電影《海洋天堂》
一個父親傾盡全力守護兒子的故事
一部深入描述家庭父子關係的好片

地點：圖書館三樓多功能廳
時間：5月9日（星期六）下午3點
　　　5月10日（星期日）下午3點

本電影適合全家觀賞
每場限50人，請在一樓櫃臺取票

(Simplified characters)

向阳区图书馆免费电影欣赏
　　电影《海洋天堂》
一个父亲倾尽全力守护儿子的故事
一部深入描述家庭父子关系的好片

地点：图书馆三楼多功能厅
时间：5月9日（星期六）下午3点
　　　5月10日（星期日）下午3点

本电影适合全家观赏
每场限50人，请在一楼柜台取票

16. Which of the following statements is TRUE about the event?

    A) No entrance ticket is required.

    B) The screening is held in a classroom.

    C) Each screening is limited to 50 people.

    D) There will be three screening sessions of the film.

17. What is the rating of the film in America?

    A) G – General Audiences

    B) PG – Parental Guidance Suggested

    C) PG-13 – Parents Strongly Cautioned

    D) R – Restricted

18. What is the theme of this film?

    A) Father-daughter relationship

    B) Family-society relationship

C) Father-son relationship
D) Family-neighbor relationship

Read this advertisement.

(Traditional characters)

<pre>
                        廣場舞大賽
參賽選手：廣場舞愛好者，年齡不限，男女均可
參賽隊伍：5～15人

比賽時間：初賽3月5日～7日，下午1點到5點
比賽時間：決賽3月14日，晚上7點到9點
比賽地點：新北中學體育館
比賽獎金：進入決賽的十支隊伍獎勵500元車馬費
         決賽獲勝隊伍最高可得獎金5,000元，並參加電視節目表演

報名截止：1月15日
申請資料：隊內所有成員的姓名、出生年月日、電話、地址、全身正面照片
報名方式：請將申請資料寄至 lovedance@community.net 新北社區中心，王明先生
</pre>

(Simplified characters)

<pre>
                        广场舞大赛
参赛选手：广场舞爱好者，年龄不限，男女均可
参赛队伍：5～15人

比赛时间：初赛3月5日～7日，下午1点到5点
比赛时间：决赛3月14日，晚上7点到9点
比赛地点：新北中学体育馆
比赛奖金：进入决赛的十支队伍奖励500元车马费
         决赛获胜队伍最高可得奖金5,000元，并参加电视节目表演

报名截止：1月15日
申请资料：队内所有成员的姓名、出生年月日、电话、地址、全身正面照片
报名方式：请将申请资料寄至 lovedance@community.net 新北社区中心，王明先生
</pre>

19. This advertisement is seeking

    A) students for a dance studio

    B) contesters for a dance competition

    C) judges for a dance competition

    D) participants for a dance TV show

20. What is a necessary step in the application process?

    A) To call Mr. Wang to apply

    B) To participate in a face-to-face interview

    C) To complete an online application form

    D) To form a team with at least five people

Read this public sign.

(Traditional characters)

今日學校舉辦籃球比賽
運動場東邊的停車場禁止停車

(Simplified characters)

今日学校举办篮球比赛
运动场东边的停车场禁止停车

21. Where would the sign most likely appear?

    A) At a bus stop

    B) At a school

    C) At an airport

    D) In a hospital

22. What is the purpose of the sign?

    A) To inform people not to park on the streets

    B) To inform people not to park in front of a gym

    C) To inform people not to park in a parking lot

    D) To inform people not to park in front of a building

Read this event brochure.

(Traditional characters)

東城小牛隊今年暑假將在小牛籃球館舉辦三期籃球夏令營，每期七天六夜。
第一期7月6日至7月12日，第二期7月13日至7月19日，第三期7月20日至7月26日。

　　　　小牛隊曾獲得美國男籃職業聯賽（NBA）三次總冠軍。自2010年開始舉辦高質量籃球夏令營，對6～12歲男學生開放。無論你是運動新手還是校隊隊員，我們都能幫你提高運動技能，讓你享受運動的快樂。

　　　　夏令營每期收費2,200美元，包括學費、食宿費及紀念品。有意報名者請在5月1日以前完成報名手續，並交付200美元訂金。

　　　　詳情請查詢小牛隊夏令營網站: http://basketball.com

(Simplified characters)

　　　　东城小牛队今年暑假将在小牛篮球馆举办三期篮球夏令营，每期七天六夜。

　　　　第一期7月6日至7月12日，第二期7月13日至7月19日，第三期7月20日至7月26日。

　　　　小牛队曾获得美国男篮职业联赛（NBA）三次总冠军。自2010年开始举办高质量篮球夏令营，对6～12岁男学生开放。无论你是运动新手还是校队队员，我们都能帮你提高运动技能，让你享受运动的快乐。

　　　　夏令营每期收费2,200美元，包括学费、食宿费及纪念品。有意报名者请在5月1日以前完成报名手续，并交付200美元订金。

　　　　详情请查询小牛队夏令营网站: http://basketball.com

23. What type of event does the brochure announce?

　　A) A summer basketball camp

　　B) A winter ski camp

　　C) A winter baseball camp

　　D) A summer football camp

24. Which of the following statements about the program is TRUE?

　　A) There will be a total of four camps.

　　B) The camp will last five days and four nights.

　　C) The camps are hosted by a professional team.

　　D) The camp goers will compete for champions.

25. According to the brochure, which of the following expenses is NOT included in the program fee?

　　A) Meals

　　B) Tuition

C) Souvenirs
D) Books

Read this journalistic article.

(Traditional characters)

森林大火無情　　野生動物遭殃

美新社4月3日報道，從去年10月到今年4月澳大利亞森林大火不斷發生，目前已經造成30人死亡，數千棟房屋被燒毀。這是澳大利亞有史以來最嚴重的森林大火。

這場持續了超過六個月的森林大火，還造成了至少30億隻動物死亡或者失去家園，其中包括哺乳動物、爬行動物、鳥類，還有蛙類。究竟有多少動物死於火災，實際的具體數目還不確定。但即使是那些從大火中成功逃生的動物，它們活下去的希望也不樂觀，因爲它們失去了食物來源，也失去了賴以生存的家。

動物專家科克教授表示："這個報道令人震驚。很難想象世界上還會有其他的事故造成這麼多的動物死亡或者無家可歸。這已經是歷史上最嚴重的野生動物災難。"他也發出警告，"森林大火會變得越來越常見"。因爲全球氣候變暖和持續的乾旱，未來這類森林火災持續的時間會更長，而且發生的頻率也會更高。如果我們不積極改善氣候變暖的問題，動物和人類的災難會繼續發生。

(Simplified characters)

森林大火无情　　野生动物遭殃

美新社4月3日报道，从去年10月到今年4月澳大利亚森林大火不断发生，目前已经造成30人死亡，数千栋房屋被烧毁。这是澳大利亚有史以来最严重的森林大火。

这场持续了超过六个月的森林大火，还造成了至少30亿只动物死亡或者失去家园，其中包括哺乳动物、爬行动物、鸟类，还有蛙类。究竟有多少动物死于火灾，实际的具体数目还不确定。但即使是那些从大火中成功逃生的动物，它们活下去的希望也不乐观，因为它们失去了食物来源，也失去了赖以生存的家。

动物专家科克教授表示："这个报道令人震惊。很难想象世界上还会有其他的事故造成这么多的动物死亡或者无家可归。这已经是历史上最严重的野生动物灾难。"他也发出警告，"森林大火会变得越来越常见"。因为全球气候变暖和持续的干旱，未来这类森林火灾持续的时间会更长，而且发生的频率也会更高。如果我们不积极改善气候变暖的问题，动物和人类的灾难会继续发生。

26. According to the article, the following types of animals were affected by the fire EXCEPT

   A) frogs

   B) insects

   C) birds

   D) snakes

27. According to the article, what is the world's largest disaster for animals?

   A) A flood

   B) An earthquake

   C) A hurricane

   D) A fire

28. What is the challenge for the survived animals?

   A) The incoming raining season

   B) Conversion of forest to fields

   C) Food sources and habitats

   D) Water supply and food sources

29. According to the article, what is a possible solution to prevent future forest fires?

   A) Controlling the global warming

   B) Preventing snowstorm damage

   C) Decreasing frequencies of tornadoes

   D) Removing old trees and plants

30. What is the warning from Professor Kirk?

   A) Wild animals will encounter more deadly disasters.

   B) Shocking news will become more common.

   C) Forest fires will become more and more frequent.

   D) A continuing drought will kill more people and animals.

Read this short story.

(Traditional characters)

點披薩外賣是很多人從小到大的共同記憶。對思文家來說，每到星期五晚上點披薩、可樂、雞翅，和家人一起坐在沙發上看電影就是最大的享受！這幾年來提供外賣的餐館兒越來越多，無論是中國餐館兒、義大利餐館兒，甚至是牛排店都有這項服務，所以她家週五晚餐的選擇就更多了。最近外賣平臺的興起更是讓一些沒有外賣送餐員的餐館兒也可以和平臺合作提供送餐服務。這個月，思文家每個人都忙著自己的工作或學習，所以他們幾乎一兩天就點一次外賣。但她家都是自己去取餐，這樣不用給小費，而且她家附近有很多飯館兒，取外賣很方便，花不了什麼時間。

一開始他們都是打電話點餐，但是有的時候電話裡面會聽不清楚。比如，他們最喜歡的披薩店也賣皮塔卷（Pita Wrap），但是點的人比較少，所以每次點皮塔都要跟接綫生重複說她們要的是皮塔不是披薩，特別麻煩。有的時候爲了說清楚要點的東西，只好去店裡點餐，還得站在店裡等。自從很多餐館兒有了自己的手機點餐軟件，這個問題就解決了。在手機上點餐再也沒有說話聽不清楚的問題，而且可以很容易地累積點數換餐，還能拿到很多折扣和優惠。

思文剛下載她最喜歡的三明治店的手機應用（App）就拿到了買一送一的優惠券。她立刻訂了她常吃的鮪魚三明治，還幫那天在家的哥哥點了餐。當她領了外賣回家，把哥哥的牛肉三明治拿給他的時候，很得意地說："我請你，不用給我錢。"其實那根本就是買一送一！

有的餐館兒把外賣的餐點放在門口的架子上，讓客人可以自己拿走；而有的餐館兒，你得請櫃臺的服務員拿給你。包裝好的食物有時候也會出點兒小問題。前幾天，她興致勃勃地想嘗試新口味，所以點了蘋果雞肉三明治，結果回到家纔發現師傅忘記放肉了，她那天中午只好吃素了。從那以後，思文就很小心了，每次一定會打開袋子看看，確認完了纔拿走。

(Simplified characters)

点披萨外卖是很多人从小到大的共同记忆。对思文家来说，每到星期五晚上点披萨、可乐、鸡翅，和家人一起坐在沙发上看电影就是最大的享受！这几年来提供外卖的餐馆儿越来越多，无论是中国餐馆儿、意大利餐馆儿，甚至是牛排店都有这项服务，所以她家周五晚餐的选择就更多了。最近外卖平台的兴起更是让一些没有外卖送餐员的餐馆儿也可以和平台合作提供送餐服务。这个月，思文家每个人都忙着自己的工作或学习，所以他们几乎一两天就点一次外卖。但她家都是自己去取餐，这样不用给小费，而且她家附近有很多饭馆儿，取外卖很方便，花不了什么时间。

一开始他们都是打电话点餐，但是有的时候电话里面会听不清楚。比如，他们最喜欢的披萨店也卖皮塔卷（Pita Wrap），但是点的人比较少，所以每次点皮塔都要跟接线生重复说她们要的是皮塔不是披萨，特别麻烦。有的时候为了说清楚要点的东西，只好去店里点餐，还得站在店里等。自从很多餐馆儿有了自己的手机点餐软件，这个问题就解决了。在手机上点餐再也没有说话听不清楚的问题，而且可以很容易地累积点数换餐，还能拿到很多折扣和优惠。

思文刚下载她最喜欢的三明治店的手机应用（App）就拿到了买一送一的优惠券。她立刻订了她常吃的鲔鱼三明治，还帮那天在家的哥哥点了餐。当她领了外卖回家，把哥哥的牛肉三明治拿给他的时候，很得意地说："我请你，不用给我钱。"其实那根本就是买一送一！

有的餐馆儿把外卖的餐点放在门口的架子上，让客人可以自己拿走；而有的餐馆儿，你得请柜台的服务员拿给你。包装好的食物有时候也会出点儿小问题。前几天，她兴致勃勃地想尝试新口味，所以点了苹果鸡肉三明治，结果回到家才发现师傅忘记放肉了，她那天中午只好吃素了。从那以后，思文就很小心了，每次一定会打开袋子看看，确认完了才拿走。

31. What does Siwen's family usually have for the Friday night dinner?

    A) Chinese carry-outs

    B) Italian food

    C) Pizza and wings

    D) Steak and salad

32. Why does Siwen's family not order food delivery?

    A) Because they can save the tip money.

    B) They don't know how to make a delivery order.

    C) Food delivery is not available in her town.

    D) They live in a very remote area.

33. Which method of ordering carry-out is NOT mentioned in the story?

    A) Making phone calls

    B) Ordering in the store

    C) Ordering on the website

    D) Using phone applications

34. What could be one of the problems of ordering food carry-out?

    A) The staff cannot hear clearly which food item you want to order.

    B) No silverware will be provided for carry-out.

C) Packaging fee will be charged for carry-out orders.

D) Customers cannot use coupons for carry-out orders.

35. According to the article, what would be an advantage of using a phone app to order food?

    A) It is easier to tip the staff.

    B) It is easier to read the menu.

    C) It is faster to complete the order.

    D) It is easier to accumulate reward points.

36. Why didn't Siwen ask her brother to pay for his sandwich?

    A) It was a free sandwich.

    B) It was his birthday.

    C) She wanted to give him a treat.

    D) Their parents paid for the food.

37. Why was there no meat on Siwen's sandwich?

    A) Because she ordered a veggie burger.

    B) Because she is a vegetarian.

    C) Because the chef forgot to put in meat.

    D) Because her brother ate it.

END OF SECTION I
YOU MAY REVIEW WORK IF THERE IS TIME LEFT.
DO NOT GO ON TO SECTION II UNTIL YOU ARE TOLD TO DO SO.

Section II: Free Response

Part A: Writing (Story Narration and E-mail Response)

Note: In this part of the exam, the student may NOT move back and forth among questions.

Writing Part Directions

You will be asked to perform two writing tasks in Chinese. In each case, you will be asked to write for a specific purpose and to a specific person. You should write in as complete and as culturally appropriate a manner as possible, taking into account the purpose and the person described.

Presentational Writing: Story Narration (15%, 15 minutes)

The four pictures present a story. Imagine you are writing the story for a friend. Narrate a complete story as suggested by the pictures. Give your story a beginning, a middle, and an end.

Interpersonal Writing: E-mail Response (10%, 15 minutes)

Read this e-mail from a friend and then type a response.

(Traditional characters)

收件箱

發件人：王麗美

收件人：李心明

郵件主題：暑假來上海玩兒

發件日期：5月30日

心明：

　　好久不見！我快要放暑假了，我打算回上海去看我的父母。你上個月跟我說你也計劃暑假的時候來上海旅行。上海有很多名勝古跡，你最想去什麼地方遊玩？爲什麼？上海也有很多好吃的飯館兒，你有什麼特別想吃的嗎？你在上海的時候可以住在我家，不用花錢住旅館，我也很期待跟你到處去遊玩。希望很快能收到你的回信。

麗美

(Simplified characters)

收件箱

发件人：王丽美

收件人：李心明

邮件主题：暑假来上海玩儿

发件日期：5月30日

心明：

　　好久不见！我快要放暑假了，我打算回上海去看我的父母。你上个月跟我说你也计划暑假的时候来上海旅行。上海有很多名胜古迹，你最想去什么地方游玩？为什么？上海也有很多好吃的饭馆儿，你有什么特别想吃的吗？你在上海的时候可以住在我家，不用花钱住旅馆，我也很期待跟你到处去游玩。希望很快能收到你的回信。

丽美

Part B: Speaking (Conversation and Cultural Presentation)

Note: In this part of the exam, you may NOT move back and forth among questions.

speaking

Speaking Part Directions: Conversation

You will participate in a simulated conversation. Each time it is your turn to speak, you will have 20 seconds to record. You should respond as fully and as appropriately as possible. There will be six times when it is your turn to speak.

Interpersonal Speaking: Conversation (10%, 4 minutes)

You and your friend Tianming are members of the Chinese Culture Club at school. You are having a video chat to discuss plans for the new school year.

Speaking Question 1 of 7
1. Record your answer. (20 seconds)

Speaking Question 2 of 7
2. Record your answer. (20 seconds)

Speaking Question 3 of 7
3. Record your answer. (20 seconds)

Speaking Question 4 of 7
4. Record your answer. (20 seconds)

Speaking Question 5 of 7
5. Record your answer. (20 seconds)

Speaking Question 6 of 7
6. Record your answer. (20 seconds

Speaking Part Directions: Cultural Presentation

You will be asked to speak in Chinese on a specific topic. Imagine you are making an oral presentation to your Chinese class. First, you will read and hear the topic for your presentation. You will have 4 minutes to prepare your presentation. Then you will have 2 minutes to record your presentation. Your presentation should be as complete as possible.

Presentational Speaking: Cultural Presentation (15%, 7 minutes)

Speaking Question 7 of 7

7. Choose ONE example of the use of technology in modern-day China (social media, online shopping, food delivery, mobile pay, bike share, ride share, robot appliances, smart homes, satellites, etc.). In your presentation, describe this use of technology and explain its significance.

You have four minutes to prepare your presentation. (240 seconds)
You have two minutes to record your presentation. (120 seconds)

YOU HAVE FINISHED THIS PART OF THE EXAM.
END OF EXAM

Student Answer Sheet 1

Section I A: Listening

1. Ⓐ Ⓑ Ⓒ Ⓓ
2. Ⓐ Ⓑ Ⓒ Ⓓ
3. Ⓐ Ⓑ Ⓒ Ⓓ
4. Ⓐ Ⓑ Ⓒ Ⓓ
5. Ⓐ Ⓑ Ⓒ Ⓓ
6. Ⓐ Ⓑ Ⓒ Ⓓ
7. Ⓐ Ⓑ Ⓒ Ⓓ
8. Ⓐ Ⓑ Ⓒ Ⓓ
9. Ⓐ Ⓑ Ⓒ Ⓓ
10. Ⓐ Ⓑ Ⓒ Ⓓ
11. Ⓐ Ⓑ Ⓒ Ⓓ
12. Ⓐ Ⓑ Ⓒ Ⓓ
13. Ⓐ Ⓑ Ⓒ Ⓓ
14. Ⓐ Ⓑ Ⓒ Ⓓ
15. Ⓐ Ⓑ Ⓒ Ⓓ
16. Ⓐ Ⓑ Ⓒ Ⓓ
17. Ⓐ Ⓑ Ⓒ Ⓓ
18. Ⓐ Ⓑ Ⓒ Ⓓ
19. Ⓐ Ⓑ Ⓒ Ⓓ
20. Ⓐ Ⓑ Ⓒ Ⓓ
21. Ⓐ Ⓑ Ⓒ Ⓓ
22. Ⓐ Ⓑ Ⓒ Ⓓ
23. Ⓐ Ⓑ Ⓒ Ⓓ
24. Ⓐ Ⓑ Ⓒ Ⓓ
25. Ⓐ Ⓑ Ⓒ Ⓓ
26. Ⓐ Ⓑ Ⓒ Ⓓ
27. Ⓐ Ⓑ Ⓒ Ⓓ
28. Ⓐ Ⓑ Ⓒ Ⓓ
29. Ⓐ Ⓑ Ⓒ Ⓓ
30. Ⓐ Ⓑ Ⓒ Ⓓ
31. Ⓐ Ⓑ Ⓒ Ⓓ
32. Ⓐ Ⓑ Ⓒ Ⓓ
33. Ⓐ Ⓑ Ⓒ Ⓓ
34. Ⓐ Ⓑ Ⓒ Ⓓ
35. Ⓐ Ⓑ Ⓒ Ⓓ

Section I B: Reading

1. Ⓐ Ⓑ Ⓒ Ⓓ
2. Ⓐ Ⓑ Ⓒ Ⓓ
3. Ⓐ Ⓑ Ⓒ Ⓓ
4. Ⓐ Ⓑ Ⓒ Ⓓ
5. Ⓐ Ⓑ Ⓒ Ⓓ
6. Ⓐ Ⓑ Ⓒ Ⓓ
7. Ⓐ Ⓑ Ⓒ Ⓓ
8. Ⓐ Ⓑ Ⓒ Ⓓ
9. Ⓐ Ⓑ Ⓒ Ⓓ
10. Ⓐ Ⓑ Ⓒ Ⓓ
11. Ⓐ Ⓑ Ⓒ Ⓓ
12. Ⓐ Ⓑ Ⓒ Ⓓ
13. Ⓐ Ⓑ Ⓒ Ⓓ
14. Ⓐ Ⓑ Ⓒ Ⓓ
15. Ⓐ Ⓑ Ⓒ Ⓓ
16. Ⓐ Ⓑ Ⓒ Ⓓ
17. Ⓐ Ⓑ Ⓒ Ⓓ
18. Ⓐ Ⓑ Ⓒ Ⓓ
19. Ⓐ Ⓑ Ⓒ Ⓓ
20. Ⓐ Ⓑ Ⓒ Ⓓ
21. Ⓐ Ⓑ Ⓒ Ⓓ
22. Ⓐ Ⓑ Ⓒ Ⓓ
23. Ⓐ Ⓑ Ⓒ Ⓓ
24. Ⓐ Ⓑ Ⓒ Ⓓ
25. Ⓐ Ⓑ Ⓒ Ⓓ
26. Ⓐ Ⓑ Ⓒ Ⓓ
27. Ⓐ Ⓑ Ⓒ Ⓓ
28. Ⓐ Ⓑ Ⓒ Ⓓ
29. Ⓐ Ⓑ Ⓒ Ⓓ
30. Ⓐ Ⓑ Ⓒ Ⓓ
31. Ⓐ Ⓑ Ⓒ Ⓓ
32. Ⓐ Ⓑ Ⓒ Ⓓ
33. Ⓐ Ⓑ Ⓒ Ⓓ
34. Ⓐ Ⓑ Ⓒ Ⓓ
35. Ⓐ Ⓑ Ⓒ Ⓓ

Student Answer Sheet 2

Section I A: Listening

1. Ⓐ Ⓑ Ⓒ Ⓓ
2. Ⓐ Ⓑ Ⓒ Ⓓ
3. Ⓐ Ⓑ Ⓒ Ⓓ
4. Ⓐ Ⓑ Ⓒ Ⓓ
5. Ⓐ Ⓑ Ⓒ Ⓓ
6. Ⓐ Ⓑ Ⓒ Ⓓ
7. Ⓐ Ⓑ Ⓒ Ⓓ
8. Ⓐ Ⓑ Ⓒ Ⓓ
9. Ⓐ Ⓑ Ⓒ Ⓓ
10. Ⓐ Ⓑ Ⓒ Ⓓ
11. Ⓐ Ⓑ Ⓒ Ⓓ
12. Ⓐ Ⓑ Ⓒ Ⓓ
13. Ⓐ Ⓑ Ⓒ Ⓓ
14. Ⓐ Ⓑ Ⓒ Ⓓ
15. Ⓐ Ⓑ Ⓒ Ⓓ
16. Ⓐ Ⓑ Ⓒ Ⓓ
17. Ⓐ Ⓑ Ⓒ Ⓓ
18. Ⓐ Ⓑ Ⓒ Ⓓ
19. Ⓐ Ⓑ Ⓒ Ⓓ
20. Ⓐ Ⓑ Ⓒ Ⓓ
21. Ⓐ Ⓑ Ⓒ Ⓓ
22. Ⓐ Ⓑ Ⓒ Ⓓ
23. Ⓐ Ⓑ Ⓒ Ⓓ
24. Ⓐ Ⓑ Ⓒ Ⓓ
25. Ⓐ Ⓑ Ⓒ Ⓓ
26. Ⓐ Ⓑ Ⓒ Ⓓ
27. Ⓐ Ⓑ Ⓒ Ⓓ
28. Ⓐ Ⓑ Ⓒ Ⓓ
29. Ⓐ Ⓑ Ⓒ Ⓓ
30. Ⓐ Ⓑ Ⓒ Ⓓ
31. Ⓐ Ⓑ Ⓒ Ⓓ
32. Ⓐ Ⓑ Ⓒ Ⓓ
33. Ⓐ Ⓑ Ⓒ Ⓓ
34. Ⓐ Ⓑ Ⓒ Ⓓ
35. Ⓐ Ⓑ Ⓒ Ⓓ

Section I B: Reading

1. Ⓐ Ⓑ Ⓒ Ⓓ
2. Ⓐ Ⓑ Ⓒ Ⓓ
3. Ⓐ Ⓑ Ⓒ Ⓓ
4. Ⓐ Ⓑ Ⓒ Ⓓ
5. Ⓐ Ⓑ Ⓒ Ⓓ
6. Ⓐ Ⓑ Ⓒ Ⓓ
7. Ⓐ Ⓑ Ⓒ Ⓓ
8. Ⓐ Ⓑ Ⓒ Ⓓ
9. Ⓐ Ⓑ Ⓒ Ⓓ
10. Ⓐ Ⓑ Ⓒ Ⓓ
11. Ⓐ Ⓑ Ⓒ Ⓓ
12. Ⓐ Ⓑ Ⓒ Ⓓ
13. Ⓐ Ⓑ Ⓒ Ⓓ
14. Ⓐ Ⓑ Ⓒ Ⓓ
15. Ⓐ Ⓑ Ⓒ Ⓓ
16. Ⓐ Ⓑ Ⓒ Ⓓ
17. Ⓐ Ⓑ Ⓒ Ⓓ
18. Ⓐ Ⓑ Ⓒ Ⓓ
19. Ⓐ Ⓑ Ⓒ Ⓓ
20. Ⓐ Ⓑ Ⓒ Ⓓ
21. Ⓐ Ⓑ Ⓒ Ⓓ
22. Ⓐ Ⓑ Ⓒ Ⓓ
23. Ⓐ Ⓑ Ⓒ Ⓓ
24. Ⓐ Ⓑ Ⓒ Ⓓ
25. Ⓐ Ⓑ Ⓒ Ⓓ
26. Ⓐ Ⓑ Ⓒ Ⓓ
27. Ⓐ Ⓑ Ⓒ Ⓓ
28. Ⓐ Ⓑ Ⓒ Ⓓ
29. Ⓐ Ⓑ Ⓒ Ⓓ
30. Ⓐ Ⓑ Ⓒ Ⓓ
31. Ⓐ Ⓑ Ⓒ Ⓓ
32. Ⓐ Ⓑ Ⓒ Ⓓ
33. Ⓐ Ⓑ Ⓒ Ⓓ
34. Ⓐ Ⓑ Ⓒ Ⓓ
35. Ⓐ Ⓑ Ⓒ Ⓓ

Student Answer Sheet 3

Section I A: Listening

1. Ⓐ Ⓑ Ⓒ Ⓓ
2. Ⓐ Ⓑ Ⓒ Ⓓ
3. Ⓐ Ⓑ Ⓒ Ⓓ
4. Ⓐ Ⓑ Ⓒ Ⓓ
5. Ⓐ Ⓑ Ⓒ Ⓓ
6. Ⓐ Ⓑ Ⓒ Ⓓ
7. Ⓐ Ⓑ Ⓒ Ⓓ
8. Ⓐ Ⓑ Ⓒ Ⓓ
9. Ⓐ Ⓑ Ⓒ Ⓓ
10. Ⓐ Ⓑ Ⓒ Ⓓ
11. Ⓐ Ⓑ Ⓒ Ⓓ
12. Ⓐ Ⓑ Ⓒ Ⓓ
13. Ⓐ Ⓑ Ⓒ Ⓓ
14. Ⓐ Ⓑ Ⓒ Ⓓ
15. Ⓐ Ⓑ Ⓒ Ⓓ
16. Ⓐ Ⓑ Ⓒ Ⓓ
17. Ⓐ Ⓑ Ⓒ Ⓓ
18. Ⓐ Ⓑ Ⓒ Ⓓ
19. Ⓐ Ⓑ Ⓒ Ⓓ
20. Ⓐ Ⓑ Ⓒ Ⓓ
21. Ⓐ Ⓑ Ⓒ Ⓓ
22. Ⓐ Ⓑ Ⓒ Ⓓ
23. Ⓐ Ⓑ Ⓒ Ⓓ
24. Ⓐ Ⓑ Ⓒ Ⓓ
25. Ⓐ Ⓑ Ⓒ Ⓓ
26. Ⓐ Ⓑ Ⓒ Ⓓ
27. Ⓐ Ⓑ Ⓒ Ⓓ
28. Ⓐ Ⓑ Ⓒ Ⓓ
29. Ⓐ Ⓑ Ⓒ Ⓓ
30. Ⓐ Ⓑ Ⓒ Ⓓ
31. Ⓐ Ⓑ Ⓒ Ⓓ
32. Ⓐ Ⓑ Ⓒ Ⓓ
33. Ⓐ Ⓑ Ⓒ Ⓓ
34. Ⓐ Ⓑ Ⓒ Ⓓ
35. Ⓐ Ⓑ Ⓒ Ⓓ

Section I B: Reading

1. Ⓐ Ⓑ Ⓒ Ⓓ
2. Ⓐ Ⓑ Ⓒ Ⓓ
3. Ⓐ Ⓑ Ⓒ Ⓓ
4. Ⓐ Ⓑ Ⓒ Ⓓ
5. Ⓐ Ⓑ Ⓒ Ⓓ
6. Ⓐ Ⓑ Ⓒ Ⓓ
7. Ⓐ Ⓑ Ⓒ Ⓓ
8. Ⓐ Ⓑ Ⓒ Ⓓ
9. Ⓐ Ⓑ Ⓒ Ⓓ
10. Ⓐ Ⓑ Ⓒ Ⓓ
11. Ⓐ Ⓑ Ⓒ Ⓓ
12. Ⓐ Ⓑ Ⓒ Ⓓ
13. Ⓐ Ⓑ Ⓒ Ⓓ
14. Ⓐ Ⓑ Ⓒ Ⓓ
15. Ⓐ Ⓑ Ⓒ Ⓓ
16. Ⓐ Ⓑ Ⓒ Ⓓ
17. Ⓐ Ⓑ Ⓒ Ⓓ
18. Ⓐ Ⓑ Ⓒ Ⓓ
19. Ⓐ Ⓑ Ⓒ Ⓓ
20. Ⓐ Ⓑ Ⓒ Ⓓ
21. Ⓐ Ⓑ Ⓒ Ⓓ
22. Ⓐ Ⓑ Ⓒ Ⓓ
23. Ⓐ Ⓑ Ⓒ Ⓓ
24. Ⓐ Ⓑ Ⓒ Ⓓ
25. Ⓐ Ⓑ Ⓒ Ⓓ
26. Ⓐ Ⓑ Ⓒ Ⓓ
27. Ⓐ Ⓑ Ⓒ Ⓓ
28. Ⓐ Ⓑ Ⓒ Ⓓ
29. Ⓐ Ⓑ Ⓒ Ⓓ
30. Ⓐ Ⓑ Ⓒ Ⓓ
31. Ⓐ Ⓑ Ⓒ Ⓓ
32. Ⓐ Ⓑ Ⓒ Ⓓ
33. Ⓐ Ⓑ Ⓒ Ⓓ
34. Ⓐ Ⓑ Ⓒ Ⓓ
35. Ⓐ Ⓑ Ⓒ Ⓓ

Student Answer Sheet 4

Section I A: Listening

1. Ⓐ Ⓑ Ⓒ Ⓓ
2. Ⓐ Ⓑ Ⓒ Ⓓ
3. Ⓐ Ⓑ Ⓒ Ⓓ
4. Ⓐ Ⓑ Ⓒ Ⓓ
5. Ⓐ Ⓑ Ⓒ Ⓓ
6. Ⓐ Ⓑ Ⓒ Ⓓ
7. Ⓐ Ⓑ Ⓒ Ⓓ
8. Ⓐ Ⓑ Ⓒ Ⓓ
9. Ⓐ Ⓑ Ⓒ Ⓓ
10. Ⓐ Ⓑ Ⓒ Ⓓ
11. Ⓐ Ⓑ Ⓒ Ⓓ
12. Ⓐ Ⓑ Ⓒ Ⓓ
13. Ⓐ Ⓑ Ⓒ Ⓓ
14. Ⓐ Ⓑ Ⓒ Ⓓ
15. Ⓐ Ⓑ Ⓒ Ⓓ
16. Ⓐ Ⓑ Ⓒ Ⓓ
17. Ⓐ Ⓑ Ⓒ Ⓓ
18. Ⓐ Ⓑ Ⓒ Ⓓ
19. Ⓐ Ⓑ Ⓒ Ⓓ
20. Ⓐ Ⓑ Ⓒ Ⓓ
21. Ⓐ Ⓑ Ⓒ Ⓓ
22. Ⓐ Ⓑ Ⓒ Ⓓ
23. Ⓐ Ⓑ Ⓒ Ⓓ
24. Ⓐ Ⓑ Ⓒ Ⓓ
25. Ⓐ Ⓑ Ⓒ Ⓓ
26. Ⓐ Ⓑ Ⓒ Ⓓ
27. Ⓐ Ⓑ Ⓒ Ⓓ
28. Ⓐ Ⓑ Ⓒ Ⓓ
29. Ⓐ Ⓑ Ⓒ Ⓓ
30. Ⓐ Ⓑ Ⓒ Ⓓ
31. Ⓐ Ⓑ Ⓒ Ⓓ
32. Ⓐ Ⓑ Ⓒ Ⓓ
33. Ⓐ Ⓑ Ⓒ Ⓓ
34. Ⓐ Ⓑ Ⓒ Ⓓ
35. Ⓐ Ⓑ Ⓒ Ⓓ

Section I B: Reading

1. Ⓐ Ⓑ Ⓒ Ⓓ
2. Ⓐ Ⓑ Ⓒ Ⓓ
3. Ⓐ Ⓑ Ⓒ Ⓓ
4. Ⓐ Ⓑ Ⓒ Ⓓ
5. Ⓐ Ⓑ Ⓒ Ⓓ
6. Ⓐ Ⓑ Ⓒ Ⓓ
7. Ⓐ Ⓑ Ⓒ Ⓓ
8. Ⓐ Ⓑ Ⓒ Ⓓ
9. Ⓐ Ⓑ Ⓒ Ⓓ
10. Ⓐ Ⓑ Ⓒ Ⓓ
11. Ⓐ Ⓑ Ⓒ Ⓓ
12. Ⓐ Ⓑ Ⓒ Ⓓ
13. Ⓐ Ⓑ Ⓒ Ⓓ
14. Ⓐ Ⓑ Ⓒ Ⓓ
15. Ⓐ Ⓑ Ⓒ Ⓓ
16. Ⓐ Ⓑ Ⓒ Ⓓ
17. Ⓐ Ⓑ Ⓒ Ⓓ
18. Ⓐ Ⓑ Ⓒ Ⓓ
19. Ⓐ Ⓑ Ⓒ Ⓓ
20. Ⓐ Ⓑ Ⓒ Ⓓ
21. Ⓐ Ⓑ Ⓒ Ⓓ
22. Ⓐ Ⓑ Ⓒ Ⓓ
23. Ⓐ Ⓑ Ⓒ Ⓓ
24. Ⓐ Ⓑ Ⓒ Ⓓ
25. Ⓐ Ⓑ Ⓒ Ⓓ
26. Ⓐ Ⓑ Ⓒ Ⓓ
27. Ⓐ Ⓑ Ⓒ Ⓓ
28. Ⓐ Ⓑ Ⓒ Ⓓ
29. Ⓐ Ⓑ Ⓒ Ⓓ
30. Ⓐ Ⓑ Ⓒ Ⓓ
31. Ⓐ Ⓑ Ⓒ Ⓓ
32. Ⓐ Ⓑ Ⓒ Ⓓ
33. Ⓐ Ⓑ Ⓒ Ⓓ
34. Ⓐ Ⓑ Ⓒ Ⓓ
35. Ⓐ Ⓑ Ⓒ Ⓓ

Student Answer Sheet 5

Section I A: Listening

1. Ⓐ Ⓑ Ⓒ Ⓓ
2. Ⓐ Ⓑ Ⓒ Ⓓ
3. Ⓐ Ⓑ Ⓒ Ⓓ
4. Ⓐ Ⓑ Ⓒ Ⓓ
5. Ⓐ Ⓑ Ⓒ Ⓓ
6. Ⓐ Ⓑ Ⓒ Ⓓ
7. Ⓐ Ⓑ Ⓒ Ⓓ
8. Ⓐ Ⓑ Ⓒ Ⓓ
9. Ⓐ Ⓑ Ⓒ Ⓓ
10. Ⓐ Ⓑ Ⓒ Ⓓ
11. Ⓐ Ⓑ Ⓒ Ⓓ
12. Ⓐ Ⓑ Ⓒ Ⓓ
13. Ⓐ Ⓑ Ⓒ Ⓓ
14. Ⓐ Ⓑ Ⓒ Ⓓ
15. Ⓐ Ⓑ Ⓒ Ⓓ
16. Ⓐ Ⓑ Ⓒ Ⓓ
17. Ⓐ Ⓑ Ⓒ Ⓓ
18. Ⓐ Ⓑ Ⓒ Ⓓ
19. Ⓐ Ⓑ Ⓒ Ⓓ
20. Ⓐ Ⓑ Ⓒ Ⓓ
21. Ⓐ Ⓑ Ⓒ Ⓓ
22. Ⓐ Ⓑ Ⓒ Ⓓ
23. Ⓐ Ⓑ Ⓒ Ⓓ
24. Ⓐ Ⓑ Ⓒ Ⓓ
25. Ⓐ Ⓑ Ⓒ Ⓓ
26. Ⓐ Ⓑ Ⓒ Ⓓ
27. Ⓐ Ⓑ Ⓒ Ⓓ
28. Ⓐ Ⓑ Ⓒ Ⓓ
29. Ⓐ Ⓑ Ⓒ Ⓓ
30. Ⓐ Ⓑ Ⓒ Ⓓ
31. Ⓐ Ⓑ Ⓒ Ⓓ
32. Ⓐ Ⓑ Ⓒ Ⓓ
33. Ⓐ Ⓑ Ⓒ Ⓓ
34. Ⓐ Ⓑ Ⓒ Ⓓ
35. Ⓐ Ⓑ Ⓒ Ⓓ

Section I B: Reading

1. Ⓐ Ⓑ Ⓒ Ⓓ
2. Ⓐ Ⓑ Ⓒ Ⓓ
3. Ⓐ Ⓑ Ⓒ Ⓓ
4. Ⓐ Ⓑ Ⓒ Ⓓ
5. Ⓐ Ⓑ Ⓒ Ⓓ
6. Ⓐ Ⓑ Ⓒ Ⓓ
7. Ⓐ Ⓑ Ⓒ Ⓓ
8. Ⓐ Ⓑ Ⓒ Ⓓ
9. Ⓐ Ⓑ Ⓒ Ⓓ
10. Ⓐ Ⓑ Ⓒ Ⓓ
11. Ⓐ Ⓑ Ⓒ Ⓓ
12. Ⓐ Ⓑ Ⓒ Ⓓ
13. Ⓐ Ⓑ Ⓒ Ⓓ
14. Ⓐ Ⓑ Ⓒ Ⓓ
15. Ⓐ Ⓑ Ⓒ Ⓓ
16. Ⓐ Ⓑ Ⓒ Ⓓ
17. Ⓐ Ⓑ Ⓒ Ⓓ
18. Ⓐ Ⓑ Ⓒ Ⓓ
19. Ⓐ Ⓑ Ⓒ Ⓓ
20. Ⓐ Ⓑ Ⓒ Ⓓ
21. Ⓐ Ⓑ Ⓒ Ⓓ
22. Ⓐ Ⓑ Ⓒ Ⓓ
23. Ⓐ Ⓑ Ⓒ Ⓓ
24. Ⓐ Ⓑ Ⓒ Ⓓ
25. Ⓐ Ⓑ Ⓒ Ⓓ
26. Ⓐ Ⓑ Ⓒ Ⓓ
27. Ⓐ Ⓑ Ⓒ Ⓓ
28. Ⓐ Ⓑ Ⓒ Ⓓ
29. Ⓐ Ⓑ Ⓒ Ⓓ
30. Ⓐ Ⓑ Ⓒ Ⓓ
31. Ⓐ Ⓑ Ⓒ Ⓓ
32. Ⓐ Ⓑ Ⓒ Ⓓ
33. Ⓐ Ⓑ Ⓒ Ⓓ
34. Ⓐ Ⓑ Ⓒ Ⓓ
35. Ⓐ Ⓑ Ⓒ Ⓓ

Student Answer Sheet 6

Section I A: Listening

1. Ⓐ Ⓑ Ⓒ Ⓓ
2. Ⓐ Ⓑ Ⓒ Ⓓ
3. Ⓐ Ⓑ Ⓒ Ⓓ
4. Ⓐ Ⓑ Ⓒ Ⓓ
5. Ⓐ Ⓑ Ⓒ Ⓓ
6. Ⓐ Ⓑ Ⓒ Ⓓ
7. Ⓐ Ⓑ Ⓒ Ⓓ
8. Ⓐ Ⓑ Ⓒ Ⓓ
9. Ⓐ Ⓑ Ⓒ Ⓓ
10. Ⓐ Ⓑ Ⓒ Ⓓ
11. Ⓐ Ⓑ Ⓒ Ⓓ
12. Ⓐ Ⓑ Ⓒ Ⓓ
13. Ⓐ Ⓑ Ⓒ Ⓓ
14. Ⓐ Ⓑ Ⓒ Ⓓ
15. Ⓐ Ⓑ Ⓒ Ⓓ
16. Ⓐ Ⓑ Ⓒ Ⓓ
17. Ⓐ Ⓑ Ⓒ Ⓓ
18. Ⓐ Ⓑ Ⓒ Ⓓ
19. Ⓐ Ⓑ Ⓒ Ⓓ
20. Ⓐ Ⓑ Ⓒ Ⓓ
21. Ⓐ Ⓑ Ⓒ Ⓓ
22. Ⓐ Ⓑ Ⓒ Ⓓ
23. Ⓐ Ⓑ Ⓒ Ⓓ
24. Ⓐ Ⓑ Ⓒ Ⓓ
25. Ⓐ Ⓑ Ⓒ Ⓓ
26. Ⓐ Ⓑ Ⓒ Ⓓ
27. Ⓐ Ⓑ Ⓒ Ⓓ
28. Ⓐ Ⓑ Ⓒ Ⓓ
29. Ⓐ Ⓑ Ⓒ Ⓓ
30. Ⓐ Ⓑ Ⓒ Ⓓ
31. Ⓐ Ⓑ Ⓒ Ⓓ
32. Ⓐ Ⓑ Ⓒ Ⓓ
33. Ⓐ Ⓑ Ⓒ Ⓓ
34. Ⓐ Ⓑ Ⓒ Ⓓ
35. Ⓐ Ⓑ Ⓒ Ⓓ

Section I B: Reading

1. Ⓐ Ⓑ Ⓒ Ⓓ
2. Ⓐ Ⓑ Ⓒ Ⓓ
3. Ⓐ Ⓑ Ⓒ Ⓓ
4. Ⓐ Ⓑ Ⓒ Ⓓ
5. Ⓐ Ⓑ Ⓒ Ⓓ
6. Ⓐ Ⓑ Ⓒ Ⓓ
7. Ⓐ Ⓑ Ⓒ Ⓓ
8. Ⓐ Ⓑ Ⓒ Ⓓ
9. Ⓐ Ⓑ Ⓒ Ⓓ
10. Ⓐ Ⓑ Ⓒ Ⓓ
11. Ⓐ Ⓑ Ⓒ Ⓓ
12. Ⓐ Ⓑ Ⓒ Ⓓ
13. Ⓐ Ⓑ Ⓒ Ⓓ
14. Ⓐ Ⓑ Ⓒ Ⓓ
15. Ⓐ Ⓑ Ⓒ Ⓓ
16. Ⓐ Ⓑ Ⓒ Ⓓ
17. Ⓐ Ⓑ Ⓒ Ⓓ
18. Ⓐ Ⓑ Ⓒ Ⓓ
19. Ⓐ Ⓑ Ⓒ Ⓓ
20. Ⓐ Ⓑ Ⓒ Ⓓ
21. Ⓐ Ⓑ Ⓒ Ⓓ
22. Ⓐ Ⓑ Ⓒ Ⓓ
23. Ⓐ Ⓑ Ⓒ Ⓓ
24. Ⓐ Ⓑ Ⓒ Ⓓ
25. Ⓐ Ⓑ Ⓒ Ⓓ
26. Ⓐ Ⓑ Ⓒ Ⓓ
27. Ⓐ Ⓑ Ⓒ Ⓓ
28. Ⓐ Ⓑ Ⓒ Ⓓ
29. Ⓐ Ⓑ Ⓒ Ⓓ
30. Ⓐ Ⓑ Ⓒ Ⓓ
31. Ⓐ Ⓑ Ⓒ Ⓓ
32. Ⓐ Ⓑ Ⓒ Ⓓ
33. Ⓐ Ⓑ Ⓒ Ⓓ
34. Ⓐ Ⓑ Ⓒ Ⓓ
35. Ⓐ Ⓑ Ⓒ Ⓓ

Student Answer Sheet 7

Section I A: Listening

1. A B C D
2. A B C D
3. A B C D
4. A B C D
5. A B C D
6. A B C D
7. A B C D
8. A B C D
9. A B C D
10. A B C D
11. A B C D
12. A B C D
13. A B C D
14. A B C D
15. A B C D
16. A B C D
17. A B C D
18. A B C D
19. A B C D
20. A B C D
21. A B C D
22. A B C D
23. A B C D
24. A B C D
25. A B C D
26. A B C D
27. A B C D
28. A B C D
29. A B C D
30. A B C D
31. A B C D
32. A B C D
33. A B C D
34. A B C D
35. A B C D

Section I B: Reading

1. A B C D
2. A B C D
3. A B C D
4. A B C D
5. A B C D
6. A B C D
7. A B C D
8. A B C D
9. A B C D
10. A B C D
11. A B C D
12. A B C D
13. A B C D
14. A B C D
15. A B C D
16. A B C D
17. A B C D
18. A B C D
19. A B C D
20. A B C D
21. A B C D
22. A B C D
23. A B C D
24. A B C D
25. A B C D
26. A B C D
27. A B C D
28. A B C D
29. A B C D
30. A B C D
31. A B C D
32. A B C D
33. A B C D
34. A B C D
35. A B C D

Student Answer Sheet 8

Section I A: Listening

1. Ⓐ Ⓑ Ⓒ Ⓓ
2. Ⓐ Ⓑ Ⓒ Ⓓ
3. Ⓐ Ⓑ Ⓒ Ⓓ
4. Ⓐ Ⓑ Ⓒ Ⓓ
5. Ⓐ Ⓑ Ⓒ Ⓓ
6. Ⓐ Ⓑ Ⓒ Ⓓ
7. Ⓐ Ⓑ Ⓒ Ⓓ
8. Ⓐ Ⓑ Ⓒ Ⓓ
9. Ⓐ Ⓑ Ⓒ Ⓓ
10. Ⓐ Ⓑ Ⓒ Ⓓ
11. Ⓐ Ⓑ Ⓒ Ⓓ
12. Ⓐ Ⓑ Ⓒ Ⓓ
13. Ⓐ Ⓑ Ⓒ Ⓓ
14. Ⓐ Ⓑ Ⓒ Ⓓ
15. Ⓐ Ⓑ Ⓒ Ⓓ
16. Ⓐ Ⓑ Ⓒ Ⓓ
17. Ⓐ Ⓑ Ⓒ Ⓓ
18. Ⓐ Ⓑ Ⓒ Ⓓ
19. Ⓐ Ⓑ Ⓒ Ⓓ
20. Ⓐ Ⓑ Ⓒ Ⓓ
21. Ⓐ Ⓑ Ⓒ Ⓓ
22. Ⓐ Ⓑ Ⓒ Ⓓ
23. Ⓐ Ⓑ Ⓒ Ⓓ
24. Ⓐ Ⓑ Ⓒ Ⓓ
25. Ⓐ Ⓑ Ⓒ Ⓓ
26. Ⓐ Ⓑ Ⓒ Ⓓ
27. Ⓐ Ⓑ Ⓒ Ⓓ
28. Ⓐ Ⓑ Ⓒ Ⓓ
29. Ⓐ Ⓑ Ⓒ Ⓓ
30. Ⓐ Ⓑ Ⓒ Ⓓ
31. Ⓐ Ⓑ Ⓒ Ⓓ
32. Ⓐ Ⓑ Ⓒ Ⓓ
33. Ⓐ Ⓑ Ⓒ Ⓓ
34. Ⓐ Ⓑ Ⓒ Ⓓ
35. Ⓐ Ⓑ Ⓒ Ⓓ

Section I B: Reading

1. Ⓐ Ⓑ Ⓒ Ⓓ
2. Ⓐ Ⓑ Ⓒ Ⓓ
3. Ⓐ Ⓑ Ⓒ Ⓓ
4. Ⓐ Ⓑ Ⓒ Ⓓ
5. Ⓐ Ⓑ Ⓒ Ⓓ
6. Ⓐ Ⓑ Ⓒ Ⓓ
7. Ⓐ Ⓑ Ⓒ Ⓓ
8. Ⓐ Ⓑ Ⓒ Ⓓ
9. Ⓐ Ⓑ Ⓒ Ⓓ
10. Ⓐ Ⓑ Ⓒ Ⓓ
11. Ⓐ Ⓑ Ⓒ Ⓓ
12. Ⓐ Ⓑ Ⓒ Ⓓ
13. Ⓐ Ⓑ Ⓒ Ⓓ
14. Ⓐ Ⓑ Ⓒ Ⓓ
15. Ⓐ Ⓑ Ⓒ Ⓓ
16. Ⓐ Ⓑ Ⓒ Ⓓ
17. Ⓐ Ⓑ Ⓒ Ⓓ
18. Ⓐ Ⓑ Ⓒ Ⓓ
19. Ⓐ Ⓑ Ⓒ Ⓓ
20. Ⓐ Ⓑ Ⓒ Ⓓ
21. Ⓐ Ⓑ Ⓒ Ⓓ
22. Ⓐ Ⓑ Ⓒ Ⓓ
23. Ⓐ Ⓑ Ⓒ Ⓓ
24. Ⓐ Ⓑ Ⓒ Ⓓ
25. Ⓐ Ⓑ Ⓒ Ⓓ
26. Ⓐ Ⓑ Ⓒ Ⓓ
27. Ⓐ Ⓑ Ⓒ Ⓓ
28. Ⓐ Ⓑ Ⓒ Ⓓ
29. Ⓐ Ⓑ Ⓒ Ⓓ
30. Ⓐ Ⓑ Ⓒ Ⓓ
31. Ⓐ Ⓑ Ⓒ Ⓓ
32. Ⓐ Ⓑ Ⓒ Ⓓ
33. Ⓐ Ⓑ Ⓒ Ⓓ
34. Ⓐ Ⓑ Ⓒ Ⓓ
35. Ⓐ Ⓑ Ⓒ Ⓓ

Student Answer Sheet 9

Section I A: Listening

1. A B C D
2. A B C D
3. A B C D
4. A B C D
5. A B C D
6. A B C D
7. A B C D
8. A B C D
9. A B C D
10. A B C D
11. A B C D
12. A B C D
13. A B C D
14. A B C D
15. A B C D
16. A B C D
17. A B C D
18. A B C D
19. A B C D
20. A B C D
21. A B C D
22. A B C D
23. A B C D
24. A B C D
25. A B C D
26. A B C D
27. A B C D
28. A B C D
29. A B C D
30. A B C D
31. A B C D
32. A B C D
33. A B C D

Section I B: Reading

1. A B C D
2. A B C D
3. A B C D
4. A B C D
5. A B C D
6. A B C D
7. A B C D
8. A B C D
9. A B C D
10. A B C D
11. A B C D
12. A B C D
13. A B C D
14. A B C D
15. A B C D
16. A B C D
17. A B C D
18. A B C D
19. A B C D
20. A B C D
21. A B C D
22. A B C D
23. A B C D
24. A B C D
25. A B C D
26. A B C D
27. A B C D
28. A B C D
29. A B C D
30. A B C D
31. A B C D
32. A B C D
33. A B C D
34. A B C D
35. A B C D
36. A B C D
37. A B C D

Student Answer Sheet 10

Section I A: Listening

1. Ⓐ Ⓑ Ⓒ Ⓓ
2. Ⓐ Ⓑ Ⓒ Ⓓ
3. Ⓐ Ⓑ Ⓒ Ⓓ
4. Ⓐ Ⓑ Ⓒ Ⓓ
5. Ⓐ Ⓑ Ⓒ Ⓓ
6. Ⓐ Ⓑ Ⓒ Ⓓ
7. Ⓐ Ⓑ Ⓒ Ⓓ
8. Ⓐ Ⓑ Ⓒ Ⓓ
9. Ⓐ Ⓑ Ⓒ Ⓓ
10. Ⓐ Ⓑ Ⓒ Ⓓ
11. Ⓐ Ⓑ Ⓒ Ⓓ
12. Ⓐ Ⓑ Ⓒ Ⓓ
13. Ⓐ Ⓑ Ⓒ Ⓓ
14. Ⓐ Ⓑ Ⓒ Ⓓ
15. Ⓐ Ⓑ Ⓒ Ⓓ
16. Ⓐ Ⓑ Ⓒ Ⓓ
17. Ⓐ Ⓑ Ⓒ Ⓓ
18. Ⓐ Ⓑ Ⓒ Ⓓ
19. Ⓐ Ⓑ Ⓒ Ⓓ
20. Ⓐ Ⓑ Ⓒ Ⓓ
21. Ⓐ Ⓑ Ⓒ Ⓓ
22. Ⓐ Ⓑ Ⓒ Ⓓ
23. Ⓐ Ⓑ Ⓒ Ⓓ
24. Ⓐ Ⓑ Ⓒ Ⓓ
25. Ⓐ Ⓑ Ⓒ Ⓓ
26. Ⓐ Ⓑ Ⓒ Ⓓ
27. Ⓐ Ⓑ Ⓒ Ⓓ
28. Ⓐ Ⓑ Ⓒ Ⓓ
29. Ⓐ Ⓑ Ⓒ Ⓓ
30. Ⓐ Ⓑ Ⓒ Ⓓ
31. Ⓐ Ⓑ Ⓒ Ⓓ
32. Ⓐ Ⓑ Ⓒ Ⓓ
33. Ⓐ Ⓑ Ⓒ Ⓓ

Section I B: Reading

1. Ⓐ Ⓑ Ⓒ Ⓓ
2. Ⓐ Ⓑ Ⓒ Ⓓ
3. Ⓐ Ⓑ Ⓒ Ⓓ
4. Ⓐ Ⓑ Ⓒ Ⓓ
5. Ⓐ Ⓑ Ⓒ Ⓓ
6. Ⓐ Ⓑ Ⓒ Ⓓ
7. Ⓐ Ⓑ Ⓒ Ⓓ
8. Ⓐ Ⓑ Ⓒ Ⓓ
9. Ⓐ Ⓑ Ⓒ Ⓓ
10. Ⓐ Ⓑ Ⓒ Ⓓ
11. Ⓐ Ⓑ Ⓒ Ⓓ
12. Ⓐ Ⓑ Ⓒ Ⓓ
13. Ⓐ Ⓑ Ⓒ Ⓓ
14. Ⓐ Ⓑ Ⓒ Ⓓ
15. Ⓐ Ⓑ Ⓒ Ⓓ
16. Ⓐ Ⓑ Ⓒ Ⓓ
17. Ⓐ Ⓑ Ⓒ Ⓓ
18. Ⓐ Ⓑ Ⓒ Ⓓ
19. Ⓐ Ⓑ Ⓒ Ⓓ
20. Ⓐ Ⓑ Ⓒ Ⓓ
21. Ⓐ Ⓑ Ⓒ Ⓓ
22. Ⓐ Ⓑ Ⓒ Ⓓ
23. Ⓐ Ⓑ Ⓒ Ⓓ
24. Ⓐ Ⓑ Ⓒ Ⓓ
25. Ⓐ Ⓑ Ⓒ Ⓓ
26. Ⓐ Ⓑ Ⓒ Ⓓ
27. Ⓐ Ⓑ Ⓒ Ⓓ
28. Ⓐ Ⓑ Ⓒ Ⓓ
29. Ⓐ Ⓑ Ⓒ Ⓓ
30. Ⓐ Ⓑ Ⓒ Ⓓ
31. Ⓐ Ⓑ Ⓒ Ⓓ
32. Ⓐ Ⓑ Ⓒ Ⓓ
33. Ⓐ Ⓑ Ⓒ Ⓓ
34. Ⓐ Ⓑ Ⓒ Ⓓ
35. Ⓐ Ⓑ Ⓒ Ⓓ
36. Ⓐ Ⓑ Ⓒ Ⓓ
37. Ⓐ Ⓑ Ⓒ Ⓓ

AP中文仿真试题集

[美]谢碧霞（Bih-hsya Hsieh）
[美]于晓华（Sunny X. Yu）　◎编著
[美]张相华（Hsiang-hua Chang）

（第二版）录音文本及参考答案

AP CHINESE LANGUAGE AND CULTURE SIMULATED TESTS (SECOND EDITION)
AUDIO SCRIPTS AND ANSWER KEYS

PEKING UNIVERSITY PRESS

目 录

Audio Scripts of AP Chinese Language and Culture Test 1 ············· 1

Audio Scripts of AP Chinese Language and Culture Test 2 ············· 12

Audio Scripts of AP Chinese Language and Culture Test 3 ············· 24

Audio Scripts of AP Chinese Language and Culture Test 4 ············· 36

Audio Scripts of AP Chinese Language and Culture Test 5 ············· 48

Audio Scripts of AP Chinese Language and Culture Test 6 ············· 59

Audio Scripts of AP Chinese Language and Culture Test 7 ············· 72

Audio Scripts of AP Chinese Language and Culture Test 8 ············· 85

Audio Scripts of AP Chinese Language and Culture Test 9 ············· 98

Audio Scripts of AP Chinese Language and Culture Test 10 ············· 109

Answer Keys ············· 120

Audio Scripts of AP Chinese Language and Culture Test 1

Section I: Multiple Choice

Part A: Listening

Rejoinders

Directions: You will hear several short conversations or parts of conversations followed by four choices, designated A, B, C, and D. Choose the one that continues or completes the conversation in a logical and culturally appropriate manner. After you have decided which of the suggested answers is best, COMPLETELY fill in the corresponding circle on the answer sheet. You will have 5 seconds to answer each question.

(Traditional characters)

1. 男：你收到大學錄取通知書了嗎？
   女：A）我還沒決定去哪個大學。
   　　B）還沒有，都快把我急死了。
   　　C）大學會把通知書寄給每個學生。
   　　D）我從來沒去過那個大學。
   　（學生答題5秒）

(Simplified characters)

1. 男：你收到大学录取通知书了吗？
   女：A）我还没决定去哪个大学。
   　　B）还没有，都快把我急死了。
   　　C）大学会把通知书寄给每个学生。
   　　D）我从来没去过那个大学。
   　（学生答题5秒）

(Traditional characters)

2. 男：蘭蘭，你的臉色看起來不太好。
   女：A）我這個人不喜歡化妝。
   　　B）我小時候比現在好看。
   　　C）今天我覺得不太舒服。
   　　D）你覺得我不漂亮嗎？
   　（學生答題5秒）

(Simplified characters)

2. 男：兰兰，你的脸色看起来不太好。
   女：A）我这个人不喜欢化妆。
   　　B）我小时候比现在好看。
   　　C）今天我觉得不太舒服。
   　　D）你觉得我不漂亮吗？
   　（学生答题5秒）

(Traditional characters)

3. 男：服務員，買單！
   女：A）好，請稍等。
   　　B）歡迎光臨！
   　　C）不用客氣！
   　　D）請慢走！
   　（學生答題5秒）

(Simplified characters)

3. 男：服务员，买单！
   女：A）好，请稍等。
   　　B）欢迎光临！
   　　C）不用客气！
   　　D）请慢走！
   　（学生答题5秒）

(Traditional characters)

4. 男：今年暑假你有什麼打算？
   女：A）暑假我可能會很忙。
   　　B）暑假時的天氣太熱了。
   　　C）去年暑假我什麼都沒做。
   　　D）我還沒決定做什麼呢。
   （學生答題 5 秒）

5. 女：你昨天看沒看 NBA 總決賽第五場的直播？
   男：A）網上看直播不如現場看氣氛好。
   　　B）錯過 NBA 的決賽是很遺憾的。
   　　C）像我這樣的忠實球迷怎麼會錯過這場球賽呢？
   　　D）NBA 總決賽每場都很精彩。
   （學生答題 5 秒）

6. 男：昨天的歷史考試考得怎麼樣？
   女：A）我很討厭歷史考試。
   　　B）歷史是我最喜歡的學科。
   　　C）考得不好也沒什麼。
   　　D）我覺得考得很一般。
   （學生答題 5 秒）

7. 女：我明明聞到你身上有菸味，你卻說你沒抽菸。
   男：A）別小題大做了！
   　　B）明明根本不會抽菸！
   　　C）抽菸不是好習慣。
   　　D）你該戒菸了，抽菸對身體不好。
   （學生答題 5 秒）

(Simplified characters)

4. 男：今年暑假你有什么打算？
   女：A）暑假我可能会很忙。
   　　B）暑假时的天气太热了。
   　　C）去年暑假我什么都没做。
   　　D）我还没决定做什么呢。
   （学生答题 5 秒）

5. 女：你昨天看没看 NBA 总决赛第五场的直播？
   男：A）网上看直播不如现场看气氛好。
   　　B）错过 NBA 的决赛是很遗憾的。
   　　C）像我这样的忠实球迷怎么会错过这场球赛呢？
   　　D）NBA 总决赛每场都很精彩。
   （学生答题 5 秒）

6. 男：昨天的历史考试考得怎么样？
   女：A）我很讨厌历史考试。
   　　B）历史是我最喜欢的学科。
   　　C）考得不好也没什么。
   　　D）我觉得考得很一般。
   （学生答题 5 秒）

7. 女：我明明闻到你身上有烟味，你却说你没抽烟。
   男：A）别小题大做了！
   　　B）明明根本不会抽烟！
   　　C）抽烟不是好习惯。
   　　D）你该戒烟了，抽烟对身体不好。
   （学生答题 5 秒）

(Traditional characters)

8. 女：你平常都喜歡做些什麼運動？
   男：A）運動對人的健康有好處。
   　　B）凡是球類運動我都喜歡。
   　　C）我常常去運動。
   　　D）我從小就喜歡運動。
   （學生答題 5 秒）

9. 男：聽說你這幾天心情不好，怎麼啦？
   女：A）我這幾天很忙。
   　　B）這幾天天氣真糟糕！
   　　C）家裡出了點兒事兒，我媽生病了。
   　　D）你的心情看起來不錯，有什麼好事兒嗎？
   （學生答題 5 秒）

10. 女：你喜歡中國的北方菜還是南方菜？
    男：A）我從來沒去過南方，你去過嗎？
    　　B）怎麼說呢？其實南方菜北方菜各有千秋。
    　　C）我有好幾個同學是南方人，但他們喜歡吃麵。
    　　D）北京菜有點兒鹹。
    （學生答題 5 秒）

11. 男：你還在那家餐館兒打工嗎？
    女：學校功課太多，所以我早就不做了。
    男：A）餐館兒的工作的確很有意思。
    　　B）我看你還是先把作業做完再去打工吧！
    　　C）那麼高的工資，辭掉太可惜了。
    　　D）那你現在在哪家餐館兒工作呢？
    （學生答題 5 秒）

(Simplified characters)

8. 女：你平常都喜欢做些什么运动？
   男：A）运动对人的健康有好处。
   　　B）凡是球类运动我都喜欢。
   　　C）我常常去运动。
   　　D）我从小就喜欢运动。
   （学生答题 5 秒）

9. 男：听说你这几天心情不好，怎么啦？
   女：A）我这几天很忙。
   　　B）这几天天气真糟糕！
   　　C）家里出了点儿事儿，我妈生病了。
   　　D）你的心情看起来不错，有什么好事儿吗？
   （学生答题 5 秒）

10. 女：你喜欢中国的北方菜还是南方菜？
    男：A）我从来没去过南方，你去过吗？
    　　B）怎么说呢？其实南方菜北方菜各有千秋。
    　　C）我有好几个同学是南方人，但他们喜欢吃面。
    　　D）北京菜有点儿咸。
    （学生答题 5 秒）

11. 男：你还在那家餐馆儿打工吗？
    女：学校功课太多，所以我早就不做了。
    男：A）餐馆儿的工作的确很有意思。
    　　B）我看你还是先把作业做完再去打工吧！
    　　C）那么高的工资，辞掉太可惜了。
    　　D）那你现在在哪家餐馆儿工作呢？
    （学生答题 5 秒）

(Traditional characters)

12. 女：聽說這位歌手現在在中國很紅。
    男：我怎麼不知道？
    女：A）你不知道他是中國人嗎？
        B）中國人很喜歡紅色。
        C）你真的沒聽過中國歌曲嗎？
        D）你大概不常聽音樂吧？
    （學生答題5秒）

(Traditional characters)

13. 男：前面車堵得這麼厲害，怎麼辦呢？
    女：真急死人了！說不定我趕不上飛機了。
    男：A）沒關係，反正我們的車開得挺慢的。
        B）我看我們還是換條道兒走吧。
        C）我們應該給老師打個電話。
        D）你幾點上班？
    （學生答題5秒）

(Traditional characters)

14. 女：最近很少見到你，忙什麼呢？
    男：期末考試快到了，每天都在開夜車。
    女：A）晚上開車不安全，要小心。
        B）我父母從不讓我夜裡開車。
        C）還是要多休息，睡眠不足也會影響考試的。
        D）考試怎麼會安排在晚上呢？
    （學生答題5秒）

(Traditional characters)

15. 女：嗨，聽說蘋果剛發佈了萬眾期待的第一款5G手機，不但外形好看，而且功能強大，我看你這個舊的該淘汰了吧？

(Simplified characters)

12. 女：听说这位歌手现在在中国很红。
    男：我怎么不知道？
    女：A）你不知道他是中国人吗？
        B）中国人很喜欢红色。
        C）你真的没听过中国歌曲吗？
        D）你大概不常听音乐吧？
    （学生答题5秒）

(Simplified characters)

13. 男：前面车堵得这么厉害，怎么办呢？
    女：真急死人了！说不定我赶不上飞机了。
    男：A）没关系，反正我们的车开得挺慢的。
        B）我看我们还是换条道儿走吧。
        C）我们应该给老师打个电话。
        D）你几点上班？
    （学生答题5秒）

(Simplified characters)

14. 女：最近很少见到你，忙什么呢？
    男：期末考试快到了，每天都在开夜车。
    女：A）晚上开车不安全，要小心。
        B）我父母从不让我夜里开车。
        C）还是要多休息，睡眠不足也会影响考试的。
        D）考试怎么会安排在晚上呢？
    （学生答题5秒）

(Simplified characters)

15. 女：嗨，听说苹果刚发布了万众期待的第一款5G手机，不但外形好看，而且功能强大，我看你这个旧的该淘汰了吧？

男：算了吧，本人從來不趕新潮，再說舊的也一樣用，父母給的錢我還是省著點兒花吧。

女：A）你父母不喜歡蘋果手機嗎？
　　B）那你可以自己打工賺錢買呀！
　　C）是的，大部分父母過日子都很節省。
　　D）我都很久沒見到你父母了！

（學生答題5秒）

Listening Selections

Directions:

You will listen to several selections in Chinese. For each selection, you will be told whether it will be played once or twice. You may take notes as you listen. Your notes will not be graded. After listening to each selection, you will see questions in English. For each question, choose the response that is best according to the selection. You will have 12 seconds to answer each question.

Selection 1: Announcement

Narrator: Now you will listen twice to a public announcement.

Woman:

(Traditional characters)

同學們請注意：

　　為了幫助低收入家庭，學校正在組織一項捐食物獻愛心的活動。請同學們回家把這次活動的意義跟父母講一講，希望得到他們的支持。捐贈的食品種類不限，只要不是新鮮的肉類、蔬菜、水果一類的就行。大米、白麵、各種罐頭，食用油、鹽什麼的都可以。希望同學們踴躍捐助。從本週一開始，每天的第四節課都會有志願者到各教室去收集食物，同學們也可以自己把帶來的食物直接放到學校辦公室外面的箱子裡。學校會在月底前把收集到的食物交到有關單位。謝謝大家的支持與合作！

(Simplified characters)

> 同学们请注意：
>
> 为了帮助低收入家庭，学校正在组织一项捐食物献爱心的活动。请同学们回家把这次活动的意义跟父母讲一讲，希望得到他们的支持。捐赠的食品种类不限，只要不是新鲜的肉类、蔬菜、水果一类的就行。大米、白面、各种罐头，食用油、盐什么的都可以。希望同学们踊跃捐助。从本周一开始，每天的第四节课都会有志愿者到各教室去收集食物，同学们也可以自己把带来的食物直接放到学校办公室外面的箱子里。学校会在月底前把收集到的食物交到有关单位。谢谢大家的支持与合作！

Narrator: Now listen again.

(Repeat)

Narrator: Now answer the questions for this selection.

(12 seconds)

(12 seconds)

(12 seconds)

(12 seconds)

Selection 2: Conversation

Narrator: Now you will listen once to a conversation between two students.

(Traditional characters)

> 男：這個星期六的晚上在學校禮堂有個舞會，你想去嗎？
> 女：我對這樣的活動從來不感興趣。
> 男：得了吧，上次舞會你不是也去了嗎？
> 女：嗨，我只是湊熱鬧去了，根本沒跳舞。
> 男：這次舞會跟以往的不同，我保證你會玩兒得很開心。
> 女：你還是找別人去吧，我實在是不想去。
> 男：算了算了，你這個人真不給面子。

(Simplified characters)

> 男：这个星期六的晚上在学校礼堂有个舞会，你想去吗？
> 女：我对这样的活动从来不感兴趣。
> 男：得了吧，上次舞会你不是也去了吗？

女：嗨，我只是凑热闹去了，根本没跳舞。
男：这次舞会跟以往的不同，我保证你会玩儿得很开心。
女：你还是找别人去吧，我实在是不想去。
男：算了算了，你这个人真不给面子。

Narrator: Now answer the questions for this selection.

(12 seconds)

(12 seconds)

(12 seconds)

Selection 3: Voice Message

Narrator: Now you will listen twice to a voice message.

Man:

(Traditional characters)

叔叔，您好！我是小明。我已經到家了。飛機早上十點半準時到達舊金山機場，我爸爸去機場接的我。謝謝您在北京招待了我那麼多天，我吃得很過癮，玩兒得也很開心！明年有機會我還想去北京看您。今天是學校春假的最後一天，明天我就得上學了。希望今天晚上能把時差倒過來，否則明天上課就慘了。好，有時間我再跟您聯繫。再見！

(Simplified characters)

叔叔，您好！我是小明。我已经到家了。飞机早上十点半准时到达旧金山机场，我爸爸去机场接的我。谢谢您在北京招待了我那么多天，我吃得很过瘾，玩儿得也很开心！明年有机会我还想去北京看您。今天是学校春假的最后一天，明天我就得上学了。希望今天晚上能把时差倒过来，否则明天上课就惨了。好，有时间我再跟您联系。再见！

Narrator: Now listen again.

(Repeat)

Narrator: Now answer the questions for this selection.

(12 seconds)

(12 seconds)

(12 seconds)
(12 seconds)

Selection 4: Instructions

Narrator: Now you will listen once to someone giving instructions.

Man:

(Traditional characters)

> 亞馬遜推出的Kindle電子書閱讀器因爲超薄、超清、超方便的優點而讓人喜愛，所以近幾年越來越流行了。Kindle和真書大小相似，點擊下面一個小按鍵或者直接觸碰觸摸屏就可以解鎖，進入主頁界面。用戶可以在主頁界面看到在亞馬遜購買的書，也可以免費直接上傳自己下載的其他的書。在Kindle上還可以看圖片格式的文件。用戶可以把喜歡的漫畫書存到裡面，直接點擊圖片就能閱讀。Kindle還可以連接無綫網，方便我們推送電子書，或者直接從亞馬遜網站上購買和下載新書。

(Simplified characters)

> 亚马逊推出的Kindle电子书阅读器因为超薄、超清、超方便的优点而让人喜爱，所以近几年越来越流行了。Kindle和真书大小相似，点击下面一个小按键或者直接触碰触摸屏就可以解锁，进入主页界面。用户可以在主页界面看到在亚马逊购买的书，也可以免费直接上传自己下载的其他的书。在Kindle上还可以看图片格式的文件。用户可以把喜欢的漫画书存到里面，直接点击图片就能阅读。Kindle还可以连接无线网，方便我们推送电子书，或者直接从亚马逊网站上购买和下载新书。

Narrator: Now answer the questions for this selection.

(12 seconds)
(12 seconds)
(12 seconds)
(12 seconds)
(12 seconds)

Selection 5: Report

Narrator: Now you will listen once to a report.

Woman:

(Traditional characters)

> 下面是今明兩天我市的天氣情況。今天白天到夜間將會有中雨，部分地區會有大雨到暴雨。受冷空氣的影響，今晚大部分地區的氣溫可降至10攝氏度，明天白天氣溫會回升到22攝氏度。望大家做好防雨準備，出門請携帶雨傘，並注意交通安全。未來幾天天氣可望轉晴，氣溫也會隨之變暖。

(Simplified characters)

> 下面是今明两天我市的天气情况。今天白天到夜间将会有中雨，部分地区会有大雨到暴雨。受冷空气的影响，今晚大部分地区的气温可降至10摄氏度，明天白天气温会回升到22摄氏度。望大家做好防雨准备，出门请携带雨伞，并注意交通安全。未来几天天气可望转晴，气温也会随之变暖。

Narrator: Now answer the questions for this selection.

(12 seconds)

(12 seconds)

(12 seconds)

(12 seconds)

Section II: Free Response

Part B: Speaking

Recording Scripts

Conversation

Directions: You will participate in a simulated conversation. Each time it is your turn to speak, you will have 20 seconds to record. You should respond as fully and as appropriately as possible. There will be six times when it is your turn to speak.

You will have a conversation with Xiaofan, your classmate, about your plan of SAT study during the summer vacation.

(Traditional characters)

小凡：聽說你準備參加一個暑假SAT補習班，是真的嗎？
（學生答題20秒）

小凡：你各科成績都夠好的啦，爲什麼還要去補習呢？
（學生答題20秒）

小凡：我覺得只要買幾套教材，自己多做題就可以了，沒有必要去上課。你是怎麼想的啊？
（學生答題20秒）

小凡：有很多SAT補習班，你爲什麼選擇離家遠的那個呢？
（學生答題20秒）

小凡：學費是多少？比其他SAT班的學費貴還是便宜？
（學生答題20秒）

小凡：聽你這麼一說，我也動心了。他們有沒有免費的講座？如果我想報名的話，都需要做些什麼？
（學生答題20秒）

(Simplified characters)

小凡：听说你准备参加一个暑假SAT补习班，是真的吗？
（学生答题20秒）

小凡：你各科成绩都够好的啦，为什么还要去补习呢？
（学生答题20秒）

小凡：我觉得只要买几套教材，自己多做题就可以了，没有必要去上课。你是怎么想的啊？
（学生答题20秒）

小凡：有很多SAT补习班，你为什么选择离家远的那个呢？
（学生答题20秒）

小凡：学费是多少？比其他SAT班的学费贵还是便宜？
（学生答题20秒）

小凡：听你这么一说，我也动心了。他们有没有免费的讲座？如果我想报名的话，都需要做些什么？
（学生答题20秒）

Cultural Presentation

Directions: You will be asked to speak in Chinese on a specific topic. Imagine you are making an oral presentation to your Chinese class. First, you will read and hear the topic for your presentation. You will have 4 minutes to prepare your presentation. Then you will have 2 minutes to record your presentation. Your presentation should be as complete as possible.

Name a Chinese movie that has left a lasting impression on you. What aspects of Chinese culture did it present? Why did you find this movie memorable? In your presentation, describe this movie and explain its significance.

Audio Scripts of AP Chinese Language and Culture Test 2

Section I: Multiple Choice

Part A: Listening

Rejoinders

Directions: You will hear several short conversations or parts of conversations followed by four choices, designated A, B, C, and D. Choose the one that continues or completes the conversation in a logical and culturally appropriate manner. After you have decided which of the suggested answers is best, COMPLETELY fill in the corresponding circle on the answer sheet. You will have 5 seconds to answer each question.

(Traditional characters)

1. 女：你對這個城市熟悉嗎？
    男：A）這個城市很漂亮。
        B）我是在這兒出生、長大的。你說呢？
        C）這兒的公共汽車和地鐵都方便得很。
        D）我想在這兒住一年。
    （學生答題 5 秒）

2. 女：你一直咳嗽，先喝點兒水再說吧。
    男：A）我對什麼都不過敏。
        B）哦，謝謝，我自己來。
        C）我媽媽昨天帶我去看大夫了。
        D）水和空氣對身體都很重要。
    （學生答題 5 秒）

3. 男：這條裙子漂亮是漂亮，可是太貴了。買那條便宜點兒的吧。
    女：A）難道你買衣服就看價錢嗎？
        B）我昨天也買了一條裙子。
        C）這家商店從來不打折。

(Simplified characters)

1. 女：你对这个城市熟悉吗？
    男：A）这个城市很漂亮。
        B）我是在这儿出生、长大的。你说呢？
        C）这儿的公共汽车和地铁都方便得很。
        D）我想在这儿住一年。
    （学生答题 5 秒）

2. 女：你一直咳嗽，先喝点儿水再说吧。
    男：A）我对什么都不过敏。
        B）哦，谢谢，我自己来。
        C）我妈妈昨天带我去看大夫了。
        D）水和空气对身体都很重要。
    （学生答题 5 秒）

3. 男：这条裙子漂亮是漂亮，可是太贵了。买那条便宜点儿的吧。
    女：A）难道你买衣服就看价钱吗？
        B）我昨天也买了一条裙子。
        C）这家商店从来不打折。

(Traditional characters)

D）不，我覺得衣服的式樣沒有價錢那麼重要。

（學生答題 5 秒）

4. 男：對不起，我們不收現金，請用手機掃二維碼支付。

　女：A）這是信用卡。

　　　B）可以用衛星導航嗎？

　　　C）糟糕，我忘了帶手機了。

　　　D）這是一百塊錢。

（學生答題 5 秒）

5. 女：怎麼？有了女朋友就把老朋友給忘了？

　男：A）我的女朋友跟你一樣漂亮。

　　　B）我們交往纔兩個星期。

　　　C）她的地址，我忘了。

　　　D）我沒忘，其實是我這幾天太忙了，對不起。

（學生答題 5 秒）

6. 男：好不容易考完試了，小王，我們這個週末一起去慶祝慶祝吧！

　女：A）好啊，我們上哪兒去慶祝？

　　　B）我覺得這次考試挺容易的。

　　　C）小王家不難找，我們週末一起去吧。

　　　D）上個週末我們在老師家慶祝春節。

（學生答題 5 秒）

(Simplified characters)

D）不，我觉得衣服的式样没有价钱那么重要。

（学生答题 5 秒）

4. 男：对不起，我们不收现金，请用手机扫二维码支付。

　女：A）这是信用卡。

　　　B）可以用卫星导航吗？

　　　C）糟糕，我忘了带手机了。

　　　D）这是一百块钱。

（学生答题 5 秒）

5. 女：怎么？有了女朋友就把老朋友给忘了？

　男：A）我的女朋友跟你一样漂亮。

　　　B）我们交往才两个星期。

　　　C）她的地址，我忘了。

　　　D）我没忘，其实是我这几天太忙了，对不起。

（学生答题 5 秒）

6. 男：好不容易考完试了，小王，我们这个周末一起去庆祝庆祝吧！

　女：A）好啊，我们上哪儿去庆祝？

　　　B）我觉得这次考试挺容易的。

　　　C）小王家不难找，我们周末一起去吧。

　　　D）上个周末我们在老师家庆祝春节。

（学生答题 5 秒）

(Traditional characters)

7. 女：聽說星期六音樂會的票很難買，你買到了嗎？

   男：A）我很想參加這次音樂會。

   　　B）我想買兩張票，一張給你。

   　　C）我早就在網上買了。

   　　D）沒問題，我星期六一定去。

   （學生答題5秒）

8. 男：這麼晚了，怎麼還不上床睡覺？明天一早還得上學呢。

   女：A）今天的作業不太多，我早就做完了。

   　　B）小明的電話號碼我不記得了。

   　　C）明天放學後沒有籃球練習。

   　　D）我們老師今天給的作業特別多，恐怕十二點半還做不完呢。

   （學生答題5秒）

9. 男：明天的考試，你準備好了沒有？我有一個問題問你一下，行嗎？

   女：A）我這個星期考試多極了，老師好像都說好了同時考試似的。

   　　B）我也有些地方不懂，我們還是一塊兒去問老師吧。

   　　C）這次的考試挺難的，你考得怎麼樣？

   　　D）說實在的，考得好不好我并不在乎。

   （學生答題5秒）

(Simplified characters)

7. 女：听说星期六音乐会的票很难买，你买到了吗？

   男：A）我很想参加这次音乐会。

   　　B）我想买两张票，一张给你。

   　　C）我早就在网上买了。

   　　D）没问题，我星期六一定去。

   （学生答题5秒）

8. 男：这么晚了，怎么还不上床睡觉？明天一早还得上学呢。

   女：A）今天的作业不太多，我早就做完了。

   　　B）小明的电话号码我不记得了。

   　　C）明天放学后没有篮球练习。

   　　D）我们老师今天给的作业特别多，恐怕十二点半还做不完呢。

   （学生答题5秒）

9. 男：明天的考试，你准备好了没有？我有一个问题问你一下，行吗？

   女：A）我这个星期考试多极了，老师好像都说好了同时考试似的。

   　　B）我也有些地方不懂，我们还是一块儿去问老师吧。

   　　C）这次的考试挺难的，你考得怎么样？

   　　D）说实在的，考得好不好我并不在乎。

   （学生答题5秒）

(Simplified characters)

10. 男：妈，几点了？
    女：七点半了，你得快点儿，要不然就迟到了。
    男：A）哎呀，糟糕，恐怕没时间吃早饭了。
        B）今天老师会不会迟到？
        C）李玫天天都迟到。
        D）你快点儿起床吧。
    （学生答题5秒）

11. 女：今天来参观的人怎么这么多？
    男：是啊，比平常多多了。
    女：A）平常参观的人更多吗？
        B）参加舞会的人我一个都不认识。
        C）啊，我知道了，今天放假，难怪人这么多。
        D）你上个月去西安参观了兵马俑，给我介绍介绍兵马俑吧。
    （学生答题5秒）

12. 男：明天我们游泳比赛，你来给我们加油，行吗？
    女：好啊，那你得好好儿游。
    男：A）那当然，还用说吗？
        B）不客气。
        C）游泳比赛几点开始？
        D）我们没油了，请你也带点儿油来。
    （学生答题5秒）

(Simplified characters)

13. 女：这家餐馆儿的菜真地道，也不贵。下回再来吧！

    男：地道是地道，就是辣了点儿。

    女：A）你也这么喜欢吃辣？跟我一样嘛。

    　　B）我不喜欢吃辣的东西。

    　　C）我是这家饭馆儿的常客。

    　　D）哦，那下次我们还是换一家吃吧！

    （学生答题5秒）

14. 男：这几天市立美术馆有个当代名画家的作品展，有没有看画儿的雅兴？我可以先去买票。

    女：兴趣有是有，不过咱们得等下回了，那个画展昨天已经闭幕了。

    男：A）哎呀，结束了？可惜错过了。

    　　B）你对哪个画家最有兴趣？

    　　C）只要是名画家的画儿，我都有兴趣。

    　　D）怪不得你一有空儿就去看画展。

    （学生答题5秒）

15. 女：请问，你们这儿有一位王先生吗？

    男：哪位王先生？我们这儿光是姓王的小伙子，就有五个。

    女：A）哦，您不认识王先生？

    　　B）是王先生要我来这儿找他的。

    　　C）他个子跟您差不多，脸圆圆的，戴黑框眼镜。

D）他約了我今天下午三點在服務
臺見面。

（學生答題 5 秒）

D）他约了我今天下午三点在服务
台见面。

（学生答题 5 秒）

Listening Selections

Directions: You will listen to several selections in Chinese. For each selection, you will be told whether it will be played once or twice. You may take notes as you listen. Your notes will not be graded. After listening to each selection, you will see questions in English. For each question, choose the response that is best according to the selection. You will have 12 seconds to answer each question.

Selection 1: Announcement

Narrator: Now you will listen twice to a public announcement.

Woman:

(Traditional characters)

> 乘坐CA3387次航班前往上海的旅客請注意：
> 您乘坐的航班將在17點10分停止辦理登機手續。乘坐本次航班還沒有辦理登機手續的旅客，請馬上到29號櫃臺辦理。謝謝！

(Simplified characters)

> 乘坐CA3387次航班前往上海的旅客请注意：
> 您乘坐的航班将在17点10分停止办理登机手续。乘坐本次航班还没有办理登机手续的旅客，请马上到29号柜台办理。谢谢！

Narrator: Now listen again.

(Repeat)

Narrator: Now answer the questions for this selection.

(12 seconds)

(12 seconds)

Selection 2: Conversation

Narrator: Now you will listen once to a conversation between two students.

(Traditional characters)

男：小文，穿得這麼漂亮，跟男朋友約會去嗎？
女：嗨，小張，我申請了一份兼職工作，現在要去面試呢！
男：是嗎？在哪兒呀？怎麼想到要打工呢？
女：就在學校附近的一家咖啡館。要是能有一點兒工作經驗，對於將來申請大學或是寫簡歷，都有好處。
男：所以你打工的目的不是為了掙錢呀！
女：可不是嗎？但是我媽媽老擔心打工會影響我的學習，今天出門前，還一直不讓我去呢！並且說缺零花錢，跟她要就是了。
男：父母都是這樣，他們總是認為當個學生把書唸好就行了，打什麼工。
女：還好最後她同意了。哎呀，我得快點兒，遲到的話，給老闆的第一印象就糟糕了。
男：祝你順利！拿到了工資，別忘了請客喲！
女：謝謝。沒問題！回頭見！

(Simplified characters)

男：小文，穿得这么漂亮，跟男朋友约会去吗？
女：嗨，小张，我申请了一份兼职工作，现在要去面试呢！
男：是吗？在哪儿呀？怎么想到要打工呢？
女：就在学校附近的一家咖啡馆。要是能有一点儿工作经验，对于将来申请大学或是写简历，都有好处。
男：所以你打工的目的不是为了挣钱呀！
女：可不是吗？但是我妈妈老担心打工会影响我的学习，今天出门前，还一直不让我去呢！并且说缺零花钱，跟她要就是了。
男：父母都是这样，他们总是认为当个学生把书念好就行了，打什么工。
女：还好最后她同意了。哎呀，我得快点儿，迟到的话，给老板的第一印象就糟糕了。
男：祝你顺利！拿到了工资，别忘了请客哟！
女：谢谢。没问题！回头见！

Narrator: Now answer the questions for this selection.

(12 seconds)

(12 seconds)

(12 seconds)

(12 seconds)

(12 seconds)

Selection 3: Instructions

Narrator: Now you will listen once to someone giving instructions.

Woman:

(Traditional characters)

> 謝謝您打電話來，您的電話對我們十分重要，請勿掛斷。如果您有事要跟校長商談，請按"1"；如果您的孩子生病要請假，請按"2"；如果您有事要我們轉達給您的孩子，請按"3"；如果您有書想要續借，請按"4"；如果您想知道各種運動比賽的時間、地點和結果，請按"5"；如果是其他要事，請按"0"。如果沒人接聽，麻煩您留下您的名字、電話及簡單的訊息，我們會儘快跟您聯絡。謝謝。

(Simplified characters)

> 谢谢您打电话来，您的电话对我们十分重要，请勿挂断。如果您有事要跟校长商谈，请按"1"；如果您的孩子生病要请假，请按"2"；如果您有事要我们转达给您的孩子，请按"3"；如果您有书想要续借，请按"4"；如果您想知道各种运动比赛的时间、地点和结果，请按"5"；如果是其他要事，请按"0"。如果没人接听，麻烦您留下您的名字、电话及简单的讯息，我们会尽快跟您联络。谢谢。

Narrator: Now answer the questions for this selection.

(12 seconds)

(12 seconds)

(12 seconds)

(12 seconds)

Selection 4: Voice Message

Narrator: Now you will listen twice to a voice message.

Woman:

(Traditional characters)

> 媽媽，我是立立，今天早上出門的時候，我怕上學遲到，匆匆忙忙的，結果忘了把今天必須交的英文讀書報告帶到學校來了。還好英文課是今天最後一節課，希望您能及時聽到我的留言。英文讀書報告在我書桌右邊書架的最上層，請您儘快帶來給我。到學校的時候，就交給坐在辦公室最前邊的李小姐。還有，我下午都有課，請發短信告訴我您到了，千萬別打我手機。媽媽，拜託了，謝謝！

(Simplified characters)

> 妈妈，我是立立，今天早上出门的时候，我怕上学迟到，匆匆忙忙的，结果忘了把今天必须交的英文读书报告带到学校来了。还好英文课是今天最后一节课，希望您能及时听到我的留言。英文读书报告在我书桌右边书架的最上层，请您尽快带来给我。到学校的时候，就交给坐在办公室最前边的李小姐。还有，我下午都有课，请发短信告诉我您到了，千万别打我手机。妈妈，拜托了，谢谢！

Narrator: Now listen again.

(Repeat)

Narrator: Now answer the questions for this selection.

(12 seconds)

(12 seconds)

(12 seconds)

(12 seconds)

Selection 5: Report

Narrator: Now you will listen once to a report.

Man:

(Traditional characters)

> 近年來，由於電腦價格普遍降低，家家都有電腦，每個家庭一般也都有網絡。不少家長擔心子女花在網絡上的時間過多，本臺記者這個星期在學校門口、購物中心以及電影院前採訪了365位高中學生，瞭解高中生上網的情況。調查的結果顯示，

將近80%的學生每晚花在網上的時間平均4個小時，18%的學生花在網上的時間每晚都超過5個小時。幾乎95%的學生表示，父母認爲他們上網的時間太長，應該多跟父母、朋友面對面溝通。但是這些學生表示，他們每天都得上網，除了查看老師佈置的作業和提交作業以外，也要看看電郵、博客什麽的。另外，有時上網還爲了找資料、做報告，或者跟同學討論課上或課外活動的問題。事實上，他們幷不是像很多父母以爲的那樣只是在網上玩兒電腦遊戲或跟朋友聊天兒。

(Simplified characters)

近年来，由于电脑价格普遍降低，家家都有电脑，每个家庭一般也都有网络。不少家长担心子女花在网络上的时间过多，本台记者这个星期在学校门口、购物中心以及电影院前采访了365位高中学生，了解高中生上网的情况。调查的结果显示，将近80%的学生每晚花在网上的时间平均4个小时，18%的学生花在网上的时间每晚都超过5个小时。几乎95%的学生表示，父母认为他们上网的时间太长，应该多跟父母、朋友面对面沟通。但是这些学生表示，他们每天都得上网，除了查看老师布置的作业和提交作业以外，也要看看电邮、博客什么的。另外，有时上网还为了找资料、做报告，或者跟同学讨论课上或课外活动的问题。事实上，他们幷不是像很多父母以为的那样只是在网上玩儿电脑游戏或跟朋友聊天儿。

Narrator: Now answer the questions for this selection.

(12 seconds)

(12 seconds)

(12 seconds)

(12 seconds)

(12 seconds)

Section II: Free Response
Part B: Speaking
Conversation

Directions:

You will participate in a simulated conversation. Each time it is your turn to speak, you will have 20 seconds to record. You should respond as fully and as appropriately as possible. There will be six times when it is your turn to speak.

You will have a conversation with Wang Zhong, your host parent, about dining at a local Chinese restaurant.

(Traditional characters)

王中：你看看菜單，想吃什麼，就點什麼，別客氣。
（學生答題20秒）
王中：他們平常上菜挺快的，今天怎麼這麼慢？你餓壞了吧？
（學生答題20秒）
王中：菜來了，來，我幫你夾。多吃點兒。味道怎麼樣，還可以吧？
（學生答題20秒）
王中：你在家時，你和家人常常去餐館兒吃飯嗎？都吃些什麼樣口味的菜？
（學生答題20秒）
王中：你媽媽會做些什麼拿手好菜？
（學生答題20秒）
王中：吃飽了嗎？菜夠不夠？要不要再來點兒什麼？
（學生答題20秒）

(Simplified characters)

王中：你看看菜单，想吃什么，就点什么，别客气。
（学生答题20秒）
王中：他们平常上菜挺快的，今天怎么这么慢？你饿坏了吧？
（学生答题20秒）
王中：菜来了，来，我帮你夹。多吃点儿。味道怎么样，还可以吧？
（学生答题20秒）
王中：你在家时，你和家人常常去餐馆儿吃饭吗？都吃些什么样口味的菜？
（学生答题20秒）
王中：你妈妈会做些什么拿手好菜？
（学生答题20秒）
王中：吃饱了吗？菜够不够？要不要再来点儿什么？
（学生答题20秒）

Cultural Presentation

You will be asked to speak in Chinese on a specific topic. Imagine you are making an oral presentation to your Chinese class. First, you will read and hear the topic for your presentation. You will have 4 minutes to prepare your presentation. Then you will have 2 minutes to record your presentation. Your presentation should be as complete as possible.

Choose ONE historical or contemporary Chinese figure. In your presentation, describe this person's background, what he/she has done, and explain his or her significance in China.

Audio Scripts of AP Chinese Language and Culture Test 3

Section I: Multiple Choice
Part A: Listening
Rejoinders

Directions: You will hear several short conversations or parts of conversations followed by four choices, designated A, B, C, and D. Choose the one that continues or completes the conversation in a logical and culturally appropriate manner. After you have decided which of the suggested answers is best, COMPLETELY fill in the corresponding circle on the answer sheet. You will have 5 seconds to answer each question.

(Traditional characters)

1. 男：小紅，剛纔跟你說話的那個人是誰啊？
   女：A）你不認識他嗎？
   　　B）她是你的朋友嗎？
   　　C）那個人不是我的同學。
   　　D）那個人很喜歡說話。
   （學生答題 5 秒）

2. 男：昨天我沒能去看那場籃球賽，哪隊贏了？
   女：A）我最不喜歡看籃球比賽了。
   　　B）這場球賽一點兒也不精彩。
   　　C）那還用問嗎，當然是我們班隊了。
   　　D）那個隊沒贏。
   （學生答題 5 秒）

3. 女：我很想找份臨時工做一做，免得老跟父母要錢花。
   男：A）對，跟父母要的錢是得省著花。
   　　B）你父母不應該花你打工掙的錢。
   　　C）我的父母花錢也很省。
   　　D）是啊，如果自己能賺點兒零用錢，就方便多了。
   （學生答題 5 秒）

(Simplified characters)

1. 男：小红，刚才跟你说话的那个人是谁啊？
   女：A）你不认识他吗？
   　　B）她是你的朋友吗？
   　　C）那个人不是我的同学。
   　　D）那个人很喜欢说话。
   （学生答题 5 秒）

2. 男：昨天我没能去看那场篮球赛，哪队赢了？
   女：A）我最不喜欢看篮球比赛了。
   　　B）这场球赛一点儿也不精彩。
   　　C）那还用问吗，当然是我们班队了。
   　　D）那个队没赢。
   （学生答题 5 秒）

3. 女：我很想找份临时工做一做，免得老跟父母要钱花。
   男：A）对，跟父母要的钱是得省着花。
   　　B）你父母不应该花你打工挣的钱。
   　　C）我的父母花钱也很省。
   　　D）是啊，如果自己能赚点儿零用钱，就方便多了。
   （学生答题 5 秒）

4. 男：春假的时候你去哪儿了，怎么连个电邮都不回？

　　女：A）我春假玩儿得很开心。

　　　　B）你开玩笑吧？我根本没收到你的电邮。

　　　　C）那个地方没有邮局，所以我没能给你回信。

　　　　D）我一到那儿就马上发电邮告诉你。

　　（学生答题 5 秒）

5. 女：听说去北京当交换学生的奖学金被你哥哥拿到了？

　　男：A）我怎么不知道你哥哥要去北京学习呢？

　　　　B）没有这回事，别听别人瞎说。

　　　　C）我也听说从北京来的交换学生都有奖学金。

　　　　D）我哥哥从来没有去过北京。

　　（学生答题 5 秒）

6. 男：咱们学校附近新开张的那家中国餐馆儿的川菜很地道，有机会你应该去尝一尝。

　　女：A）我最讨厌四川菜，太辣了！

　　　　B）那家餐馆儿开的时间不太长。

　　　　C）咱们学校餐厅的川菜是很地道。

　　　　D）在学校附近开个餐馆儿对我们来说很方便。

　　（学生答题 5 秒）

(Traditional characters)

7. 女：我這個人很怕吵，所以我常常喜歡待在圖書館裡看書，因爲那裡最安靜，你呢？

   男：A）很多人都喜歡去圖書館借書。

   B）在圖書館學習是要安靜。

   C）看來咱倆性格差不多，我也愛去圖書館看書。

   D）我也覺得圖書館有時候很吵。

   （學生答題5秒）

(Traditional characters)

8. 女：爸爸，寒假時我想跟朋友去上海旅遊，你覺得我們坐飛機去好還是坐高鐵去好呢？

   男：A）坐高鐵比坐動車稍微貴一點兒。

   B）這麼大的雨，你哥哥的飛機恐怕要晚點了。

   C）到了上海別忘了給你媽媽買個禮物回來。

   D）咱家離高鐵站這麼近，多方便啊！

   （學生答題5秒）

(Traditional characters)

9. 男：小紅，剛五月你家怎麼就這麼熱呢？

   女：A）老房子了，沒有空調。

   B）這個房子的設備比較齊全。

   C）夏天恐怕不會很熱。

   D）每年都會熱上五個月。

   （學生答題5秒）

(Traditional characters)

10. 女：哥哥，哪天把你的女朋友帶到家裡讓我們看一看。

(Simplified characters)

7. 女：我这个人很怕吵，所以我常常喜欢待在图书馆里看书，因为那里最安静，你呢？

   男：A）很多人都喜欢去图书馆借书。

   B）在图书馆学习是要安静。

   C）看来咱俩性格差不多，我也爱去图书馆看书。

   D）我也觉得图书馆有时候很吵。

   （学生答题5秒）

(Simplified characters)

8. 女：爸爸，寒假时我想跟朋友去上海旅游，你觉得我们坐飞机去好还是坐高铁去好呢？

   男：A）坐高铁比坐动车稍微贵一点儿。

   B）这么大的雨，你哥哥的飞机恐怕要晚点了。

   C）到了上海别忘了给你妈妈买个礼物回来。

   D）咱家离高铁站这么近，多方便啊！

   （学生答题5秒）

(Simplified characters)

9. 男：小红，刚五月你家怎么就这么热呢？

   女：A）老房子了，没有空调。

   B）这个房子的设备比较齐全。

   C）夏天恐怕不会很热。

   D）每年都会热上五个月。

   （学生答题5秒）

(Simplified characters)

10. 女：哥哥，哪天把你的女朋友带到家里让我们看一看。

男：A）我覺得我的女朋友是很好看。
　　B）她不好意思來咱們家。
　　C）我一定會帶你去她家。
　　D）她已經帶我去過她家了。
（學生答題 5 秒）

(Traditional characters)

11. 男：你原來不是很喜歡化學嗎？怎麼上大學以後決定讀英文專業呢？
　　女：其實這兩科我都喜歡，所以沒選化學專業我也覺得有點兒可惜。
　　男：A）我也覺得科學更有意思。
　　　　B）英語的確是很難讀的專業。
　　　　C）沒關係，反正上學以後還可以改專業。
　　　　D）我父母也不支持我學英文。
（學生答題 5 秒）

(Traditional characters)

12. 女：你吃過北京全聚德的烤鴨嗎？
　　男：聽說過，但還沒吃過。
　　女：A）味道好極了！跟一般的烤鴨不一樣。
　　　　B）大部分中國人都不喜歡吃。
　　　　C）你真的不知道全聚德嗎？
　　　　D）很遺憾你不喜歡吃烤鴨。
（學生答題 5 秒）

(Traditional characters)

13. 男：這件襯衫夠便宜的啦，還猶豫什麼呢？
　　女：價錢還可以，可是我穿不太合身。
　　男：A）好，我們再看看有沒有更便宜的吧。

男：A）我觉得我的女朋友是很好看。
　　B）她不好意思来咱们家。
　　C）我一定会带你去她家。
　　D）她已经带我去过她家了。
（学生答题 5 秒）

(Simplified characters)

11. 男：你原来不是很喜欢化学吗？怎么上大学以后决定读英文专业呢？
　　女：其实这两科我都喜欢，所以没选化学专业我也觉得有点儿可惜。
　　男：A）我也觉得科学更有意思。
　　　　B）英语的确是很难读的专业。
　　　　C）没关系，反正上学以后还可以改专业。
　　　　D）我父母也不支持我学英文。
（学生答题 5 秒）

(Simplified characters)

12. 女：你吃过北京全聚德的烤鸭吗？
　　男：听说过，但还没吃过。
　　女：A）味道好极了！跟一般的烤鸭不一样。
　　　　B）大部分中国人都不喜欢吃。
　　　　C）你真的不知道全聚德吗？
　　　　D）很遗憾你不喜欢吃烤鸭。
（学生答题 5 秒）

(Simplified characters)

13. 男：这件衬衫够便宜的啦，还犹豫什么呢？
　　女：价钱还可以，可是我穿不太合身。
　　男：A）好，我们再看看有没有更便宜的吧。

B）那我們再去別的店看看吧。

C）這家店的東西是不怎麼樣。

D）沒關係，錢不夠的話我可以借給你。

（學生答題 5 秒）

B）那我们再去别的店看看吧。

C）这家店的东西是不怎么样。

D）没关系，钱不够的话我可以借给你。

（学生答题 5 秒）

(Traditional characters)

14. 女：好幾次游泳練習你都沒去，怎麼啦?

    男：學校的作業太多，壓得我都喘不過氣來了。

    女：A）你應該去看醫生。

    　　B）怪不得你沒去上學。

    　　C）不能只顧學習，鍛煉身體也很重要。

    　　D）別生氣，我也覺得老師應該多給些作業。

（學生答題 5 秒）

(Simplified characters)

14. 女：好几次游泳练习你都没去，怎么啦?

    男：学校的作业太多，压得我都喘不过气来了。

    女：A）你应该去看医生。

    　　B）怪不得你没去上学。

    　　C）不能只顾学习，锻炼身体也很重要。

    　　D）别生气，我也觉得老师应该多给些作业。

（学生答题 5 秒）

(Traditional characters)

15. 男：你跟你的男朋友不是相處得挺好嗎? 怎麼說分手就分手了呢?

    女：我們其實只是一般的朋友，所以也算不上什麼分手不分手。

    男：A）不是朋友就應該分手。

    　　B）哦,看來大家誤會你們的關係了。

    　　C）你男朋友長得挺好的。

    　　D）真的沒說什麼就分手了嗎?

（學生答題 5 秒）

(Simplified characters)

15. 男：你跟你的男朋友不是相处得挺好吗? 怎么说分手就分手了呢?

    女：我们其实只是一般的朋友，所以也算不上什么分手不分手。

    男：A）不是朋友就应该分手。

    　　B）哦,看来大家误会你们的关系了。

    　　C）你男朋友长得挺好的。

    　　D）真的没说什么就分手了吗?

（学生答题 5 秒）

Listening Selections

Directions: You will listen to several selections in Chinese. For each selection, you will be told whether it will be played once or twice. You may take notes as you listen. Your notes will not be graded. After listening to each selection, you will see questions in English. For each question, choose the response that is best according to the selection. You will have 12 seconds to answer each question.

Selection 1: Conversation

Narrator: Now you will listen once to a conversation between two students.

(Traditional characters)

> 男：下週四晚上在學校召開一個關於怎樣申請大學的咨詢會，聽說很多大學負責招生的人都會來。我很想參加，因為有些問題我在網上找不到答案，正好可以趁這個機會問問他們。你想去嗎？
>
> 女：我其實很想去，但是那天晚上我還有別的事要做。麻煩你把重要的資料幫我帶回來，或者用電子郵件發給我也行。拜託你了！

(Simplified characters)

> 男：下周四晚上在学校召开一个关于怎样申请大学的咨询会，听说很多大学负责招生的人都会来。我很想参加，因为有些问题我在网上找不到答案，正好可以趁这个机会问问他们。你想去吗？
>
> 女：我其实很想去，但是那天晚上我还有别的事要做。麻烦你把重要的资料帮我带回来，或者用电子邮件发给我也行。拜托你了！

Narrator: Now answer the questions for this selection.

(12 seconds)

(12 seconds)

(12 seconds)

(12 seconds)

Selection 2: Announcement

Narrator: Now you will listen twice to an announcement.

Woman:

(Traditional characters)

> 為了慶祝教師節，中文俱樂部的同學準備在本週四舉辦一個尊師愛校的活動。中午12點到1點，在學生中心門前將會有中國城黃河藝術團表演的中國功夫及歌舞，學校會為全校師生提供一份免費的中式午餐。另外，請每個學生給自己最喜愛的老師寫一張卡片來表達你對老師的感激之情，并將卡片直接放到老師的信箱裡。你也可以附上一份小小的禮物。謝謝大家的支持！

(Simplified characters)

> 为了庆祝教师节，中文俱乐部的同学准备在本周四举办一个尊师爱校的活动。中午12点到1点，在学生中心门前将会有中国城黄河艺术团表演的中国功夫及歌舞，学校会为全校师生提供一份免费的中式午餐。另外，请每个学生给自己最喜爱的老师写一张卡片来表达你对老师的感激之情，并将卡片直接放到老师的信箱里。你也可以附上一份小小的礼物。谢谢大家的支持！

Narrator: Now listen again.

(Repeat)

Narrator: Now answer the questions for this selection.

(12 seconds)

(12 seconds)

(12 seconds)

Selection 3: Voice Message

Narrator: Now you will listen twice to a voice message.

Woman:

(Traditional characters)

> 王老師：您好！我是李曉美。我已經告訴我媽媽我們班下週去亞洲博物館的事了，她說可以開車送我們去。我媽媽的車很大，可以坐六個人，但問題是我媽媽中午要去機場接人，她把我們送到博物館後就得先走，不能送我們回學校。其實我們幾個坐地鐵回來也很方便。您有事可以打電話跟我媽媽聯繫，她的手機號碼是（520）820-7070。再見！

(Simplified characters)

> 王老师：您好！我是李晓美。我已经告诉我妈妈我们班下周去亚洲博物馆的事了，她说可以开车送我们去。我妈妈的车很大，可以坐六个人，但问题是我妈妈中午要去机场接人，她把我们送到博物馆后就得先走，不能送我们回学校。其实我们几个坐地铁回来也很方便。您有事可以打电话跟我妈妈联系，她的手机号码是（520）820-7070。再见！

Narrator: Now listen again.

(Repeat)

Narrator: Now answer the questions for this selection.

(12 seconds)

(12 seconds)

(12 seconds)

Selection 4: Instructions

Narrator: Now you will listen once to someone giving instructions.

Man:

(Traditional characters)

> 全校師生請注意：
> 　　因學校正門前面在修路，所以明天防火練習的路綫有所改變。聽到防火警報時，請所有師生馬上從學校後門出去，沿著左邊的那條小路往前走，一直走到社區中心前面的草地上。各班的集合地點不變，請在那兒等候所有的同學到來。請各位老師記住帶急救包，並在集合的地點點名。

(Simplified characters)

> 全校师生请注意：
> 　　因学校正门前面在修路，所以明天防火练习的路线有所改变。听到防火警报时，请所有师生马上从学校后门出去，沿着左边的那条小路往前走，一直走到社区中心前面的草地上。各班的集合地点不变，请在那儿等候所有的同学到来。请各位老师记住带急救包，并在集合的地点点名。

Narrator: Now answer the questions for this selection.

(12 seconds)

(12 seconds)

(12 seconds)

(12 seconds)

Selection 5: Report

Narrator: Now you will listen once to a report.

Woman:

(Traditional characters)

> 同學們：
> 　　我校一年一度的大學專業咨詢活動昨天圓滿結束了，共有12位往屆畢業生參加了這次活動。他們以自己的親身經歷向同學們介紹了他們所從事工作的特點，並就同學們的提問給以解答。同學們都覺得這次活動增加了他們對許多職業的瞭解，這對大學專業的選擇以及未來可能從事的工作有很大的幫助。昨天沒能參加活動的同學，可以通過電郵和這幾位演講者聯繫。

(Simplified characters)

> 同学们：
> 　　我校一年一度的大学专业咨询活动昨天圆满结束了，共有12位往届毕业生参加了这次活动。他们以自己的亲身经历向同学们介绍了他们所从事工作的特点，并就同学们的提问给以解答。同学们都觉得这次活动增加了他们对许多职业的了解，这对大学专业的选择以及未来可能从事的工作有很大的帮助。昨天没能参加活动的同学，可以通过电邮和这几位演讲者联系。

Narrator: Now answer the questions for this selection.

(12 seconds)

(12 seconds)

(12 seconds)

Selection 6: Conversation

Narrator: Now you will listen once to a conversation between two students.

(Traditional characters)

> 男：我下個月要去西安旅遊，最近正在準備辦簽證的事兒。以前都是我父母幫我辦，可是不巧他們都到外地開會去了。我聽說你這方面很有經驗，所以想問問你辦簽證都需要什麼手續。
>
> 女：首先你要確定你的護照是有效的，然後你要準備一張二寸正面照片，再上網下載一份簽證申請表，填好後一起交到領事館。最後取簽證時要交$130，不管幾次入境，簽證費都是一樣的。

男：簽證要等幾天纔能取？
女：通常是五個工作日，不過也有加急服務，但是要多付些錢。
男：嗯，知道了，那我還是早點兒辦吧。謝謝你！
女：不客氣！

(Simplified characters)

男：我下个月要去西安旅游，最近正在准备办签证的事儿。以前都是我父母帮我办，可是不巧他们都到外地开会去了。我听说你这方面很有经验，所以想问问你办签证都需要什么手续。
女：首先你要确定你的护照是有效的，然后你要准备一张二寸正面照片，再上网下载一份签证申请表，填好后一起交到领事馆。最后取签证时要交$130，不管几次入境，签证费都是一样的。
男：签证要等几天才能取？
女：通常是五个工作日，不过也有加急服务，但是要多付些钱。
男：嗯，知道了，那我还是早点儿办吧。谢谢你！
女：不客气！

Narrator: Now answer the questions for this selection.

(12 seconds)

(12 seconds)

(12 seconds)

Section II: Free Response
Part B: Speaking
Recording Scripts
Conversation

Directions: You will participate in a simulated conversation. Each time it is your turn to speak, you will have 20 seconds to record. You should respond as fully and as appropriately as possible. There will be six times when it is your turn to speak.

You have been invited to have dinner with a Chinese family. You will have a conversation with a member of the family at the dinner table.

(Traditional characters)

> 中國家庭：這些都是家常菜，可能做得不夠好，不知合不合你的口味？
> （學生答題20秒）
> 中國家庭：吃得慣中餐嗎？你常吃的中餐有哪些？
> （學生答題20秒）
> 中國家庭：你瞭解中國的八大菜系嗎？你最喜歡什麼地方風味的菜？
> （學生答題20秒）
> 中國家庭：你在家裡或在中文班上學沒學過包餃子？喜歡吃餃子嗎？
> （學生答題20秒）
> 中國家庭：美國人平常都吃什麼？
> （學生答題20秒）
> 中國家庭：你的老家在哪兒？那兒的菜肴有什麼特色？教我做一道你的家鄉菜吧！
> （學生答題20秒）

(Simplified characters)

> 中国家庭：这些都是家常菜，可能做得不够好，不知合不合你的口味？
> （学生答题20秒）
> 中国家庭：吃得惯中餐吗？你常吃的中餐有哪些？
> （学生答题20秒）
> 中国家庭：你了解中国的八大菜系吗？你最喜欢什么地方风味的菜？
> （学生答题20秒）
> 中国家庭：你在家里或在中文班上学没学过包饺子？喜欢吃饺子吗？
> （学生答题20秒）
> 中国家庭：美国人平常都吃什么？
> （学生答题20秒）
> 中国家庭：你的老家在哪儿？那儿的菜肴有什么特色？教我做一道你的家乡菜吧！
> （学生答题20秒）

Cultural Presentation

Directions: You will be asked to speak in Chinese on a specific topic. Imagine you are making an oral presentation to your Chinese class. First, you will read and hear the topic for your presentation. You will have 4 minutes to prepare your presentation. Then you will have 2 minutes to record your presentation. Your presentation should be as complete as possible.

The concept of "一日为师，终身为父" (一日為師，終身為父) ("A teacher for one day, and a father forever") has always been valued in China. In your presentation, share your thoughts on this concept and explain its significance, compare and contrast it with the Western cultural attitudes toward the role of teachers, and toward education as a whole.

Audio Scripts of AP Chinese Language and Culture Test 4

Section I: Multiple Choice

Part A: Listening

Rejoinders

Directions: You will hear several short conversations or parts of conversations followed by four choices, designated A, B, C, and D. Choose the one that continues or completes the conversation in a logical and culturally appropriate manner. After you have decided which of the suggested answers is best, COMPLETELY fill in the corresponding circle on the answer sheet. You will have 5 seconds to answer each question.

(Simplified characters)

1. 女：今年暑假，你做什么有意思的事儿了？说来听听啊！

   男：A）我暑假想去中国旅行。

   　　B）我妈妈不让我开车上学。

   　　C）没做什么，整天就吃饭、睡觉。

   　　D）暑假太长了，真没意思，怎么办？

   （学生答题5秒）

2. 女：嗨，小王！听说昨天的篮球赛你们赢了。

   男：A）可不是？68比67，把我们对手给气死了。

   　　B）我们每天放学以后都练球。

   　　C）我们今年可能连赢一场的希望都没有。

   　　D）打篮球比踢足球容易多了。

   （学生答题5秒）

3. 女：站在小李旁边的那个帅哥是谁呀？是不是她的新男朋友？

   男：A）小李的新男朋友是刚从华盛顿转学到这儿的。

B）啊，哪個？哦，那是我弟弟，待會兒我給你們介紹介紹。
C）參加晚會的人真多。
D）小李今天晚上真漂亮，喜歡她的男孩子可真不少呢。

（學生答題5秒）

(Traditional characters)

4. 男：你本來不是想選電腦課的嗎？怎麼學生名單上沒有你的名字？
   女：A）想選是想選，但是電腦課花的時間多，我想了想，還是等下個學期不太忙時再選吧。
   B）我發現自己對電腦課的興趣可大著呢。
   C）我打的那份工也需要電腦方面的知識。
   D）我以後電腦課有問題，可以問你嗎？

（學生答題5秒）

(Traditional characters)

5. 女：對不起，你音樂開得聲太大了，能不能小聲點兒？我沒法兒專心看書了。
   男：A）我喜歡一邊聽音樂，一邊看書。
   B）要是你不喜歡這個音樂，我可以換別的音樂。
   C）不喜歡？那你可以出去。
   D）哎呀，對不起，對不起，我沒注意到屋子裡還有人。

（學生答題5秒）

B）啊，哪个？哦，那是我弟弟，待会儿我给你们介绍介绍。
C）参加晚会的人真多。
D）小李今天晚上真漂亮，喜欢她的男孩子可真不少呢。

（学生答题5秒）

(Simplified characters)

4. 男：你本来不是想选电脑课的吗？怎么学生名单上没有你的名字？
   女：A）想选是想选，但是电脑课花的时间多，我想了想，还是等下个学期不太忙时再选吧。
   B）我发现自己对电脑课的兴趣可大着呢。
   C）我打的那份工也需要电脑方面的知识。
   D）我以后电脑课有问题，可以问你吗？

（学生答题5秒）

(Simplified characters)

5. 女：对不起，你音乐开得声太大了，能不能小声点儿？我没法儿专心看书了。
   男：A）我喜欢一边听音乐，一边看书。
   B）要是你不喜欢这个音乐，我可以换别的音乐。
   C）不喜欢？那你可以出去。
   D）哎呀，对不起，对不起，我没注意到屋子里还有人。

（学生答题5秒）

(Traditional characters)

6. 男：到了北京，要記得馬上給我們發個短信報平安，別讓我們擔心。

    女：A）你的手機真酷，讓我瞧瞧。

    B）我晚上八點會到北京。

    C）現在的飛機都很準時，你不用擔心飛機晚點。

    D）那當然，一定，一定。

    （學生答題5秒）

(Traditional characters)

7. 女：你的行李看起來挺重的，我來幫你提吧！

    男：A）那怎麼好意思？我自己來，沒事兒的！

    B）我的行李是我媽媽幫我收拾的。

    C）我的行李超重了，上飛機時還多交了五十塊錢。

    D）我的行李裡面有很多書。

    （學生答題5秒）

(Traditional characters)

8. 男：中秋節快到了，你打算自己做月餅嗎？

    女：A）中秋節大家都吃月餅，我也不例外。

    B）我沒吃過月餅。好吃嗎？

    C）我們家月餅都是在商店買的，我根本不會做。

    D）中秋節我們一起賞月、吃月餅吧！

    （學生答題5秒）

(Simplified characters)

6. 男：到了北京，要记得马上给我们发个短信报平安，别让我们担心。

    女：A）你的手机真酷，让我瞧瞧。

    B）我晚上八点会到北京。

    C）现在的飞机都很准时，你不用担心飞机晚点。

    D）那当然，一定，一定。

    （学生答题5秒）

(Simplified characters)

7. 女：你的行李看起来挺重的，我来帮你提吧！

    男：A）那怎么好意思？我自己来，没事儿的！

    B）我的行李是我妈妈帮我收拾的。

    C）我的行李超重了，上飞机时还多交了五十块钱。

    D）我的行李里面有很多书。

    （学生答题5秒）

(Simplified characters)

8. 男：中秋节快到了，你打算自己做月饼吗？

    女：A）中秋节大家都吃月饼，我也不例外。

    B）我没吃过月饼。好吃吗？

    C）我们家月饼都是在商店买的，我根本不会做。

    D）中秋节我们一起赏月、吃月饼吧！

    （学生答题5秒）

9. 女：請問，新生在哪兒辦註冊手續？
   男：A）老生在圖書館辦註冊手續。
   　　B）註冊手續？我已經辦好了。
   　　C）在學生活動中心。
   　　D）新生明天纔辦註冊手續。
   （學生答題5秒）

10. 男：快放假了，你有什麼計劃？
    女：我要麼到中國去玩兒，要麼去快餐店打工。你呢？
    男：A）中國各地，我都去過。
    　　B）可能會上暑期學校。
    　　C）我比較喜歡放寒假。
    　　D）暑假太長了，真無聊。
    （學生答題5秒）

11. 女：那個新電影不錯，聽說看的人挺多的，你看了嗎？
    男：現在去是人擠人，過一陣子再說吧。
    女：A）等你想看的時候，給我打個電話，我們一塊兒去。
    　　B）我們下課以後就一起去看吧。
    　　C）沒想到看電影的人這麼多。
    　　D）要排隊買票嗎？
    （學生答題5秒）

12. 男：你平常幫不幫你媽媽做家務？
    女：我媽媽白天上班，忙得很，家裡都是我和妹妹輪流打掃房子、倒垃圾。

---

9. 女：请问，新生在哪儿办注册手续？
   男：A）老生在图书馆办注册手续。
   　　B）注册手续？我已经办好了。
   　　C）在学生活动中心。
   　　D）新生明天才办注册手续。
   （学生答题5秒）

10. 男：快放假了，你有什么计划？
    女：我要么到中国去玩儿，要么去快餐店打工。你呢？
    男：A）中国各地，我都去过。
    　　B）可能会上暑期学校。
    　　C）我比较喜欢放寒假。
    　　D）暑假太长了，真无聊。
    （学生答题5秒）

11. 女：那个新电影不错，听说看的人挺多的，你看了吗？
    男：现在去是人挤人，过一阵子再说吧。
    女：A）等你想看的时候，给我打个电话，我们一块儿去。
    　　B）我们下课以后就一起去看吧。
    　　C）没想到看电影的人这么多。
    　　D）要排队买票吗？
    （学生答题5秒）

12. 男：你平常帮不帮你妈妈做家务？
    女：我妈妈白天上班，忙得很，家里都是我和妹妹轮流打扫房子、倒垃圾。

男：A）你媽媽可真忙！

　　B）我父母都不上班，他們經常一起跳廣場舞。

　　C）是嗎？你媽媽有你們這樣的女兒真好。

　　D）打掃房子多沒意思啊，你明天再做吧！

（學生答題 5 秒）

(Traditional characters)

13. 女：起來，起來，別待在家裡看電視了，我們出去走走吧！

　　男：外面下著雨呢。

　　女：A）天氣預報說明天也會下雨。

　　　　B）下雨走路要小心。

　　　　C）我們可以帶傘呀，走吧！

　　　　D）這個電視節目真好看。

（學生答題 5 秒）

(Traditional characters)

14. 男：你怎麼不說話？看上去好像有什麼心事似的。

　　女：我男朋友的父母請我明天晚上去他們家吃飯，這是我們第一次見面，我很緊張，不知該帶什麼樣的禮物去。

　　男：A）我緊張的時候常常說不出話來。

　　　　B）原來你煩的是這個。給你出個好主意吧，帶一束鮮花去是再好不過的了。

　　　　C）你吃飯時最好不要吃太多。吃太多會給人很差的印象。

　　　　D）不用擔心送什麼禮物給我，只要是你送的，我都喜歡。

（學生答題 5 秒）

男：A）你妈妈可真忙！

　　B）我父母都不上班，他们经常一起跳广场舞。

　　C）是吗？你妈妈有你们这样的女儿真好。

　　D）打扫房子多没意思啊，你明天再做吧！

（学生答题 5 秒）

(Simplified characters)

13. 女：起来，起来，别待在家里看电视了，我们出去走走吧！

　　男：外面下着雨呢。

　　女：A）天气预报说明天也会下雨。

　　　　B）下雨走路要小心。

　　　　C）我们可以带伞呀，走吧！

　　　　D）这个电视节目真好看。

（学生答题 5 秒）

(Simplified characters)

14. 男：你怎么不说话？看上去好像有什么心事似的。

　　女：我男朋友的父母请我明天晚上去他们家吃饭，这是我们第一次见面，我很紧张，不知该带什么样的礼物去。

　　男：A）我紧张的时候常常说不出话来。

　　　　B）原来你烦的是这个。给你出个好主意吧，带一束鲜花去是再好不过的了。

　　　　C）你吃饭时最好不要吃太多。吃太多会给人很差的印象。

　　　　D）不用担心送什么礼物给我，只要是你送的，我都喜欢。

（学生答题 5 秒）

(Traditional characters) | (Simplified characters)

15. 女：我上個月報名申請當夏令營的輔導員，剛剛接到了錄取通知，我樂壞了。

男：我也被錄取了，不過我媽不讓我去，她認爲我還不夠獨立，怎麼能輔導別人！

女：A）這次錄取的人并不多，我們可夠幸運的。

B）我媽媽認爲當輔導員不必那麼獨立。

C）夏令營有很多好玩兒的活動，小孩子肯定會非常喜歡。

D）你跟你媽媽多溝通溝通，她自然就會改變她的想法了。

（學生答題5秒）

---

15. 女：我上个月报名申请当夏令营的辅导员，刚刚接到了录取通知，我乐坏了。

男：我也被录取了，不过我妈不让我去，她认为我还不够独立，怎么能辅导别人！

女：A）这次录取的人并不多，我们可够幸运的。

B）我妈妈认为当辅导员不必那么独立。

C）夏令营有很多好玩儿的活动，小孩子肯定会非常喜欢。

D）你跟你妈妈多沟通沟通，她自然就会改变她的想法了。

（学生答题5秒）

Listening Selections

Directions:

You will listen to several selections in Chinese. For each selection, you will be told whether it will be played once or twice. You may take notes as you listen. Your notes will not be graded. After listening to each selection, you will see questions in English. For each question, choose the response that is best according to the selection. You will have 12 seconds to answer each question.

Selection 1: Announcement

Narrator: Now you will listen twice to a public announcement.

Woman:

(Traditional characters)

前往北京的旅客請注意：
　　我們很抱歉地通知各位，您乘坐的MU7765次航班由於颱風來襲，風雨太大，視綫不佳，不能按時起飛。在此我們深表歉意。請您先在候機廳休息，等候通知。如果您有什麼需要，請與服務臺聯繫。謝謝！

(Simplified characters)

> 前往北京的旅客请注意：
> 　　我们很抱歉地通知各位，您乘坐的MU7765次航班由于台风来袭，风雨太大，视线不佳，不能按时起飞。在此我们深表歉意。请您先在候机厅休息，等候通知。如果您有什么需要，请与服务台联系。谢谢！

Narrator: Now listen again.

(Repeat)

Narrator: Now answer the questions for this selection.

(12 seconds)

(12 seconds)

Selection 2: Conversation

Narrator: Now you will listen once to a conversation between two students.

(Traditional characters)

> 女：這家飯館兒你來過嗎？他們的菜怎麼樣？
> 男：我沒來過，不過，我同屋是這兒的常客。Yelp和谷歌顧客點評都是五顆星，而且電視新聞也曾經報道過。
> 女：是嗎？那記者說他們師傅哪些菜最拿手？
> 男：聽說魚香肉絲、麻婆豆腐什麼的，都十分地道，他們的水煮魚也是大家常常點的。
> 女：這些菜聽起來似乎都辣得很，我不太吃辣，換一家吧？
> 男：既來之，則安之。我們讓師傅少放辣椒不就得了。
> 女：說的也是。除了辣椒以外，千萬別忘了讓他們別放味精、少放點兒鹽。
> 男：放心吧！你看，菜單上不是清清楚楚地寫著"請安心食用，我們不用味精"嗎？
> 女：好，那咱們可以點菜了吧？我餓壞了。

(Simplified characters)

> 女：这家饭馆儿你来过吗？他们的菜怎么样？
> 男：我没来过，不过，我同屋是这儿的常客。Yelp和谷歌顾客点评都是五颗星，而且电视新闻也曾经报道过。
> 女：是吗？那记者说他们师傅哪些菜最拿手？

男：听说鱼香肉丝、麻婆豆腐什么的，都十分地道，他们的水煮鱼也是大家常常点的。
女：这些菜听起来似乎都辣得很，我不太吃辣，换一家吧？
男：既来之，则安之。我们让师傅少放辣椒不就得了。
女：说的也是。除了辣椒以外，千万别忘了让他们别放味精、少放点儿盐。
男：放心吧！你看，菜单上不是清清楚楚地写着"请安心食用，我们不用味精"吗？
女：好，那咱们可以点菜了吧？我饿坏了。

Narrator: Now answer the questions for this selection.

(12 seconds)

(12 seconds)

(12 seconds)

(12 seconds)

Selection 3: Instructions

Narrator: Now you will listen once to someone giving instructions.

Woman:

(Traditional characters)

你不用擔心，你的病沒什麼要緊的，只是季節性的感冒，不是新流感，不用住院隔離觀察。我給你開兩種藥，你去藥房取藥。比較大的那種藥，一天吃三次，一次吃兩片，飯前吃，要按時吃。比較小的那種，你咳嗽不停的時候吃，一次吃一粒，飯前、飯後服用都可以，但必須間隔六個小時，一天不能超過四粒。

(Simplified characters)

你不用担心，你的病没什么要紧的，只是季节性的感冒，不是新流感，不用住院隔离观察。我给你开两种药，你去药房取药。比较大的那种药，一天吃三次，一次吃两片，饭前吃，要按时吃。比较小的那种，你咳嗽不停的时候吃，一次吃一粒，饭前、饭后服用都可以，但必须间隔六个小时，一天不能超过四粒。

Narrator: Now answer the questions for this selection.

(12 seconds)

(12 seconds)

(12 seconds)

(12 seconds)

Selection 4: Voice Message

Narrator: Now you will listen twice to a voice message.

Man:

(Traditional characters)

> 小鵬，給你打了好幾次電話，可是一直占綫，好不容易通了，你又不接。怎麼回事？你都在忙些什麼？是這樣的，我剛看到學校的通知，4月底學生會要舉辦一場才藝表演。你還記得我們去年表演的相聲是多麼受大家的歡迎嗎？想不想在畢業前再合作一次，爲我們的高中生活留個美好的回憶？給我回個電話，我們好好兒商量商量！雖然離演出的時間還有6個星期，但是越早準備越好，再説我們還得向王老師借説相聲的長袍，是吧？我等你電話。

(Simplified characters)

> 小鹏，给你打了好几次电话，可是一直占线，好不容易通了，你又不接。怎么回事？你都在忙些什么？是这样的，我刚看到学校的通知，4月底学生会要举办一场才艺表演。你还记得我们去年表演的相声是多么受大家的欢迎吗？想不想在毕业前再合作一次，为我们的高中生活留个美好的回忆？给我回个电话，我们好好儿商量商量！虽然离演出的时间还有6个星期，但是越早准备越好，再说我们还得向王老师借说相声的长袍，是吧？我等你电话。

Narrator: Now listen again.

(Repeat)

Narrator: Now answer the questions for this selection.

(12 seconds)

(12 seconds)

(12 seconds)

(12 seconds)

(12 seconds)

Selection 5: Report

Narrator: Now you will listen once to a report.

Man:

(Traditional characters)

> 尊敬的校長、各位老師、各位同學：
>
> 　　大家好！現在我代表我們小組來匯報一下上學期我們調查十一、十二年級學生課餘打工的情況。一共有234位同學接受了我們的電話訪問調查，其中有70%的學生都有打工的經歷。60%的同學平均每週工作10個小時，只有不到5%的學生每週打工超過20個小時。74%的同學都表示，打工除了爲了挣點兒零用錢，還爲了增加一點兒工作經驗。有7%的學生打工是因爲家境需要，課餘打工來貼補家用。這些學生一般每週打工至少15個小時。所有的同學都表示，學習比挣錢重要，如果打工影響學業的話，他們就會把工作辭掉。
>
> 　　以上是我們的調查報告，謝謝。

(Simplified characters)

> 尊敬的校长、各位老师、各位同学：
>
> 　　大家好！现在我代表我们小组来汇报一下上学期我们调查十一、十二年级学生课余打工的情况。一共有234位同学接受了我们的电话访问调查，其中有70%的学生都有打工的经历。60%的同学平均每周工作10个小时，只有不到5%的学生每周打工超过20个小时。74%的同学都表示，打工除了为了挣点儿零用钱，还为了增加一点儿工作经验。有7%的学生打工是因为家境需要，课余打工来贴补家用。这些学生一般每周打工至少15个小时。所有的同学都表示，学习比挣钱重要，如果打工影响学业的话，他们就会把工作辞掉。
>
> 　　以上是我们的调查报告，谢谢。

Narrator: Now answer the questions for this selection.

(12 seconds)

(12 seconds)

(12 seconds)

(12 seconds)

(12 seconds)

Section II: Free Response

Part B: Speaking

Recording Scripts

Conversation

Directions: You will participate in a simulated conversation. Each time it is your turn to speak, you will have 20 seconds to record. You should respond as fully and as appropriately as possible. There will be six times when it is your turn to speak.

Xiaomei just came to the United States from China as an exchange student at your school. She would like to ask you some questions about studying and living in the United States.

(Traditional characters)

> 小美：你好！請問，除了學習以外，你課外都參加些什麼活動？
> （學生答題20秒）
> 小美：學校有哪些運動隊和社團呢？要怎麼參加呢？
> （學生答題20秒）
> 小美：聽說美國高中生都得抽空做些社區服務，你都做過些什麼呢？會不會影響學習？
> （學生答題20秒）
> 小美：我也想做義工，你能不能告訴我做什麼好？做義工要注意些什麼？
> （學生答題20秒）
> 小美：在美國這段時間，除了學習，我也想到各處走走，看看美國的名勝古跡，體驗一下美國人的生活和文化。在旅遊上，你可不可以給我一些建議？
> （學生答題20秒）
> 小美：你還有什麼建議能讓我在美國這一年收穫更多，過得更有意義？
> （學生答題20秒）

(Simplified characters)

> 小美：你好！请问，除了学习以外，你课外都参加些什么活动？
> （学生答题20秒）
> 小美：学校有哪些运动队和社团呢？要怎么参加呢？
> （学生答题20秒）

小美：听说美国高中生都得抽空做些社区服务，你都做过些什么呢？会不会影响学习？

（学生答题20秒）

小美：我也想做义工，你能不能告诉我做什么好？做义工要注意些什么？

（学生答题20秒）

小美：在美国这段时间，除了学习，我也想到各处走走，看看美国的名胜古迹，体验一下美国人的生活和文化。在旅游上，你可不可以给我一些建议？

（学生答题20秒）

小美：你还有什么建议能让我在美国这一年收获更多，过得更有意义？

（学生答题20秒）

Cultural Presentation

Directions: You will be asked to speak in Chinese on a specific topic. Imagine you are making an oral presentation to your Chinese class. First, you will read and hear the topic for your presentation. You will have 4 minutes to prepare your presentation. Then you will have 2 minutes to record your presentation. Your presentation should be as complete as possible.

Choose ONE celebration of the Chinese festivals, such as the Spring Festival, Dragon Boat Festival, Mid-Autumn Festival, etc.. In your presentation, describe the festival, how Chinese celebrate it, and explain its significance.

Audio Scripts of AP Chinese Language and Culture Test 5

Section I: Multiple Choice

Part A: Listening

Rejoinders

Directions: You will hear several short conversations or parts of conversations followed by four choices, designated A, B, C, and D. Choose the one that continues or completes the conversation in a logical and culturally appropriate manner. After you have decided which of the suggested answers is best, COMPLETELY fill in the corresponding circle on the answer sheet. You will have 5 seconds to answer each question.

(Traditional characters)

1. 男：你參加學校游泳隊纔幾個月，就游得這麼棒，你是怎麼練的呢？
   女：A）我們學校的游泳隊真的很棒。
   　　B）游泳訓練很無聊。
   　　C）我每天早上和下午都練習兩個小時。
   　　D）游泳的確很有意思。
   （學生答題5秒）

2. 男：售貨員，我昨天買的這雙鞋質量有點兒問題，我想把它退了。
   女：A）這雙鞋的樣子過時了，很少有人買。
   　　B）收據帶來了嗎？
   　　C）這雙鞋夠便宜的了，不能再打折了。
   　　D）你還要買些什麼？
   （學生答題5秒）

3. 男：玲玲，我好幾天沒來上學，落下了很多課。可不可以借你的筆記看一下？
   女：A）好幾天沒見到你了。

(Simplified characters)

1. 男：你参加学校游泳队才几个月，就游得这么棒，你是怎么练的呢？
   女：A）我们学校的游泳队真的很棒。
   　　B）游泳训练很无聊。
   　　C）我每天早上和下午都练习两个小时。
   　　D）游泳的确很有意思。
   （学生答题5秒）

2. 男：售货员，我昨天买的这双鞋质量有点儿问题，我想把它退了。
   女：A）这双鞋的样子过时了，很少有人买。
   　　B）收据带来了吗？
   　　C）这双鞋够便宜的了，不能再打折了。
   　　D）你还要买些什么？
   （学生答题5秒）

3. 男：玲玲，我好几天没来上学，落下了很多课。可不可以借你的笔记看一下？
   女：A）好几天没见到你了。

B）你的作業找不到了嗎?

C）這個筆記本多少錢?

D）沒問題,就是我的筆記很亂。

（學生答題 5 秒）

4. 女：哎呀,外面下大雨了!今天的足球賽恐怕得取消了。

   男：A）我看足球賽時一定得吃爆米花。

   B）千萬不要呀!那樣就太掃興了。

   C）不用擔心,咱們學校的足球隊肯定會贏。

   D）現在喜歡足球的人越來越少了。

（學生答題 5 秒）

5. 女：嗨,下個月就要高中畢業了,想不想幫學校做點兒什麼來表示感謝?

   男：A）好主意,讓我想一想。

   B）我們這幾年學到了很多東西。

   C）沒問題,我們是應該開個舞會。

   D）你猜猜學校會送畢業生什麼禮物呢。

（學生答題 5 秒）

6. 男：下週我有個工作面試,我打算去買套西裝。

   女：A）穿西裝上班很得體。

   B）逛街很有意思。

   C）賣西裝的工作不好做,因為現在穿西裝的人很少。

   D）現在經濟這麼差你還能有面試的機會,運氣不錯啊。

（學生答題 5 秒）

(Simplified characters)

7. 女：大山，你父母说英文好像没有什么口音。

男：A）他们都是第二代移民了。
　　B）有些父母不会说英文。
　　C）我父母英文的发音是不太标准。
　　D）我父母说话声音都很小。

（学生答题5秒）

8. 女：我们这个周末要去做义工，你有没有空儿和我们一块儿去？

男：A）我觉得做义工很有意义。
　　B）你每个星期都做义工吗？
　　C）好啊！是不是去海边捡垃圾？
　　D）我从小就喜欢做义工。

（学生答题5秒）

9. 男：真倒霉！我三次驾驶考试都没过。

女：你大概太紧张了吧？要不然你肯定考得过。

男：A）考试不应该紧张。
　　B）你怎么知道我不紧张呢？
　　C）有一点儿，下次考试时我得放轻松点儿。
　　D）我开得够好的了，不用再练了。

（学生答题5秒）

10. 女：你去过中国的云南省吗？听说那个地方很有意思。

男：跟我家人去过一次。那儿住着很多少数民族，文化非常丰富。

女：A）爲什麼很少人住在那兒呢？
　　B）這個問題我不清楚。
　　C）這麼說我一定得去看一看。
　　D）雲南只有少數人很富有。
（學生答題5秒）

(Traditional characters)

11. 男：我覺得我們開錯路了，大偉家肯定沒這麼遠。
　　女：那我們把車停在右邊那個加油站去問一問路吧。
　　男：A）這兒怎麼連個加油站都沒有呢？
　　　　B）我的車是今天早上剛加的油。
　　　　C）來不及了，這裡不讓右轉。
　　　　D）大偉現在不在家，找他也幫不上忙。
（學生答題5秒）

(Traditional characters)

12. 男：今天我們在中文課上看了一部關於大熊貓的紀錄片，好看極了！
　　女：你見過真正的熊貓嗎？
　　男：A）前年我去聖地亞哥動物園，看到了剛從中國來的大熊貓。
　　　　B）我覺得我們應該保護自然環境，讓熊貓有好的生存環境。
　　　　C）熊貓是瀕臨絕種的珍稀動物。
　　　　D）成龍演的那部熊貓電影真好玩兒。
（學生答題5秒）

(Traditional characters)

13. 男：蘭蘭，你昨天去中國城看遊行了？
　　女：我去了，人太多，簡直都擠死了。

女：A）为什么很少人住在那儿呢？
　　B）这个问题我不清楚。
　　C）这么说我一定得去看一看。
　　D）云南只有少数人很富有。
（学生答题5秒）

(Simplified characters)

11. 男：我觉得我们开错路了，大伟家肯定没这么远。
　　女：那我们把车停在右边那个加油站去问一问路吧。
　　男：A）这儿怎么连个加油站都没有呢？
　　　　B）我的车是今天早上刚加的油。
　　　　C）来不及了，这里不让右转。
　　　　D）大伟现在不在家，找他也帮不上忙。
（学生答题5秒）

(Simplified characters)

12. 男：今天我们在中文课上看了一部关于大熊猫的纪录片，好看极了！
　　女：你见过真正的熊猫吗？
　　男：A）前年我去圣地亚哥动物园，看到了刚从中国来的大熊猫。
　　　　B）我觉得我们应该保护自然环境，让熊猫有好的生存坏境。
　　　　C）熊猫是濒临绝种的珍稀动物。
　　　　D）成龙演的那部熊猫电影真好玩儿。
（学生答题5秒）

(Simplified characters)

13. 男：兰兰，你昨天去中国城看游行了吗？
　　女：我去了，人太多，简直都挤死了。

男：A）幸虧我沒去，在家看電視轉播其實更舒服。
B）我的天哪！擠死了幾個人呀？
C）中國城有很多旅遊的人。
D）我要是參加遊行就好了。
（學生答題5秒）

(Traditional characters)

14. 男：嗨，小麗，我昨晚做了個夢，夢見我 AP 中文考試得了個 5。
女：有意思！真是個美夢。
男：A）你也做過同樣的夢啊？
B）做夢沒有意思。
C）但願美夢成真。
D）我不喜歡 AP 中文在晚上考。
（學生答題5秒）

(Traditional characters)

15. 女：我外婆手特巧，幾下子就能剪出個花鳥什麼的。
男：剪紙是中國的傳統藝術，你應該跟你外婆學一學。
女：A）好，我讓我外婆教你。
B）我外婆的剪紙很酷。
C）嗯，不過看著容易，學起來很難。
D）你看到我的剪刀了嗎？
（學生答題5秒）

Listening Selections

Directions:

You will listen to several selections in Chinese. For each selection, you will be told whether it will be played once or twice. You may take notes as you listen. Your notes will not be graded. After listening to each selection, you will see questions in English. For each question, choose the response that is best according to the selection. You will have 12 seconds to answer each question.

Selection 1: Announcement

Narrator: Now you will listen twice to a public announcement.

Woman:

(Traditional characters)

> 旅客們請注意：
> 　　由於氣流的緣故，飛機顛簸得很厲害。請您馬上回到您的座位，并繫好安全帶。洗手間暫停使用。機艙乘務員也請就坐，待安全指示燈顯示後，再繼續您的工作。謝謝大家的合作！

(Simplified characters)

> 旅客们请注意：
> 　　由于气流的缘故，飞机颠簸得很厉害。请您马上回到您的座位，并系好安全带。洗手间暂停使用。机舱乘务员也请就坐，待安全指示灯显示后，再继续您的工作。谢谢大家的合作！

Narrator: Now listen again.

(Repeat)

Narrator: Now answer the questions for this selection.

(12 seconds)

(12 seconds)

(12 seconds)

Selection 2: Voice Message

Narrator: Now you will listen twice to a voice message.

Woman:

(Traditional characters)

> 　　英英，我是紫薇。咱們小組星期六的活動我去不了了。我爺爺被車撞了，星期六我得和我父母去醫院看望他，大概很晚纔能回來。如果能把小組活動改到星期天最好了，要不然我就只好缺席了。分給我的那部分，我一定會完成，絕不會影響咱們小組星期一的報告。麻煩你代我向大家道個歉。有事請打我的手機。謝謝！再見！

(Simplified characters)

> 英英，我是紫薇。咱们小组星期六的活动我去不了了。我爷爷被车撞了，星期六我得和我父母去医院看望他，大概很晚才能回来。如果能把小组活动改到星期天最好了，要不然我就只好缺席了。分给我的那部分，我一定会完成，绝不会影响咱们小组星期一的报告。麻烦你代我向大家道个歉。有事请打我的手机。谢谢！再见！

Narrator: Now listen again.

(Repeat)

Narrator: Now answer the questions for this selection.

(12 seconds)

(12 seconds)

(12 seconds)

Selection 3: Conversation

Narrator: Now you will listen once to a conversation between two students.

(Traditional characters)

> 男：美雲，下週三學校體操隊有個選拔賽，你想去試試嗎？
> 女：我很想去，可是我的腳傷還沒全好呢，去了恐怕也選不上。你應該去啊！
> 男：我覺得練體操很累，而且這學期我選的課都很難，真是有點兒力不從心。
> 女：那你也不應該半途而廢。你從小就學體操，都練了這麼多年了，扔了太可惜了。
> 男：你說的倒也是，讓我想想吧，可我還是覺得你也應該去。
> 女：你去我就去！
> 男：好，一言爲定！

(Simplified characters)

> 男：美云，下周三学校体操队有个选拔赛，你想去试试吗？
> 女：我很想去，可是我的脚伤还没全好呢，去了恐怕也选不上。你应该去啊！
> 男：我觉得练体操很累，而且这学期我选的课都很难，真是有点儿力不从心。
> 女：那你也不应该半途而废。你从小就学体操，都练了这么多年了，扔了太可惜了。
> 男：你说的倒也是，让我想想吧，可我还是觉得你也应该去。

女：你去我就去！
男：好，一言为定！

Narrator: Now answer the questions for this selection.

(12 seconds)

(12 seconds)

(12 seconds)

(12 seconds)

Selection 4: Instructions

Narrator: Now you will listen once to someone giving instructions.

Man:

(Traditional characters)

電腦促銷退款說明

　　凡是在2020年6月28日至10月11日期間購買本公司電腦的客戶均可享受50美元的退款優惠。用戶必須在購買日期之後的45天以內，登錄本公司網站填寫退款申請表。所需的信息包括：（1）客戶姓名、住址及聯繫方式；（2）購買產品的收據或網上購買的付款記錄；（3）產品的型號、電腦的序列號以及郵寄公司的送貨號。如信息齊全，您會在提交退款申請表後24小時內收到客服郵件，告知您收到退款的日期。通常退款到您的賬戶只需3天，郵寄退款支票需5到10天。本優惠只限美國境內客戶，希望您對我們的服務滿意。如有疑問，請撥打我們的免費咨詢電話：（888）666-9999。

(Simplified characters)

电脑促销退款说明

　　凡是在2020年6月28日至10月11日期间购买本公司电脑的客户均可享受50美元的退款优惠。用户必须在购买日期之后的45天以内，登录本公司网站填写退款申请表。所需的信息包括：（1）客户姓名、住址及联系方式；（2）购买产品的收据或网上购买的付款记录；（3）产品的型号、电脑的序列号以及邮寄公司的送货号。如信息齐全，您会在提交退款申请表后24小时内收到客服邮件，告知您收到退款的日期。通常退款到您的账户只需3天，邮寄退款支票需5到10天。本优惠只限美国境内客户，希望您对我们的服务满意。如有疑问，请拨打我们的免费咨询电话：（888）666-9999。

Narrator: Now answer the questions for this selection.

(12 seconds)

(12 seconds)

(12 seconds)

(12 seconds)

Selection 5: Report

Narrator: Now you will listen once to a report.

Man:

(Traditional characters)

> 上海氣象臺於2020年7月12日18時08分發佈雷電黃色預警信號：預計1到3小時內本市自西向東會有雷電活動，可能造成雷電災害事故。政府及相關部門會按照規定做好防雷工作，市民應密切注意天氣，儘量避免戶外活動。如有事故發生，請撥打120或999求助。

(Simplified characters)

> 上海气象台于2020年7月12日18时08分发布雷电黄色预警信号：预计1到3小时内本市自西向东会有雷电活动，可能造成雷电灾害事故。政府及相关部门会按照规定做好防雷工作，市民应密切注意天气，尽量避免户外活动。如有事故发生，请拨打120或999求助。

Narrator: Now answer the questions for this selection.

(12 seconds)

(12 seconds)

(12 seconds)

(12 seconds)

(12 seconds)

Section II: Free Response
Part B: Speaking
Recording Scripts
Conversation
Directions:

You will participate in a simulated conversation. Each time it is your turn to speak, you will have 20 seconds to record. You should respond as fully and as appropriately as possible. There will be six times when it is your turn to speak.

You will have a conversation with Li Long, a Chinese student you met on the Great Wall, about your experiences in China.

(Traditional characters)

> 李龍：很高興認識你，你的中文講得這麼好，還有點兒北京口音，你在北京生活過嗎？
> （學生答題20秒）
> 李龍：我看你登長城很輕鬆，你大概經常運動吧？你都喜歡些什麼運動？
> （學生答題20秒）
> 李龍：你們外國人是怎樣理解"不到長城非好漢"這句話的呢？
> （學生答題20秒）
> 李龍：這次中國之行你還打算去哪些地方？
> （學生答題20秒）
> 李龍：北京有很多有名的小吃，你都吃過哪些？
> （學生答題20秒）
> 李龍：過一段時間我要去美國旅遊，可以給我介紹一些好玩兒的地方嗎？
> （學生答題20秒）

(Simplified characters)

> 李龙：很高兴认识你，你的中文讲得这么好，还有点儿北京口音，你在北京生活过吗？
> （学生答题20秒）
> 李龙：我看你登长城很轻松，你大概经常运动吧？你都喜欢些什么运动？
> （学生答题20秒）
> 李龙：你们外国人是怎样理解"不到长城非好汉"这句话的呢？
> （学生答题20秒）

李龙：这次中国之行你还打算去哪些地方？

（学生答题20秒）

李龙：北京有很多有名的小吃，你都吃过哪些？

（学生答题20秒）

李龙：过一段时间我要去美国旅游，可以给我介绍一些好玩儿的地方吗？

（学生答题20秒）

Cultural Presentation

Directions: You will be asked to speak in Chinese on a specific topic. Imagine you are making an oral presentation to your Chinese class. First, you will read and hear the topic for your presentation. You will have 4 minutes to prepare your presentation. Then you will have 2 minutes to record your presentation. Your presentation should be as complete as possible.

Choose ONE contemporary Chinese celebrity (athlete, musician, actor, politician, etc.) and describe the reason for his or her popularity, his or her achievements, and any influence he or she has had on Chinese culture at large or on your life.

Audio Scripts of AP Chinese Language and Culture Test 6

Section I: Multiple Choice

Part A: Listening

Rejoinders

Directions:

Directions: You will hear several short conversations or parts of conversations followed by four choices, designated A, B, C, and D. Choose the one that continues or completes the conversation in a logical and culturally appropriate manner. After you have decided which of the suggested answers is best, COMPLETELY fill in the corresponding circle on the answer sheet. You will have 5 seconds to answer each question.

(Simplified characters)

1. 男：我们家的洗衣机、烘干机都坏了，这几天又一直下雨，衣服干不了，真讨厌。

   女：A）你可以来用我们家的。

   　　B）下雨才好呢，要不然，今年夏天就缺水了。

   　　C）你不洗衣服吗？

   　　D）我们家的衣服都是我洗的。

   （学生答题5秒）

2. 女：小林的生日晚会，你要是不去，那我也不去。

   男：A）他去年的生日晚会邀请了很多亲朋好友。

   　　B）你知道哪些人去了吗？

   　　C）我是因为第二天有考试才不去的，你没什么事儿的话还是去吧！

   　　D）小林再过三天就十八岁了。

   （学生答题5秒）

(Traditional characters)

3. 男：今天晚上的電視節目，不是球賽就是動畫片，沒什麼好看的。

   女：A）現在的電視節目都做得不錯。

   B）我妹妹現在在學動畫製作，聽說挺有意思的。

   C）那你怎麼還一直坐在電視機前面盯著電視看呢？

   D）今天下午的球賽非常精彩，你去看了沒有？

   （學生答題 5 秒）

(Traditional characters)

4. 女：我們前兩天剛搬進了新家，這回我總算有自己的房間了。

   男：A）我家離學校很近，非常方便。

   B）你喜歡跟你妹妹住同一個房間嗎？

   C）我們最好經常打掃和收拾自己的房間。

   D）太好了！你們是自己搬的家，還是請搬家公司幫的忙？

   （學生答題 5 秒）

(Traditional characters)

5. 男：這種藥還不錯，你試試看！

   女：A）我已經試過五六種藥了，都沒用，明天還得再去看醫生。

   B）我沒有健康保險，所以從不去看醫生，也不吃藥。

   C）謝謝你的關心，希望吃了這個藥病就好了。

   D）我家附近的藥店也不錯。

   （學生答題 5 秒）

(Simplified characters)

3. 男：今天晚上的电视节目，不是球赛就是动画片，没什么好看的。

   女：A）现在的电视节目都做得不错。

   B）我妹妹现在在学动画制作，听说挺有意思的。

   C）那你怎么还一直坐在电视机前面盯着电视看呢？

   D）今天下午的球赛非常精彩，你去看了没有？

   （学生答题 5 秒）

(Simplified characters)

4. 女：我们前两天刚搬进了新家，这回我总算有自己的房间了。

   男：A）我家离学校很近，非常方便。

   B）你喜欢跟你妹妹住同一个房间吗？

   C）我们最好经常打扫和收拾自己的房间。

   D）太好了！你们是自己搬的家，还是请搬家公司帮的忙？

   （学生答题 5 秒）

(Simplified characters)

5. 男：这种药还不错，你试试看！

   女：A）我已经试过五六种药了，都没用，明天还得再去看医生。

   B）我没有健康保险，所以从不去看医生，也不吃药。

   C）谢谢你的关心，希望吃了这个药病就好了。

   D）我家附近的药店也不错。

   （学生答题 5 秒）

(Traditional characters)

6. 女：你出門以前,先幫我把碗、盤洗了吧！
   男：A）我比較喜歡洗車。
   　　B）哎呀,碗、盤那麼多,等我回來再說吧！
   　　C）我要出門去買東西。
   　　D）碗、盤在哪兒？我不知道。
   　（學生答題5秒）

(Traditional characters)

7. 女：你要是真想吃就吃吧,但是減肥失敗了,可別怪別人喲！
   男：A）好了,好了,我吃就是了,何必不高興呢？
   　　B）哪有這樣的事？為了你減肥,我就不能吃東西了？
   　　C）要說不怕胖是假的,但是美食當前,胖就胖吧,吃了再說。
   　　D）你這麼胖下去怎麼得了？
   　（學生答題5秒）

(Traditional characters)

8. 男：今年這個棒球隊表現傑出,尤其是他們的當家投手,很少有人打得到他的球。
   女：A）籃球賽比棒球賽精彩多了。
   　　B）真沒想到你棒球打得這麼好,你是怎麼練的？
   　　C）他們的水平不行,所以今年常常輸球。
   　　D）他可值錢呢,聽說一年可以賺上兩百萬美金。
   　（學生答題5秒）

(Simplified characters)

6. 女：你出门以前,先帮我把碗、盘洗了吧！
   男：A）我比较喜欢洗车。
   　　B）哎呀,碗、盘那么多,等我回来再说吧！
   　　C）我要出门去买东西。
   　　D）碗、盘在哪儿？我不知道。
   　（学生答题5秒）

(Simplified characters)

7. 女：你要是真想吃就吃吧,但是减肥失败了,可别怪别人哟！
   男：A）好了,好了,我吃就是了,何必不高兴呢？
   　　B）哪有这样的事？为了你减肥,我就不能吃东西了？
   　　C）要说不怕胖是假的,但是美食当前,胖就胖吧,吃了再说。
   　　D）你这么胖下去怎么得了？
   　（学生答题5秒）

(Simplified characters)

8. 男：今年这个棒球队表现杰出,尤其是他们的当家投手,很少有人打得到他的球。
   女：A）篮球赛比棒球赛精彩多了。
   　　B）真没想到你棒球打得这么好,你是怎么练的？
   　　C）他们的水平不行,所以今年常常输球。
   　　D）他可值钱呢,听说一年可以赚上两百万美金。
   　（学生答题5秒）

(Traditional characters) | (Simplified characters)

9. 男：沒想到這次考試會這麼難，恐怕我會不及格。

   女：你父母會罵你嗎？

   男：A）那倒不至於，不過，我自己會挺難過的。

   B）希望下星期的考試容易些。

   C）我父母希望我考上名牌大學。

   D）我父母經常嘮叨，說我不用功，可是我不聽他們的。

   （學生答題5秒）

9. 男：没想到这次考试会这么难，恐怕我会不及格。

   女：你父母会骂你吗？

   男：A）那倒不至于，不过，我自己会挺难过的。

   B）希望下星期的考试容易些。

   C）我父母希望我考上名牌大学。

   D）我父母经常唠叨，说我不用功，可是我不听他们的。

   （学生答题5秒）

10. 女：你今年生日過得怎麼樣？

    男：哎，別提了，收到了兩件一模一樣的禮物。

    女：A）你今年生日是怎麼過的？

    B）你今年多大了？

    C）我非常喜歡你送我的生日禮物。

    D）那你可以拿到商店去退換呀。

    （學生答題5秒）

10. 女：你今年生日过得怎么样？

    男：哎，别提了，收到了两件一模一样的礼物。

    女：A）你今年生日是怎么过的？

    B）你今年多大了？

    C）我非常喜欢你送我的生日礼物。

    D）那你可以拿到商店去退换呀。

    （学生答题5秒）

11. 男：這個學期的課外活動，你決定參加什麼了沒有？

    女：我對羽毛球和網球都非常感興趣，還不知道該選什麼纔好。

    男：A）我可以跟你一起練習。

    B）別說了，我也不行。

    C）你看看球隊練習的時間再決定吧。

    D）我和小美約好了明天一起打羽毛球，你想加入嗎？

    （學生答題5秒）

11. 男：这个学期的课外活动，你决定参加什么了没有？

    女：我对羽毛球和网球都非常感兴趣，还不知道该选什么才好。

    男：A）我可以跟你一起练习。

    B）别说了，我也不行。

    C）你看看球队练习的时间再决定吧。

    D）我和小美约好了明天一起打羽毛球，你想加入吗？

    （学生答题5秒）

(Traditional characters)

12. 女：這家商店在大減價，我們進去看看有什麼便宜的。
    男：打折的衣服常常大小不合適，樣子也不好。
    女：A）我最喜歡打折的時候買東西了。
    　　B）這家商店難得大減價，你不買點兒嗎？
    　　C）那也不見得。
    　　D）你看，打七折呢，真便宜。
    （學生答題5秒）

(Traditional characters)

13. 男：對不起，我來晚了，路上堵車，平常十分鐘的路，足足開了一個小時。
    女：怎麼了，有人出車禍了？
    男：A）大概是吧，有兩輛車停在馬路中間，旁邊圍著四五個警察。
    　　B）一出車禍，保險費馬上就跟著漲了。
    　　C）現在開車的人沒什麼耐心，交通事故比前幾年頻繁多了。
    　　D）我的車平常挺快的，大概是出了什麼毛病了，過兩天得送去修修。
    （學生答題5秒）

(Traditional characters)

14. 女：你看那隻貓，多可愛啊，真想求媽媽讓我養一隻貓，可是我知道她絕對不會答應的。
    男：你又沒問，怎麼知道你媽媽絕對不會答應？

(Simplified characters)

12. 女：这家商店在大减价，我们进去看看有什么便宜的。
    男：打折的衣服常常大小不合适，样子也不好。
    女：A）我最喜欢打折的时候买东西了。
    　　B）这家商店难得大减价，你不买点儿吗？
    　　C）那也不见得。
    　　D）你看，打七折呢，真便宜。
    （学生答题5秒）

(Simplified characters)

13. 男：对不起，我来晚了，路上堵车，平常十分钟的路，足足开了一个小时。
    女：怎么了，有人出车祸了？
    男：A）大概是吧，有两辆车停在马路中间，旁边围着四五个警察。
    　　B）一出车祸，保险费马上就跟着涨了。
    　　C）现在开车的人没什么耐心，交通事故比前几年频繁多了。
    　　D）我的车平常挺快的，大概是出了什么毛病了，过两天得送去修修。
    （学生答题5秒）

(Simplified characters)

14. 女：你看那只猫，多可爱啊，真想求妈妈让我养一只猫，可是我知道她绝对不会答应的。
    男：你又没问，怎么知道你妈妈绝对不会答应？

(Traditional characters)

女：A）因爲對貓過敏的人一天到晚打噴嚏。
　　B）因爲我們家鄰居也有一隻貓，常常上我們家來玩兒。
　　C）因爲我媽媽嫌貓髒，也怕傢具被貓抓壞了。
　　D）因爲我每天都花很多時間上網看貓的圖片。
（學生答題5秒）

15. 女：小陳，是你呀，這麼巧！
    男：啊，小茵，你不是說最近挺忙的嗎？今天怎麼有空兒來逛商場呢？
    女：A）今天是什麼日子，商場擠得人山人海的。
    　　B）母親節快到了，我想給媽媽挑個別致的禮物。
    　　C）要是買的東西不合適，這個商場讓不讓顧客退換？
    　　D）聽說這個商場的工作人員買東西有很好的折扣。
    （學生答題5秒）

(Simplified characters)

女：A）因为对猫过敏的人一天到晚打喷嚏。
　　B）因为我们家邻居也有一只猫，常常上我们家来玩儿。
　　C）因为我妈妈嫌猫脏，也怕家具被猫抓坏了。
　　D）因为我每天都花很多时间上网看猫的图片。
（学生答题5秒）

15. 女：小陈，是你呀，这么巧！
    男：啊，小茵，你不是说最近挺忙的吗？今天怎么有空儿来逛商场呢？
    女：A）今天是什么日子，商场挤得人山人海的。
    　　B）母亲节快到了，我想给妈妈挑个别致的礼物。
    　　C）要是买的东西不合适，这个商场让不让顾客退换？
    　　D）听说这个商场的工作人员买东西有很好的折扣。
    （学生答题5秒）

Listening Selections

Directions:

You will listen to several selections in Chinese. For each selection, you will be told whether it will be played once or twice. You may take notes as you listen. Your notes will not be graded. After listening to each selection, you will see questions in English. For each question, choose the response that is best according to the selection. You will have 12 seconds to answer each question.

Selection 1: Announcement

Narrator: Now you will listen twice to a public announcement.

Woman:

(Traditional characters)

> 各位旅客請注意：
> 　　本次列車的終點站——上海——馬上就要到了，請您拿好隨身攜帶的行李，準備下車。要前往南京的旅客，請到三號站臺轉乘到南京的火車；前往蘇州的旅客，請到五號站臺等候上車。謝謝各位旅客搭乘本次列車，若有服務不周的地方，請您多多包涵。

(Simplified characters)

> 各位旅客请注意：
> 　　本次列车的终点站——上海——马上就要到了，请您拿好随身携带的行李，准备下车。要前往南京的旅客，请到三号站台转乘到南京的火车；前往苏州的旅客，请到五号站台等候上车。谢谢各位旅客搭乘本次列车，若有服务不周的地方，请您多多包涵。

Narrator: Now listen again.

(Repeat)

Narrator: Now answer the questions for this selection.

(12 seconds)

(12 seconds)

Selection 2: Conversation

Narrator: Now you will listen once to a conversation between two students.

(Traditional characters)

> 男：明明，後天晚上的畢業舞會你去嗎？
> 女：去是肯定會去的，可是不知道該穿哪件衣服。這兩天功課忙，又沒有時間去買衣服。
> 男：你上次參加小莉生日舞會時穿的那件連衣裙不是挺好的嗎？很漂亮，非常適合你。
> 女：哪件？
> 男：就是那件藍底帶小白花兒的。
> 女：那件啊，不行，那件是我姐姐的。上次跟她借，結果呢，喝咖啡時不小心，濺了幾滴在上頭。我姐姐簡直氣炸了，一連三天都沒理我。

男：你姐姐脾氣那麼大啊？
女：不管她了！你說我該怎麼辦？
男：那跟小平借吧！她的衣服多，個子又跟你差不多，你穿肯定合身。
女：好主意！那我現在就給她打電話。

(Simplified characters)

男：明明，后天晚上的毕业舞会你去吗？
女：去是肯定会去的，可是不知道该穿哪件衣服。这两天功课忙，又没有时间去买衣服。
男：你上次参加小莉生日舞会时穿的那件连衣裙不是挺好的吗？很漂亮，非常适合你。
女：哪件？
男：就是那件蓝底带小白花儿的。
女：那件啊，不行，那件是我姐姐的。上次跟她借，结果呢，喝咖啡时不小心，溅了几滴在上头。我姐姐简直气炸了，一连三天都没理我。
男：你姐姐脾气那么大啊？
女：不管她了！你说我该怎么办？
男：那跟小平借吧！她的衣服多，个子又跟你差不多，你穿肯定合身。
女：好主意！那我现在就给她打电话。

Narrator: Now answer the questions for this selection.

(12 seconds)

(12 seconds)

(12 seconds)

(12 seconds)

(12 seconds)

Selection 3: Instructions

Narrator: Now you will listen once to someone giving instructions.

Woman:

(Traditional characters)

> 凡是本市居民或在本市就讀的學生都可申請辦理借書證。如果是本市的學生，您需要帶學生證和兩張一寸的免冠黑白照片，親自到市立圖書館的櫃臺辦理。如果不是學生，除了帶兩張照片以外，您還必須帶一個上面有本市地址的信封，以及一種身份證明文件，例如駕照或護照，進行辦理。您也可以託別人代辦。辦理當天發證，您當天就可以借書。

(Simplified characters)

> 凡是本市居民或在本市就读的学生都可申请办理借书证。如果是本市的学生，您需要带学生证和两张一寸的免冠黑白照片，亲自到市立图书馆的柜台办理。如果不是学生，除了带两张照片以外，您还必须带一个上面有本市地址的信封，以及一种身份证明文件，例如驾照或护照，进行办理。您也可以托别人代办。办理当天发证，您当天就可以借书。

Narrator: Now answer the questions for this selection.

(12 seconds)

(12 seconds)

(12 seconds)

(12 seconds)

Selection 4: Voice Message

Narrator: Now you will listen twice to a voice message.

Woman:

(Traditional characters)

> 爸爸，對不起，剛剛教練說，因為這個週末就要比賽了，可是我們表現得還不夠好，所以他要我們留下來再多練習一個小時，要不然比賽的結果可能會不太理想。我們羽毛球隊的隊員對這次比賽都非常重視，希望能獲得冠軍，所以大家都很樂意留下來練習。本來我練完球是要坐公共汽車回家的，但是如果我坐車回家，就趕不上七點的小提琴課了。能不能麻煩您六點半開車來接我？謝謝！我們學校正門口見。

(Simplified characters)

> 爸爸，对不起，刚刚教练说，因为这个周末就要比赛了，可是我们表现得还不够好，所以他要我们留下来再多练习一个小时，要不然比赛的结果可能会不太理想。我们羽毛球队的队员对这次比赛都非常重视，希望能获得冠军，所以大家都很乐意留下来练习。本来我练完球是要坐公共汽车回家的，但是如果我坐车回家，就赶不上七点的小提琴课了。能不能麻烦您六点半开车来接我？谢谢！我们学校正门口见。

Narrator: Now listen again.

(Repeat)

Narrator: Now answer the questions for this selection.

(12 seconds)

(12 seconds)

(12 seconds)

(12 seconds)

Selection 5: Report

Narrator: Now you will listen once to a report.

Man:

(Traditional characters)

> 尊敬的校長、各位老師、各位同學：
> 　　大家好！我是王大爲，代表學生會來匯報我們這次交通工具問卷調查的結果。我們總共發出500份問卷，收回450份，謝謝所有參與問卷調查的同學。根據這450份問卷的統計結果，60%的同學自己上下學，完全不用父母接送；25%的學生上學、放學都是靠父母開車接送；剩餘的15%有時候自己上下學，有時候父母開車接送。自己上下學的同學，有的坐校車，有的坐公共汽車，有的騎車，有的走路，還有的自己開車。有父母接送的同學比自己上下學的同學遲到的比例高得多。他們表示，遲到的原因往往不在他們自己，而是父母的動作太慢。
> 　　我的報告結束，謝謝。

(Simplified characters)

尊敬的校长、各位老师、各位同学：

大家好！我是王大为，代表学生会来汇报我们这次交通工具问卷调查的结果。我们总共发出500份问卷，收回450份，谢谢所有参与问卷调查的同学。根据这450份问卷的统计结果，60%的同学自己上下学，完全不用父母接送；25%的学生上学、放学都是靠父母开车接送；剩余的15%有时候自己上下学，有时候父母开车接送。自己上下学的同学，有的坐校车，有的坐公共汽车，有的骑车，有的走路，还有的自己开车。有父母接送的同学比自己上下学的同学迟到的比例高得多。他们表示，迟到的原因往往不在他们自己，而是父母的动作太慢。

我的报告结束，谢谢。

Narrator: Now answer the questions for this selection.

(12 seconds)

(12 seconds)

(12 seconds)

(12 seconds)

(12 seconds)

Section II: Free Response

Part B: Speaking

Recording Scripts

Conversation

Directions:

You will participate in a simulated conversation. Each time it is your turn to speak, you will have 20 seconds to record. You should respond as fully and as appropriately as possible. There will be six times when it is your turn to speak.

You will have a conversation with Chen Chong, the community service director, about your applying for volunteering to tutor English to the new immigrant Chinese students at the local elementary schools.

(Traditional characters)

陳沖：你為什麼對幫助小學生學英語有興趣？
（學生答題20秒）

陳沖：你以前做過義工嗎？有沒有輔導英語或其他的教學經驗？
（學生答題20秒）

陳沖：如果小朋友上課不聽話，你會怎麼辦？
（學生答題20秒）

陳沖：你會怎樣提升小學生學習英語的興趣？
（學生答題20秒）

陳沖：我們的上課時間是星期一到星期五下午三點半到晚上六點，星期六上午八點到下午五點。你一個星期哪幾天，從幾點到幾點可以來輔導小學生學習？
（學生答題20秒）

陳沖：你覺得課外來輔導小學生學英語，對你學校的功課會不會有什麼影響？
（學生答題20秒）

(Simplified characters)

陈冲：你为什么对帮助小学生学英语有兴趣？
（学生答题20秒）

陈冲：你以前做过义工吗？有没有辅导英语或其他的教学经验？
（学生答题20秒）

陈冲：如果小朋友上课不听话，你会怎么办？
（学生答题20秒）

陈冲：你会怎样提升小学生学习英语的兴趣？
（学生答题20秒）

陈冲：我们的上课时间是星期一到星期五下午三点半到晚上六点，星期六上午八点到下午五点。你一个星期哪几天，从几点到几点可以来辅导小学生学习？
（学生答题20秒）

陈冲：你觉得课外来辅导小学生学英语，对你学校的功课会不会有什么影响？
（学生答题20秒）

Cultural Presentation

Directions:

You will be asked to speak in Chinese on a specific topic. Imagine you are making an oral presentation to your Chinese class. First, you will read and hear the topic for your presentation. You will have 4 minutes to prepare your presentation. Then you will have 2 minutes to record your presentation. Your presentation should be as complete as possible.

Choose ONE "成语故事"（成語故事），such as "守株待兔"（守株待兔）"画龙点睛"（畫龍點睛）"自相矛盾"（自相矛盾）"亡羊补牢"（亡羊補牢）"拔苗助长"（拔苗助長）"南辕北辙"（南轅北轍）"望梅止渴"（望梅止渴）"买椟还珠"（買櫝還珠）"夜郎自大"（夜郎自大）"滥竽充数"（濫竽充數），etc.. In your presentation, describe the original story of the expression, what the expression means, give an example to explain how the expression is used, and explain its significance.

Audio Scripts of AP Chinese Language and Culture Test 7

Section I: Multiple Choice

Part A: Listening

Rejoinders

Directions:

Directions: You will hear several short conversations or parts of conversations followed by four choices, designated A, B, C, and D. Choose the one that continues or completes the conversation in a logical and culturally appropriate manner. After you have decided which of the suggested answers is best, COMPLETELY fill in the corresponding circle on the answer sheet. You will have 5 seconds to answer each question.

(Simplified characters)

1. 男：唉，这几天因为选大学专业的事儿跟我父母吵了一架，他们不同意我报考哲学专业，可明天就得交申请表了，我真不知道该怎么办才好。

   女：A）填写大学申请表很费时间。

   B）我听说生物专业很难念，也许你应该尊重你父母的意见。

   C）哦，既然如此，那你就再考虑几天吧，反正不急。

   D）我觉得你应该心平气和地再跟你父母好好儿谈谈。

   （学生答题5秒）

2. 女：今天上中文课时，老师教我们打太极拳，挺有意思的，可是不太好学。

   男：A）我也学过，其实难倒是不难，就是需要有耐心。

   B）我们的中文课也挺有意思的，就是有时听不太懂。

   C）慢性子的人学不了太极拳。

   D）打太极拳的确是又难又没意思。

   （学生答题5秒）

(Traditional characters)

3. 男：蘭蘭，告訴你一個好消息，咱們今年的畢業典禮將在市體育館舉行！

　女：A）那兒的場地非常適合體育訓練。

　　　B）畢業以後你有什麼打算呢？

　　　C）那太好了！同學們知道了一定會很高興！

　　　D）你決定上哪個大學了嗎？

（學生答題5秒）

(Traditional characters)

4. 女：樂樂，你去夏令營那麼長時間，怎麼一直都沒跟我聯繫呢？

　男：A）你說得沒錯，夏令營的時間是有點兒太長了。

　　　B）那個地方既不能上網，也不能打電話。

　　　C）我在夏令營交了很多新朋友，過得很快樂。

　　　D）時間過得真快，夏令營很快就要結束了。

（學生答題5秒）

(Traditional characters)

5. 女：嗨，算上新來的那個印度同學，咱們班現在一共有11個從不同國家來的學生了。

　男：A）每個國家的人都有自己的語言。

　　　B）印度離中國比美國離中國近。

　　　C）咱們班都快成一個小聯合國了。

　　　D）我從來沒去過印度。

（學生答題5秒）

(Simplified characters)

3. 男：兰兰，告诉你一个好消息，咱们今年的毕业典礼将在市体育馆举行！

　女：A）那儿的场地非常适合体育训练。

　　　B）毕业以后你有什么打算呢？

　　　C）那太好了！同学们知道了一定会很高兴！

　　　D）你决定上哪个大学了吗？

（学生答题5秒）

(Simplified characters)

4. 女：乐乐，你去夏令营那么长时间，怎么一直都没跟我联系呢？

　男：A）你说得没错，夏令营的时间是有点儿太长了。

　　　B）那个地方既不能上网，也不能打电话。

　　　C）我在夏令营交了很多新朋友，过得很快乐。

　　　D）时间过得真快，夏令营很快就要结束了。

（学生答题5秒）

(Simplified characters)

5. 女：嗨，算上新来的那个印度同学，咱们班现在一共有11个从不同国家来的学生了。

　男：A）每个国家的人都有自己的语言。

　　　B）印度离中国比美国离中国近。

　　　C）咱们班都快成一个小联合国了。

　　　D）我从来没去过印度。

（学生答题5秒）

(Traditional characters)

6. 男：一看你家牆上掛的那些字畫，就知道你爸爸的毛筆字功底很深，你知道他是怎麼學的嗎？

   女：A）毛筆字是中國傳統文化藝術的一種，很多外國人也喜歡學。

   B）聽奶奶說我爸爸像我這麼大時就開始學了。

   C）我爸爸字畫的水平，一般人比不了。

   D）有些人是跟老師學，有些人是自學的。

   （學生答題5秒）

7. 女：嗨，漢語橋美英中學生夏令營不是在北京嗎？你怎麼跑山東去了呢？

   男：A）山東是個旅遊的好地方，我很喜歡。

   B）不都是去北京，有去山東的，還有去上海的。

   C）山東離北京可遠了，我們是坐飛機去的。

   D）夏令營活動在中美青少年之間架起了一座友誼的橋樑。

   （學生答題5秒）

8. 女：以後上課時你可千萬別給我發短信了，弄得我心神不定的，今天差點兒被老師發現。

   男：A）如果你上課時覺得不舒服，要馬上告訴老師。

(Simplified characters)

6. 男：一看你家墙上挂的那些字画，就知道你爸爸的毛笔字功底很深，你知道他是怎么学的吗？

   女：A）毛笔字是中国传统文化艺术的一种，很多外国人也喜欢学。

   B）听奶奶说我爸爸像我这么大时就开始学了。

   C）我爸爸字画的水平，一般人比不了。

   D）有些人是跟老师学，有些人是自学的。

   （学生答题5秒）

7. 女：嗨，汉语桥美英中学生夏令营不是在北京吗？你怎么跑山东去了呢？

   男：A）山东是个旅游的好地方，我很喜欢。

   B）不都是去北京，有去山东的，还有去上海的。

   C）山东离北京可远了，我们是坐飞机去的。

   D）夏令营活动在中美青少年之间架起了一座友谊的桥梁。

   （学生答题5秒）

8. 女：以后上课时你可千万别给我发短信了，弄得我心神不定的，今天差点儿被老师发现。

   男：A）如果你上课时觉得不舒服，要马上告诉老师。

B）謝謝你提醒我，以後咱們上課應該專心點兒。

C）發短信在青少年中很流行，因為比發電郵方便。

D）要是我早知道你心情不好，我一定會給你發短信的。

（學生答題5秒）

(Traditional characters)

9. 男：咱們學校外語系上週組織的那個演出，你去看了嗎？我們班唱周傑倫歌兒的那個同學得了一等獎。

 女：A）周傑倫的確唱得不錯，得一等獎是應該的。

 B）我不信周傑倫會到你們學校來表演。

 C）我去看了，那個同學唱得是很棒，而且他的歌兒也選得好。

 D）這個學期我沒選外語課，因為我的學分已經夠了。

（學生答題5秒）

(Traditional characters)

10. 女：大偉，你今天走路看起來怪怪的，怎麼了？

 男：昨天踢足球把腳扭傷了，不過醫生說沒大事兒，休息幾天就好了。

 女：A）這麼多天還沒好啊？

 B）今天放學後我們一起去游泳，好嗎？

 C）我也是個足球迷，不過我沒你踢得好。

 D）那這幾天上下學要不要我接送你一下？

（學生答題5秒）

B）谢谢你提醒我，以后咱们上课应该专心点儿。

C）发短信在青少年中很流行，因为比发电邮方便。

D）要是我早知道你心情不好，我一定会给你发短信的。

（学生答题5秒）

(Simplified characters)

9. 男：咱们学校外语系上周组织的那个演出，你去看了吗？我们班唱周杰伦歌儿的那个同学得了一等奖。

 女：A）周杰伦的确唱得不错，得一等奖是应该的。

 B）我不信周杰伦会到你们学校来表演。

 C）我去看了，那个同学唱得是很棒，而且他的歌儿也选得好。

 D）这个学期我没选外语课，因为我的学分已经够了。

（学生答题5秒）

(Simplified characters)

10. 女：大伟，你今天走路看起来怪怪的，怎么了？

 男：昨天踢足球把脚扭伤了，不过医生说没大事儿，休息几天就好了。

 女：A）这么多天还没好啊？

 B）今天放学后我们一起去游泳，好吗？

 C）我也是个足球迷，不过我没你踢得好。

 D）那这几天上下学要不要我接送你一下？

（学生答题5秒）

(Traditional characters)

11. 男：媽媽，我還有半個鐘頭就練完球了，今天晚飯我們可不可以吃韭菜餡兒的餃子？

    女：我正包著呢！等你回來時就差不多包完了。

    男：A）我不喜歡吃蒸包子，咱們家最近老吃包子。

    　　B）太好了！我都快餓死了！

    　　C）餃子做起來很麻煩，但吃起來很香。

    　　D）北方人都很喜歡吃餃子。

    （學生答題5秒）

12. 男：老師，我這學期一直很努力，可成績就是上不去，您看我是哪方面的問題？

    女：光靠努力還不夠，也要注意學習方法，我覺得你課後應該多複習。

    男：A）知道了，我放學回家後多花點兒時間複習。

    　　B）謝謝你，我一定努力學習中文和中國的文化。

    　　C）我覺得一個學生的學習成績是很重要的。

    　　D）我們應該活到老學到老。

    （學生答題5秒）

13. 女：樂樂，媽媽在學校門口等了都快半個小時了，以後放了學快點兒出來。

    男：A）我放學已經半個小時了，您怎麼纔到呢？

(Simplified characters)

11. 男：妈妈，我还有半个钟头就练完球了，今天晚饭我们可不可以吃韭菜馅儿的饺子？

    女：我正包着呢！等你回来时就差不多包完了。

    男：A）我不喜欢吃蒸包子，咱们家最近老吃包子。

    　　B）太好了！我都快饿死了！

    　　C）饺子做起来很麻烦，但吃起来很香。

    　　D）北方人都很喜欢吃饺子。

    （学生答题5秒）

12. 男：老师，我这学期一直很努力，可成绩就是上不去，您看我是哪方面的问题？

    女：光靠努力还不够，也要注意学习方法，我觉得你课后应该多复习。

    男：A）知道了，我放学回家后多花点儿时间复习。

    　　B）谢谢你，我一定努力学习中文和中国的文化。

    　　C）我觉得一个学生的学习成绩是很重要的。

    　　D）我们应该活到老学到老。

    （学生答题5秒）

13. 女：乐乐，妈妈在学校门口等了都快半个小时了，以后放了学快点儿出来。

    男：A）我放学已经半个小时了，您怎么才到呢？

(Traditional characters)

B）對不起,今天學生會有事兒,耽誤了一會兒。

C）您怎麼來得這麼晚呢?

D）您用了半個多小時纔開到學校,是不是路上堵車啊?

（學生答題 5 秒）

(Simplified characters)

B）对不起,今天学生会有事儿,耽误了一会儿。

C）您怎么来得这么晚呢?

D）您用了半个多小时才开到学校,是不是路上堵车啊?

（学生答题 5 秒）

(Traditional characters)

14. 男：嗨,小玲,差點兒沒認出你來。今天怎麼想起穿旗袍上學了?

    女：今天中文課有一個關於中國傳統服裝的報告,我就把我媽媽的旗袍穿來了。

    男：A）中國有五千年的悠久歷史。

    B）現在的中國人已經不太穿旗袍了。

    C）旗袍是中國傳統服裝的一種。

    D）你這身打扮肯定會給你的報告增色不少。

    （學生答題 5 秒）

(Simplified characters)

14. 男：嗨,小玲,差点儿没认出你来。今天怎么想起穿旗袍上学了?

    女：今天中文课有一个关于中国传统服装的报告,我就把我妈妈的旗袍穿来了。

    男：A）中国有五千年的悠久历史。

    B）现在的中国人已经不太穿旗袍了。

    C）旗袍是中国传统服装的一种。

    D）你这身打扮肯定会给你的报告增色不少。

    （学生答题 5 秒）

(Traditional characters)

15. 女：馬東,你發現沒有,最近我們學校餐廳的飯菜好像越來越豐盛了。

    男：真是英雄所見略同,我也覺得飯菜種類多了很多。

    女：A）我這個人中餐西餐都喜歡吃。

    B）這說明學校很重視我們的飲食健康。

    C）飯菜好的學校不一定是好學校。

    D）價錢便宜是好事,我可以省下錢來買書。

    （學生答題 5 秒）

(Simplified characters)

15. 女：马东,你发现没有,最近我们学校餐厅的饭菜好像越来越丰盛了。

    男：真是英雄所见略同,我也觉得饭菜种类多了很多。

    女：A）我这个人中餐西餐都喜欢吃。

    B）这说明学校很重视我们的饮食健康。

    C）饭菜好的学校不一定是好学校。

    D）价钱便宜是好事,我可以省下钱来买书。

    （学生答题 5 秒）

Listening Selections

Directions:

You will listen to several selections in Chinese. For each selection, you will be told whether it will be played once or twice. You may take notes as you listen. Your notes will not be graded. After listening to each selection, you will see questions in English. For each question, choose the response that is best according to the selection. You will have 12 seconds to answer each question.

Selection 1: Announcement

Narrator: Now you will listen twice to a public announcement.

Man:

(Traditional characters)

> 同學們請注意：
> 　　昨天下午，有位同學在學校操場上撿到了一個藍色的運動袋，裡面有一套運動服、一雙球鞋、一個手機、幾本書和一個錢包，還有少量現金。請丟失此物的同學速到校辦公室認領。

(Simplified characters)

> 同学们请注意：
> 　　昨天下午，有位同学在学校操场上捡到了一个蓝色的运动袋，里面有一套运动服、一双球鞋、一个手机、几本书和一个钱包，还有少量现金。请丢失此物的同学速到校办公室认领。

Narrator: Now listen again.

(Repeat)

Narrator: Now answer the questions for this selection.

(12 seconds)

(12 seconds)

(12 seconds)

Selection 2: Voice Message

Narrator: Now you will listen twice to a voice message.

Woman:

(Traditional characters)

> 王老師：您好！我是您中文三班學生李帥帥的媽媽。帥帥回家跟我提到您班上要組織一個討論會，想請家長去講講在美國奮鬥的經歷和感受。我和我先生都非常願意參加這次討論會，但是有幾個問題想問問您，比如，每個家長可以講多長時間，用中文還是用英文講，是否需要我們把講稿事先給每個學生印一份，等等。麻煩您有時間給我回個電話：(415) 541-6969。謝謝！

(Simplified characters)

> 王老师：您好！我是您中文三班学生李帅帅的妈妈。帅帅回家跟我提到您班上要组织一个讨论会，想请家长去讲讲在美国奋斗的经历和感受。我和我先生都非常愿意参加这次讨论会，但是有几个问题想问问您，比如，每个家长可以讲多长时间，用中文还是用英文讲，是否需要我们把讲稿事先给每个学生印一份，等等。麻烦您有时间给我回个电话：(415) 541-6969。谢谢！

Narrator: Now listen again.

(Repeat)

Narrator: Now answer the questions for this selection.

(12 seconds)

(12 seconds)

(12 seconds)

Selection 3: Conversation

Narrator: Now you will listen once to a conversation between a girl and her younger brother.

(Traditional characters)

> 男：姐姐，剛纔你的一個同學打電話找你。他說今晚你們學校有舞會，你要去做他的舞伴。
> 女：他還說什麼啦？
> 男：他說等你準備好了，就馬上給他打個電話，他會開車來接你。
> 女：知道了，謝謝你。
> 男：可不可以帶我一起去啊？我一個人在家真無聊。
> 女：哎呀，我真希望爸媽去上海開會時把你也帶著。好了好了，趕緊準備吧。

男：爲什麼今天學校有舞會呢？今天既不是週末，也不是什麼節日。
女：你去了就知道了，快換衣服吧，別囉唆了！

(Simplified characters)

男：姐姐，刚才你的一个同学打电话找你。他说今晚你们学校有舞会，你要去做他的舞伴。
女：他还说什么啦？
男：他说等你准备好了，就马上给他打个电话，他会开车来接你。
女：知道了，谢谢你。
男：可不可以带我一起去啊？我一个人在家真无聊。
女：哎呀，我真希望爸妈去上海开会时把你也带着。好了好了，赶紧准备吧。
男：为什么今天学校有舞会呢？今天既不是周末，也不是什么节日。
女：你去了就知道了，快换衣服吧，别啰唆了！

Narrator: Now answer the questions for this selection.

(12 seconds)

(12 seconds)

(12 seconds)

(12 seconds)

Selection 4: Instructions

Narrator: Now you will listen once to someone giving instructions.

Man:

(Traditional characters)

東華大學關於新生辦理入學手續的說明

歡迎各位同學來到東華大學學習，爲方便各位同學快速辦理入學手續，請遵循以下程序：入學手續辦理時間爲8月28日，地點在學校行政大樓一樓。請先到新生註冊中心辦理入學登記手續，向學院提交入學通知書，同時領取新生選課手冊、體檢表和校園卡。學生們需在開學一週內在校園卡上預存學費，同時在校園網站上註冊自己的賬户和電子郵件地址。這樣便於學校直接從卡上扣取學費、食宿費等。

8月30日午休後，請同學們先去學校操場參加開學典禮，下午1點正式開始；然後參加新生年級大會和隨後的課程介紹及輔導。請同學們在開學後的第一週務必到校園網站註冊本學期選修的課程并到學校圖書館購買教科書。有問題請跟新生聯絡處聯繫。

　　祝願各位同學在東華大學度過美好的大學時光！

(Simplified characters)

东华大学关于新生办理入学手续的说明

　　欢迎各位同学来到东华大学学习，为方便各位同学快速办理入学手续，请遵循以下程序：入学手续办理时间为8月28日，地点在学校行政大楼一楼。请先到新生注册中心办理入学登记手续，向学院提交入学通知书，同时领取新生选课手册、体检表和校园卡。学生们需在开学一周内在校园卡上预存学费，同时在校园网站上注册自己的账户和电子邮件地址。这样便于学校直接从卡上扣取学费、食宿费等。

　　8月30日午休后，请同学们先去学校操场参加开学典礼，下午1点正式开始；然后参加新生年级大会和随后的课程介绍及辅导。请同学们在开学后的第一周务必到校园网站注册本学期选修的课程并到学校图书馆购买教科书。有问题请跟新生联络处联系。

　　祝愿各位同学在东华大学度过美好的大学时光！

Narrator: Now answer the questions for this selection.

(12 seconds)

(12 seconds)

(12 seconds)

(12 seconds)

Selection 5: Report

Narrator: Now you will listen once to a report.

Man:

(Traditional characters)

　　大家好！

　　我代表我們小組的四名同學向大家匯報一下我們這次就環保展開的調查活動的結果。本次調查共發放問卷223份，收回問卷率爲90%，85%的學生對問卷進行了認真填寫。調查結果顯示，76%的同學已經認識到環境保護的重要性，并會主動監督自己的行爲；18%的同學認爲他們的環保意識還可以，但做得還不夠；6%的同學覺得他們沒有什麽環保意識，幷承認有破壞環境的行爲。當問到如果在公共場所看到有人亂扔垃圾他們會怎麽做時，87%的同學說他們雖然知道那樣做不對，但不會去管別人，認爲只要自己不去扔就行了；9%的同學說他們會告訴那些人把垃圾撿起來；4%的同學覺得無所謂，反正有清潔工處理垃圾。

以上是我們小組的調查報告，謝謝大家！

(Simplified characters)

大家好！

我代表我们小组的四名同学向大家汇报一下我们这次就环保展开的调查活动的结果。本次调查共发放问卷223份，收回问卷率为90%，85%的学生对问卷进行了认真填写。调查结果显示，76%的同学已经认识到环境保护的重要性，并会主动监督自己的行为；18%的同学认为他们的环保意识还可以，但做得还不够；6%的同学觉得他们没有什么环保意识，并承认有破坏环境的行为。当问到如果在公共场所看到有人乱扔垃圾他们会怎么做时，87%的同学说他们虽然知道那样做不对，但不会去管别人，认为只要自己不去扔就行了；9%的同学说他们会告诉那些人把垃圾捡起来；4%的同学觉得无所谓，反正有清洁工处理垃圾。

以上是我们小组的调查报告，谢谢大家！

Narrator: Now answer the questions for this selection.

(12 seconds)

(12 seconds)

(12 seconds)

(12 seconds)

(12 seconds)

Section II: Free Response

Part B: Speaking

Recording Scripts

Conversation

Directions: You will participate in a simulated conversation. Each time it is your turn to speak, you will have 20 seconds to record. You should respond as fully and as appropriately as possible. There will be six times when it is your turn to speak.

You will have a conversation with Xiaoliang, a Chinese student you met for the first time at a summer program in China, about American schools.

(Traditional characters)

> 小亮：聽說美國學校的聚會特別多，你們學校是這樣嗎？
> （學生答題20秒）
> 小亮：一般來說，學校爲什麽有聚會呢？
> (學生答題20秒）
> 小亮：聚會通常都有哪些形式？你們都做些什麽？
> （學生答題20秒）
> 小亮：你覺得參加聚會對你的學習、生活有什麽影響？
> （學生答題20秒）
> 小亮：聽說美國不允許青少年喝酒，如果學生在聚會上喝了酒，學校會怎麽處理？
> （學生答題20秒）
> 小亮：咱們暑期班最後一天有個文化交流聚會，我們可以一起表演個節目，你有什麽好主意嗎？
> （學生答題20秒）

(Simplified characters)

> 小亮：听说美国学校的聚会特别多，你们学校是这样吗？
> （学生答题20秒）
> 小亮：一般来说，学校为什么有聚会呢？
> (学生答题20秒）
> 小亮：聚会通常都有哪些形式？你们都做些什么？
> （学生答题20秒）
> 小亮：你觉得参加聚会对你的学习、生活有什么影响？
> （学生答题20秒）

> 小亮：听说美国不允许青少年喝酒，如果学生在聚会上喝了酒，学校会怎么处理？
>
> （学生答题20秒）
>
> 小亮：咱们暑期班最后一天有个文化交流聚会，我们可以一起表演个节目，你有什么好主意吗？
>
> （学生答题20秒）

Cultural Presentation

Directions: You will be asked to speak in Chinese on a specific topic. Imagine you are making an oral presentation to your Chinese class. First, you will read and hear the topic for your presentation. You will have 4 minutes to prepare your presentation. Then you will have 2 minutes to record your presentation. Your presentation should be as complete as possible.

Please describe the culinary diversity in China in terms of the various food styles and geographic regions. Choose ONE specific culinary style, and talk about its popular dishes, commonly used ingredients, and unique cooking techniques, and explain its significance.

Audio Scripts of AP Chinese Language and Culture Test 8

Section I: Multiple Choice

Part A: Listening

Rejoinders

Directions:

Directions: You will hear several short conversations or parts of conversations followed by four choices, designated A, B, C, and D. Choose the one that continues or completes the conversation in a logical and culturally appropriate manner. After you have decided which of the suggested answers is best, COMPLETELY fill in the corresponding circle on the answer sheet. You will have 5 seconds to answer each question.

(Traditional characters)

1. 男：趕快把電視打開，現在正轉播世界杯籃球賽呢！

   女：A）你今天就歇著吧，咱們家的電視壞了。

   B）我們公司下個星期有一場籃球賽，我該不該報名參加呢？

   C）比賽什麼時候開始？

   D）想不想出去練籃球？明天不是有比賽嗎？

   （學生答題5秒）

(Simplified characters)

1. 男：赶快把电视打开，现在正转播世界杯篮球赛呢！

   女：A）你今天就歇着吧，咱们家的电视坏了。

   B）我们公司下个星期有一场篮球赛，我该不该报名参加呢？

   C）比赛什么时候开始？

   D）想不想出去练篮球？明天不是有比赛吗？

   （学生答题5秒）

(Traditional characters)

2. 女：你急什麼啊？瞧你滿頭大汗的。

   男：A）哎呀，熱死了，熱死了！我買一瓶礦泉水！

   B）我的登機牌不見了，剛纔還在這兒的。

   C）這兒的夏天就是這樣，常常熱得讓人滿頭大汗。

   D）我今天的作業早就做好了，所以我一點兒也不急。

   （學生答題5秒）

(Simplified characters)

2. 女：你急什么啊？瞧你满头大汗的。

   男：A）哎呀，热死了，热死了！我买一瓶矿泉水！

   B）我的登机牌不见了，刚才还在这儿的。

   C）这儿的夏天就是这样，常常热得让人满头大汗。

   D）我今天的作业早就做好了，所以我一点儿也不急。

   （学生答题5秒）

(Simplified characters)

3. 男：这是昨天买的那台电脑的收据，快收好，别丢了。

   女：A）大家都说那个牌子的电脑质量很好，售后服务也很不错。

   B）你把收据放到哪儿去了？怎么转眼就不见了？

   C）这个收据是谁签的名？我一点儿都看不出来。

   D）你尽管放心，连十年前的收据我都保存得好好的。

   （学生答题5秒）

4. 女：大大超市旁边新开了一家中国饭馆儿，他们的广告上说，这个星期六中午前一百名顾客可以免费享用自助餐，咱们要不要去碰碰运气？

   男：A）既然你做东，我当然去。

   B）那星期六一早就得去排队了，值得吗？

   C）自助餐最好是能吃多少拿多少，拿多了吃不完，实在浪费。

   D）这家饭馆儿很会招待客人，服务特别好，我们运气不错。

   （学生答题5秒）

5. 男：你的选课表上还少了导师的签字，注册组恐怕不会接受。

   女：A）这位导师开的课极受学生的欢迎。

   B）注册组这个星期忙着学生选课的事儿，不会给我签字的。

(Traditional characters)

C）我的導師這兩天去別的城市開會去了，怎麽辦？

D）我的導師認爲我選的課太多了，要我少選一門。

（學生答題5秒）

6. 女：你們這個小區公共設施非常齊全，在這兒生活很方便吧？

　男：A）這個小區的房子看起來都差不多，相當高級。

　　　B）我們家住十六層，視野非常好。

　　　C）只可惜沒有游泳池，未免美中不足。

　　　D）這兒的住戶都有正當的工作。

（學生答題5秒）

7. 男：你高中畢業以後，打算工作還是上大學？

　女：A）我早就申請好大學了。

　　　B）其實工作賺多少錢并不重要，夠用就行了。

　　　C）我沒有什麽工作經驗，簡歷不好寫。

　　　D）畢業以後，我會常和朋友們聯繫。

（學生答題5秒）

8. 男：你一天到晚坐在電腦前，不怕腰酸背痛嗎？最好時不時站起來走走。

　女：A）腰酸背痛得去看醫生，太麻煩了。

　　　B）你的建議很好，就怕我一專心工作就忘了。

(Simplified characters)

C）我的导师这两天去别的城市开会去了，怎么办？

D）我的导师认为我选的课太多了，要我少选一门。

（学生答题5秒）

6. 女：你们这个小区公共设施非常齐全，在这儿生活很方便吧？

　男：A）这个小区的房子看起来都差不多，相当高级。

　　　B）我们家住十六层，视野非常好。

　　　C）只可惜没有游泳池，未免美中不足。

　　　D）这儿的住户都有正当的工作。

（学生答题5秒）

7. 男：你高中毕业以后，打算工作还是上大学？

　女：A）我早就申请好大学了。

　　　B）其实工作赚多少钱并不重要，够用就行了。

　　　C）我没有什么工作经验，简历不好写。

　　　D）毕业以后，我会常和朋友们联系。

（学生答题5秒）

8. 男：你一天到晚坐在电脑前，不怕腰酸背痛吗？最好时不时站起来走走。

　女：A）腰酸背痛得去看医生，太麻烦了。

　　　B）你的建议很好，就怕我一专心工作就忘了。

C）我的電腦桌是特別設計的，手指不容易受傷。

D）我們可以上網去查查對着電腦和腰酸背痛有什麽關係。

（學生答題 5 秒）

(Traditional characters)

9. 女：小白上課的時候常常偷偷跟我傳紙條。

   男：A）紙條雖短，但是很有趣。

   B）難得這次他記得把作業帶來了。

   C）原來他健康狀況不好，難怪常常請病假。

   D）你不怕老師發現嗎？

（學生答題5秒）

(Traditional characters)

10. 男：美國好大學比比皆是，我不理解媽媽爲什麽一定要我跟別人去擠所謂的名牌大學。

    女：A）除非你的功課太差，否則你不用擔心上不了大學。

    B）名牌大學的校園裡人很多嗎？

    C）那樣你的心理負擔可重了，是吧？

    D）這個大學的教授素質和教學設備都比別的大學好。

（學生答題 5 秒）

(Traditional characters)

11. 女：真氣人，屋裡的空調又壞了。

    男：天氣這麽熱，趕緊找工人來修吧！

    女：A）咱們家的空調開關在哪兒？

C）我的电脑桌是特别设计的，手指不容易受伤。

D）我们可以上网去查查对着电脑和腰酸背痛有什么关系。

（学生答题 5 秒）

(Simplified characters)

9. 女：小白上课的时候常常偷偷跟我传纸条。

   男：A）纸条虽短，但是很有趣。

   B）难得这次他记得把作业带来了。

   C）原来他健康状况不好，难怪常常请病假。

   D）你不怕老师发现吗？

（学生答题 5 秒）

(Simplified characters)

10. 男：美国好大学比比皆是，我不理解妈妈为什么一定要我跟别人去挤所谓的名牌大学。

    女：A）除非你的功课太差，否则你不用担心上不了大学。

    B）名牌大学的校园里人很多吗？

    C）那样你的心理负担可重了，是吧？

    D）这个大学的教授素质和教学设备都比别的大学好。

（学生答题 5 秒）

(Simplified characters)

11. 女：真气人，屋里的空调又坏了。

    男：天气这么热，赶紧找工人来修吧！

    女：A）咱们家的空调开关在哪儿？

B）已经打了电话了，可是他们今天没空儿，明天下午才能来。

C）把温度调高点儿吧，可以省点儿电费。

D）修车厂的工人都忙得很，找他们来修，恐怕得等上一阵子。

（学生答题5秒）

(Simplified characters)

12. 男：你这是什么打扮？男不男女不女的，穿出去像话吗？

    女：爸，这你就不懂了，这叫流行。我走了，拜拜！

    男：A）现在你的同学中都流行看什么电视节目？

    B）我对流行再熟悉不过了。

    C）你今天不把你这身衣服换下来，就别出门。

    D）你现在不听流行音乐了吗？也好，我乐得清静清静。

（学生答题5秒）

(Simplified characters)

13. 女：你怎么闷闷不乐的，有什么心事吗？

    男：我跟我女朋友为了一点儿小事儿闹翻了，现在觉得挺后悔的。

    女：A）与其在这儿后悔，还不如给她打个电话赔个不是吧。

    B）哦，你的女朋友有新男朋友了？

    C）你说的话要算话，别说了又后悔了。

    D）你一定不会后悔的，你的女朋友肯定会喜欢的。

（学生答题5秒）

(Traditional characters)

14. 男：從十年級以來，老師生怕我們閑著似的，每天給我們的作業寫都寫不完。

    女：那你怎麼有足夠的時間睡覺呢？

    男：A）小李上課常打瞌睡，挨老師罵。

    　　B）明天要考試，我今天晚上得熬夜準備，沒時間睡覺。

    　　C）所以我上課的時候常常累得睜不開眼睛。

    　　D）作業太多了，幾點可以上床睡覺呢？

    （學生答題5秒）

(Traditional characters)

15. 女：現在父母要求孩子全面發展，既要學習好，又要琴棋書畫樣樣都行，真不容易。

    男：有些父母對孩子的期望太高了。

    女：A）這就叫愛之深，責之切啊。

    　　B）這就叫望子成龍、望女成鳳啊。

    　　C）這就叫子不教父之過啊。

    　　D）這就叫天下無不是的父母啊。

    （學生答題5秒）

(Simplified characters)

14. 男：从十年级以来，老师生怕我们闲着似的，每天给我们的作业写都写不完。

    女：那你怎么有足够的时间睡觉呢？

    男：A）小李上课常打瞌睡，挨老师骂。

    　　B）明天要考试，我今天晚上得熬夜准备，没时间睡觉。

    　　C）所以我上课的时候常常累得睁不开眼睛。

    　　D）作业太多了，几点可以上床睡觉呢？

    （学生答题5秒）

(Simplified characters)

15. 女：现在父母要求孩子全面发展，既要学习好，又要琴棋书画样样都行，真不容易。

    男：有些父母对孩子的期望太高了。

    女：A）这就叫爱之深，责之切啊。

    　　B）这就叫望子成龙、望女成凤啊。

    　　C）这就叫子不教父之过啊。

    　　D）这就叫天下无不是的父母啊。

    （学生答题5秒）

Listening Selections

Directions:

You will listen to several selections in Chinese. For each selection, you will be told whether it will be played once or twice. You may take notes as you listen. Your notes will not be graded. After listening to each selection, you will see questions in English. For each question, choose the response that is best according to the selection. You will have 12 seconds to answer each question.

Selection 1: Announcement

Narrator: Now you will listen twice to a public announcement.

Woman:

(Traditional characters)

> 各位同學！從明天早上八點到大後天下午四點，十一年級的學生將在大禮堂展示他們歷史課的作品。這次展覽，主要是他們這兩個月研究、訪談的成果。他們每個人在學期初選定一個跟自己的文化有關的題目，然後找資料、照片，寫文章，並設計自己的展板。就我所知，每個學生都下了極大的功夫來完成這個項目，他們也從中學習到了很多。爲了方便各位同學觀看和學習，學校決定明天早上開放給家長參觀，明天下午九年級學生，後天十年級，大後天十二年級，家長和各年級學生可按時前往觀覽。

(Simplified characters)

> 各位同学！从明天早上八点到大后天下午四点，十一年级的学生将在大礼堂展示他们历史课的作品。这次展览，主要是他们这两个月研究、访谈的成果。他们每个人在学期初选定一个跟自己的文化有关的题目，然后找资料、照片，写文章，并设计自己的展板。就我所知，每个学生都下了极大的功夫来完成这个项目，他们也从中学习到了很多。为了方便各位同学观看和学习，学校决定明天早上开放给家长参观，明天下午九年级学生，后天十年级，大后天十二年级，家长和各年级学生可按时前往观览。

Narrator: Now listen again.

(Repeat)

Narrator: Now answer the questions for this selection.

(12 seconds)

(12 seconds)

(12 seconds)

(12 seconds)

(12 seconds)

Selection 2: Conversation

Narrator: Now you will listen once to a conversation between two students.

(Traditional characters)

男：蘭蘭，心情不好啊，怎麼看起來這麼鬱悶？
女：唉，我爸爸媽媽最近在鬧離婚，家裡氣氛非常糟糕，我真不想回家。
男：我可以理解你的心情。去年我媽媽離家出走的那幾個星期，我爸爸整天不停地喝酒，醉了就摔杯子，還罵我，拿我出氣。
女：我都不知道你們家這些事，你當時怎麼沒跟我說呢？後來呢？
男：後來我媽媽又回來了，家纔又有了家的樣子，我媽媽甚至比以前更關心我，爸爸也把酒戒了。
女：唉！我不懂為什麼大人鬧不愉快，非得把小孩兒扯進去不可？我都不知道該聽誰的。
男：依照我的經驗，你最好什麼話都別說，要不然，他們可能會生你的氣，拿你出氣。
女：唉，我寧可他們生我的氣，要是他們把氣都出在我身上，從此就和好、不離婚了，那不是很值得嗎？

(Simplified characters)

男：兰兰，心情不好啊，怎么看起来这么郁闷？
女：唉，我爸爸妈妈最近在闹离婚，家里气氛非常糟糕，我真不想回家。
男：我可以理解你的心情。去年我妈妈离家出走的那几个星期，我爸爸整天不停地喝酒，醉了就摔杯子，还骂我，拿我出气。
女：我都不知道你们家这些事，你当时怎么没跟我说呢？后来呢？
男：后来我妈妈又回来了，家才又有了家的样子，我妈妈甚至比以前更关心我，爸爸也把酒戒了。
女：唉！我不懂为什么大人闹不愉快，非得把小孩儿扯进去不可？我都不知道该听谁的。
男：依照我的经验，你最好什么话都别说，要不然，他们可能会生你的气，拿你出气。
女：唉，我宁可他们生我的气，要是他们把气都出在我身上，从此就和好、不离婚了，那不是很值得吗？

Narrator: Now answer the questions for this selection.

(12 seconds)

(12 seconds)

(12 seconds)
(12 seconds)

Selection 3: Instructions

Narrator: Now you will listen once to someone giving instructions.

Woman:

(Traditional characters)

> 媽媽，謝謝您不嫌麻煩，答應幫我照顧我的熱帶魚。我跟我們學校的足球隊到芝加哥去參加全州高中聯盟總決賽的這段時間，您就多費心了。小瓶裡的魚食，一天喂兩次或三次都行，每次喂三四顆，千萬別給太多，因爲魚是給多少吃多少，吃太多可能會撐死。魚缸的水每七天換一次，先把水龍頭的水調到室溫，把一些水放到一個乾淨的碗裡，用漁網把魚撈起來，放到碗裡，再把魚缸裡的水倒掉，用熱水沖洗魚缸和魚缸裡的石頭，最後往魚缸加水到七八分滿，再滴一兩滴大瓶裡的營養水，就可以把魚放回魚缸裡了。媽媽，看到魚在水裡游來游去非常快樂的樣子，您肯定也會非常快樂的。

(Simplified characters)

> 妈妈，谢谢您不嫌麻烦，答应帮我照顾我的热带鱼。我跟我们学校的足球队到芝加哥去参加全州高中联盟总决赛的这段时间，您就多费心了。小瓶里的鱼食，一天喂两次或三次都行，每次喂三四颗，千万别给太多，因为鱼是给多少吃多少，吃太多可能会撑死。鱼缸的水每七天换一次，先把水龙头的水调到室温，把一些水放到一个干净的碗里，用渔网把鱼捞起来，放到碗里，再把鱼缸里的水倒掉，用热水冲洗鱼缸和鱼缸里的石头，最后往鱼缸加水到七八分满，再滴一两滴大瓶里的营养水，就可以把鱼放回鱼缸里了。妈妈，看到鱼在水里游来游去非常快乐的样子，您肯定也会非常快乐的。

Narrator: Now answer the questions for this selection.

(12 seconds)
(12 seconds)
(12 seconds)
(12 seconds)

Selection 4: Voice Message

Narrator: Now you will listen twice to a voice message.

Woman:

(Traditional characters)

> 慧心，我是可文。你的手機大概是關機了吧？響了一聲就跳到你的語音信箱了，希望你能及時聽到我的留言。我們原先不是約好了今天放學後一起留在學校討論英文小說的問題嗎？很不巧，早上起床的時候，牙套有點兒鬆了，剛纔我媽媽打電話來，說是幫我預約了今天下午四點去看牙醫。要是方便，明天五點到我家來吧！我們可以那時候再一起討論英文小說的問題，你也可以順便在我家吃晚飯，我媽媽會做你最喜歡的紅燒獅子頭。儘快給我回電或發個短信吧。

(Simplified characters)

> 慧心，我是可文。你的手机大概是关机了吧？响了一声就跳到你的语音信箱了，希望你能及时听到我的留言。我们原先不是约好了今天放学后一起留在学校讨论英文小说的问题吗？很不巧，早上起床的时候，牙套有点儿松了，刚才我妈妈打电话来，说是帮我预约了今天下午四点去看牙医。要是方便，明天五点到我家来吧！我们可以那时候再一起讨论英文小说的问题，你也可以顺便在我家吃晚饭，我妈妈会做你最喜欢的红烧狮子头。尽快给我回电或发个短信吧。

Narrator: Now listen again.

(Repeat)

Narrator: Now answer the questions for this selection.

(12 seconds)

(12 seconds)

(12 seconds)

Selection 5: Report

Narrator: Now you will listen once to a report.

Man:

(Traditional characters)

老師好，同學們好！現在我代表我們的三人小組來匯報一下我們這次問卷調查的結果。我們的問卷是調查同學們使用Snapchat、推特、臉書等社交媒體的情況。我們一共發出了300份問卷，收回了290份。所有答卷的同學至少都有兩個社交媒體的賬戶。75%的同學每天都會上網更新生活動態，也有60%的同學每天查看社交媒體新動態的次數在25次到30次之間。90%以上的同學看了以後會點贊，只有不到10%的同學通常只看而不做任何反應。雖然學校不准學生在上課時使用手機，但有1/3的學生承認，他們都有在上課時上社交平臺查看朋友新動態的經歷。他們認爲只要不被老師發覺，就沒有什麼大不了的。

以上是我們小組的報告，謝謝。

(Simplified characters)

老师好，同学们好！现在我代表我们的三人小组来汇报一下我们这次问卷调查的结果。我们的问卷是调查同学们使用Snapchat、推特、脸书等社交媒体的情况。我们一共发出了300份问卷，收回了290份。所有答卷的同学至少都有两个社交媒体的账户。75%的同学每天都会上网更新生活动态，也有60%的同学每天查看社交媒体新动态的次数在25次到30次之间。90%以上的同学看了以后会点赞，只有不到10%的同学通常只看而不做任何反应。虽然学校不准学生在上课时使用手机，但有1/3的学生承认，他们都有在上课时上社交平台查看朋友新动态的经历。他们认为只要不被老师发觉，就没有什么大不了的。

以上是我们小组的报告，谢谢。

Narrator: Now answer the questions for this selection.

(12 seconds)

(12 seconds)

(12 seconds)

(12 seconds)

Section II: Free Response
Part B: Speaking
Recording Scripts
Conversation

Directions:

You will participate in a simulated conversation. Each time it is your turn to speak, you will have 20 seconds to record. You should respond as fully and as appropriately as possible. There will be six times when it is your turn to speak.

You will have a conversation with Jiang Ning, a passenger sitting next to you on the bus, about your experience in learning Chinese.

(Traditional characters)

姜寧：你來中國多久了？是來學習的嗎？
（學生答題20秒）
姜寧：你中文說得這麼好，學了幾年了？在哪兒學的？你是怎麼對中文產生興趣的？
（學生答題20秒）
姜寧：你覺得中文難不難學？你有沒有什麼學中文的有趣經驗？
（學生答題20秒）
姜寧：我現在正在學英文，你覺得我要怎麼做纔能把英文學好？
（學生答題20秒）
姜寧：除了學習以外，你平常都做些什麼？
（學生答題20秒）
姜寧：跟你聊天兒真有意思，我能不能跟你做個朋友？我們以後怎麼聯繫？
（學生答題20秒）

(Simplified characters)

姜宁：你来中国多久了？是来学习的吗？
（学生答题20秒）
姜宁：你中文说得这么好，学了几年了？在哪儿学的？你是怎么对中文产生兴趣的？
（学生答题20秒）
姜宁：你觉得中文难不难学？你有没有什么学中文的有趣经验？
（学生答题20秒）

姜宁：我现在正在学英文，你觉得我要怎么做才能把英文学好？

（学生答题20秒）

姜宁：除了学习以外，你平常都做些什么？

（学生答题20秒）

姜宁：跟你聊天儿真有意思，我能不能跟你做个朋友？我们以后怎么联系？

（学生答题20秒）

Cultural Presentation

Directions:

You will be asked to speak in Chinese on a specific topic. Imagine you are making an oral presentation to your Chinese class. First, you will read and hear the topic for your presentation. You will have 4 minutes to prepare your presentation. Then you will have 2 minutes to record your presentation. Your presentation should be as complete as possible.

Choose ONE of your favorite Chinese writers, ancient or contemporary. In your presentation, describe this writer's background, name one of his/her most famous works and introduce its form and content, and explain the writer's significance in the history of Chinese literature.

Audio Scripts of AP Chinese Language and Culture Test 9

Section I: Multiple Choice

Part A: Listening

Rejoinders

Directions:

Directions: You will hear several short conversations or parts of conversations followed by four choices, designated A, B, C, and D. Choose the one that continues or completes the conversation in a logical and culturally appropriate manner. After you have decided which of the suggested answers is best, COMPLETELY fill in the corresponding circle on the answer sheet. You will have 5 seconds to answer each question.

(Traditional characters)

1. 男：作業這麼多，我都快累死了。
   女：A）你每天做一點兒，就不會那麼累了。
   　　B）你做什麼了，怎麼看起來這麼累?
   　　C）你整天玩兒遊戲，當然累了!
   　　D）這道題我不會,你可以幫幫我嗎?
   （學生答題 5 秒）

(Simplified characters)

1. 男：作业这么多，我都快累死了。
   女：A）你每天做一点儿，就不会那么累了。
   　　B）你做什么了，怎么看起来这么累?
   　　C）你整天玩儿游戏，当然累了!
   　　D）这道题我不会，你可以帮帮我吗?
   （学生答题 5 秒）

(Traditional characters)

2. 女：弟弟把我的手機拿走了，害我找了半天。
   男：A）你弟弟的手機常常沒電嗎?
   　　B）我玩兒手機玩兒了半天了。
   　　C）你又把手機落在教室了。
   　　D）哎呀! 他怎麼沒告訴你?
   （學生答題 5 秒）

(Simplified characters)

2. 女：弟弟把我的手机拿走了，害我找了半天。
   男：A）你弟弟的手机常常没电吗?
   　　B）我玩儿手机玩儿了半天了。
   　　C）你又把手机落在教室了。
   　　D）哎呀! 他怎么没告诉你?
   （学生答题 5 秒）

(Traditional characters)

3. 男：我這個學期很忙，幾乎一個月沒給奶奶發短信了。
   女：A）她一定很想你。
   　　B）老人不會發短信。

(Simplified characters)

3. 男：我这个学期很忙，几乎一个月没给奶奶发短信了。
   女：A）她一定很想你。
   　　B）老人不会发短信。

C）我這個學期不忙。

D）這就是我爺爺和奶奶的照片。

（學生答題5秒）

(Traditional characters)

4. 女：我一看見人多就緊張得說不出話來。

   男：A）別緊張，多說話就好了。

   B）別緊張，放輕鬆。

   C）別擔心，時間不多了。

   D）怎麼辦？人太多了！

   （學生答題5秒）

(Traditional characters)

5. 男：這次考試我的壓力很大。

   女：A）放輕鬆，我們一起準備。

   B）我上次考試也考得不好。

   C）我的經濟壓力也很大。

   D）明天的演講比賽你參加嗎？

   （學生答題5秒）

(Traditional characters)

6. 女：你在網上看什麼呢？

   男：A）網球場上有很多人。

   B）網上垃圾新聞很多。

   C）看網球賽很無聊。

   D）我想在網上買下個學期的課本。

   （學生答題5秒）

(Traditional characters)

7. 女：你一邊打工一邊學習會影響成績吧？

   男：A）可是，打工不要求我有工作經驗。

   B）可是，我打工掙的錢很少。

   C）不會，我一個星期只打一天工。

   D）對啊，我不喜歡學習，成績不好。

   （學生答題5秒）

C）我这个学期不忙。

D）这就是我爷爷和奶奶的照片。

（学生答题5秒）

(Simplified characters)

4. 女：我一看见人多就紧张得说不出话来。

   男：A）别紧张，多说话就好了。

   B）别紧张，放轻松。

   C）别担心，时间不多了。

   D）怎么办？人太多了！

   （学生答题5秒）

(Simplified characters)

5. 男：这次考试我的压力很大。

   女：A）放轻松，我们一起准备。

   B）我上次考试也考得不好。

   C）我的经济压力也很大。

   D）明天的演讲比赛你参加吗？

   （学生答题5秒）

(Simplified characters)

6. 女：你在网上看什么呢？

   男：A）网球场上有很多人。

   B）网上垃圾新闻很多。

   C）看网球赛很无聊。

   D）我想在网上买下个学期的课本。

   （学生答题5秒）

(Simplified characters)

7. 女：你一边打工一边学习会影响成绩吧？

   男：A）可是，打工不要求我有工作经验。

   B）可是，我打工挣的钱很少。

   C）不会，我一个星期只打一天工。

   D）对啊，我不喜欢学习，成绩不好。

   （学生答题5秒）

8. 男：你真会做菜，居然连糖醋鱼都会做。

女：哪里，哪里，其实一点儿都不难。

男：A）是啊，我觉得做中国菜很难。

　　B）真的？那你教我怎么做，好吗？

　　C）真的！你做的糖醋鱼太好吃了。

　　D）是啊，我也喜欢自己做糖醋鱼。

（学生答题5秒）

9. 男：学生的生活离不开电脑。

女：是啊，要是没电就糟糕了。

男：A）要是没电，你就休息一下，别用电脑了。

　　B）要是电脑坏了，我可以帮你修理。

　　C）要是电脑中心停电，就不会开放。

　　D）我的新电脑是打折的时候买的。

（学生答题5秒）

10. 女：他常常麻烦别人，可是一点儿也不愿意帮助别人。

男：难怪他一个朋友也没有。

女：A）我的朋友常常帮助我。

　　B）是啊，朋友就应该互相帮助。

　　C）我很乐意成为你的朋友。

　　D）对，多交朋友对他帮助很大。

（学生答题5秒）

11. 女：这份工作快把我累死了，怎么有这么多问题？！

男：把你的问题说出来，我们大家帮你解决。

女：A）謝謝！我先把我的問題整理一下。
　　B）可以！你可以去問老師問題。
　　C）不行！你不懂我的問題。
　　D）太好了！我沒有問題了。
　（學生答題 5 秒）

女：A）谢谢！我先把我的问题整理一下。
　　B）可以！你可以去问老师问题。
　　C）不行！你不懂我的问题。
　　D）太好了！我没有问题了。
　（学生答题 5 秒）

(Traditional characters)

12. 女：你覺得學校餐廳的菜怎麼樣？
　　男：我覺得不好吃，所以我不是叫外賣，就是去飯館兒吃。
　　女：A）我也不想做飯，我們叫個外賣吧？
　　　　B）我昨天晚上也是去飯館兒吃的，吃了川菜。
　　　　C）可是那樣太花錢了！
　　　　D）聽說學校餐廳要重新裝修了。
　　（學生答題 5 秒）

(Simplified characters)

12. 女：你觉得学校餐厅的菜怎么样？
　　男：我觉得不好吃，所以我不是叫外卖，就是去饭馆儿吃。
　　女：A）我也不想做饭，我们叫个外卖吧？
　　　　B）我昨天晚上也是去饭馆儿吃的，吃了川菜。
　　　　C）可是那样太花钱了！
　　　　D）听说学校餐厅要重新装修了。
　　（学生答题 5 秒）

(Traditional characters)

13. 男：我女朋友快過生日了，你覺得我送什麼禮物比較好？
　　女：買花兒送她最好不過了。
　　男：A）我從不過生日。
　　　　B）我不送她禮物。
　　　　C）我想也是。
　　　　D）她不愛吃蛋糕。
　　（學生答題 5 秒）

(Simplified characters)

13. 男：我女朋友快过生日了，你觉得我送什么礼物比较好？
　　女：买花儿送她最好不过了。
　　男：A）我从不过生日。
　　　　B）我不送她礼物。
　　　　C）我想也是。
　　　　D）她不爱吃蛋糕。
　　（学生答题 5 秒）

(Traditional characters)

14. 男：我這個學期上的課，作業特別多，我都忙得沒時間睡覺了。
　　女：上什麼課這麼累？

(Simplified characters)

14. 男：我这个学期上的课，作业特别多，我都忙得没时间睡觉了。
　　女：上什么课这么累？

男：A）金融和數學，我不喜歡和數字打交道。
　　B）數學課對我來說很容易。
　　C）我常常累得睡不著覺。
　　D）我整天不是寫作業，就是睡覺。
（學生答題5秒）

(Traditional characters)

15. 男：糟糕，我又忘了帶錢包了。
    女：唉，那只好我付錢了。
    男：A）謝謝，這頓飯很便宜。
    　　B）謝謝，我明天把錢還給你。
    　　C）謝謝，你真有錢。
    　　D）謝謝，下次別來這家飯館兒了。
（學生答題5秒）

(Simplified characters)

男：A）金融和数学，我不喜欢和数字打交道。
　　B）数学课对我来说很容易。
　　C）我常常累得睡不着觉。
　　D）我整天不是写作业，就是睡觉。
（学生答题5秒）

15. 男：糟糕，我又忘了带钱包了。
    女：唉，那只好我付钱了。
    男：A）谢谢，这顿饭很便宜。
    　　B）谢谢，我明天把钱还给你。
    　　C）谢谢，你真有钱。
    　　D）谢谢，下次别来这家饭馆儿了。
（学生答题5秒）

Listening Selections

Directions:

You will listen to several selections in Chinese. For each selection, you will be told whether it will be played once or twice. You may take notes as you listen. Your notes will not be graded. After listening to each selection, you will see questions in English. For each question, choose the response that is best according to the selection. You will have 12 seconds to answer each question.

Selection 1: Transportation Announcement

Narrator: Now you will listen twice to a transportation announcement.

Man:

(Traditional characters)

女士們、先生們：
　　早上好，飛往紐約的國航CA789次航班現在開始登機了！請旅客們拿好您的護照、登機牌和行李到12號登機口的國航櫃臺依次排隊等候上飛機，謝謝！

(Simplified characters)

> 女士们、先生们：
> 　　早上好，飞往纽约的国航CA789次航班现在开始登机了！请旅客们拿好您的护照、登机牌和行李到12号登机口的国航柜台依次排队等候上飞机，谢谢！

Narrator: Now listen again.

(Repeat)

Narrator: Now answer the questions for this selection.

(12 seconds)

(12 seconds)

Selection 2: Voice Message

Narrator: Now you will listen twice to a voice message.

Woman:

(Traditional characters)

> 　　小安，我是娜娜，你今天沒到學校上課，給你發短信，你也沒回復。我很擔心你。你生病了嗎？還是因為天氣不好沒辦法到學校？因為今天早上的大風雪，有一些同學也沒有來上課，所以老師今天沒有給我們生詞小考，改成下個星期一考。本來今天要交的第三課的語法作業，也可以下個星期一再交。你聽到留言就給我發個短信或者打個電話，好嗎？

(Simplified characters)

> 　　小安，我是娜娜，你今天没到学校上课，给你发短信，你也没回复。我很担心你。你生病了吗？还是因为天气不好没办法到学校？因为今天早上的大风雪，有一些同学也没有来上课，所以老师今天没有给我们生词小考，改成下个星期一考。本来今天要交的第三课的语法作业，也可以下个星期一再交。你听到留言就给我发个短信或者打个电话，好吗？

Narrator: Now listen again.

(Repeat)

Narrator: Now answer the questions for this selection.

(12 seconds)

(12 seconds)

(12 seconds)

Selection 3: School Conversation

Narrator: Now you will listen once to a school conversation.

(Traditional characters)

> 女：家明，後天就要考試了，你怎麼現在纔開始背生詞？我真爲你著急。
> 男：蘭蘭，你説，我現在開始複習生詞、語法、課文還來得及嗎？
> 女：時間不多了。我看很難！
> 男：哎呀，看來我得加油啦！要是這次考試考不好，我媽媽下個月就不給我零用錢了。你幫幫忙吧！
> 女：好吧，那我幫你複習吧！
> 男：你人真好！

(Simplified characters)

> 女：家明，后天就要考试了，你怎么现在才开始背生词？我真为你着急。
> 男：兰兰，你说，我现在开始复习生词、语法、课文还来得及吗？
> 女：时间不多了。我看很难！
> 男：哎呀，看来我得加油啦！要是这次考试考不好，我妈妈下个月就不给我零用钱了。你帮帮忙吧！
> 女：好吧，那我帮你复习吧！
> 男：你人真好！

Narrator: Now answer the questions for this selection.

(12 seconds)

(12 seconds)

(12 seconds)

Selection 4: Radio Report

Narrator: Now you will listen once to a radio report.

Woman:

(Traditional characters)

> 歡迎收聽本臺最新新聞。交通部最新消息，今年春節期間，全國高速公路將對七人座及以下的小客車開放免費通行，免費通行時間爲1月25日到1月30日。在此提醒各位聽衆，春節期間小心開車，祝您旅途平安！

(Simplified characters)

> 欢迎收听本台最新新闻。交通部最新消息，今年春节期间，全国高速公路将对七人座及以下的小客车开放免费通行，免费通行时间为1月25日到1月30日。在此提醒各位听众，春节期间小心开车，祝您旅途平安！

Narrator: Now answer the questions for this selection.

(12 seconds)

(12 seconds)

(12 seconds)

Selection 5: Instructions

Narrator: Now you will listen once to someone giving instructions.

Man:

(Traditional characters)

> 親愛的顧客您好，感謝您光臨文華書店！今天下午兩點，氣象預報發出了陸上颱風警報，很快就會有大風大雨。爲了大家的安全，本書店決定今天四點關門，需要結賬的顧客請您儘快到櫃臺結賬。很抱歉給您造成不便，請諒解。祝您回家一路平安。

(Simplified characters)

> 亲爱的顾客您好，感谢您光临文华书店！今天下午两点，气象预报发出了陆上台风警报，很快就会有大风大雨。为了大家的安全，本书店决定今天四点关门，需要结账的顾客请您尽快到柜台结账。很抱歉给您造成不便，请谅解。祝您回家一路平安。

Narrator: Now answer the questions for this selection.

(12 seconds)

(12 seconds)

(12 seconds)

Selection 6: Conversation

Narrator: Now you will listen once to a conversation.

(Traditional characters)

> 女：小高，我想去美國的大城市上大學，你有什麼建議?
> 男：我覺得去紐約最好不過了。那裡是美國的文化和經濟中心。
> 女：我也喜歡紐約。那裡有很多有名的大學，而且有很多好玩兒的地方。
> 男：可惜，我打算在家附近上大學，不會申請紐約的學校。
> 女：沒關係，你可以來找我玩兒。
> 男：好啊！要是你去紐約上大學，我放假就去找你，我們去中國城吃烤鴨。
> 女：就這麼說定了！

(Simplified characters)

> 女：小高，我想去美国的大城市上大学，你有什么建议?
> 男：我觉得去纽约最好不过了。那里是美国的文化和经济中心。
> 女：我也喜欢纽约。那里有很多有名的大学，而且有很多好玩儿的地方。
> 男：可惜，我打算在家附近上大学，不会申请纽约的学校。
> 女：没关系，你可以来找我玩儿。
> 男：好啊！要是你去纽约上大学，我放假就去找你，我们去中国城吃烤鸭。
> 女：就这么说定了！

Narrator: Now answer the questions for this selection.

(12 seconds)

(12 seconds)

(12 seconds)

(12 seconds)

Section II: Free Response

Part B: Speaking

Recording Scripts

Conversation

Directions:

You will participate in a simulated conversation. Each time it is your turn to speak, you will have 20 seconds to record. You should respond as fully and as appropriately as possible. There will be six times when it is your turn to speak.

Faculty adviser Tianzhen is interviewing you for a volunteer position in a Student Internet Committee at your school. The goal of the committee is to promote correct use of the internet.

(Traditional characters)

> 天真：你好，你爲什麼對參加學生網絡小組感興趣？
> （學生答題20秒）
> 天真：你上網常做些什麼？爲什麼？
> （學生答題20秒）
> 天真：你覺得網絡改善人們的生活了嗎？爲什麼？
> （學生答題20秒）
> 天真：你覺得在網上工作或者上課有什麼好處和壞處？
> （學生答題20秒）
> 天真：你認爲網絡能夠幫助學生學習嗎？爲什麼？
> （學生答題20秒）
> 天真：網絡會帶來什麼問題？上網的時候應該注意什麼？
> （學生答題20秒）

(Simplified characters)

> 天真：你好，你为什么对参加学生网络小组感兴趣？
> （学生答题20秒）
> 天真：你上网常做些什么？为什么？
> （学生答题20秒）
> 天真：你觉得网络改善人们的生活了吗？为什么？
> （学生答题20秒）

天真：你觉得在网上工作或者上课有什么好处和坏处？

（学生答题20秒）

天真：你认为网络能够帮助学生学习吗？为什么？

（学生答题20秒）

天真：网络会带来什么问题？上网的时候应该注意什么？

（学生答题20秒）

Cultural Presentation

Directions:

You will be asked to speak in Chinese on a specific topic. Imagine you are making an oral presentation to your Chinese class. First, you will read and hear the topic for your presentation. You will have 4 minutes to prepare your presentation. Then you will have 2 minutes to record your presentation. Your presentation should be as complete as possible.

Choose ONE Chinese art form (calligraphy, painting, paper cutting, jade jewelry, porcelain pottery, Beijing Opera, etc.). In your presentation, describe this art form and explain its significance.

Audio Scripts of AP Chinese Language and Culture Test 10

Section I: Multiple Choice

Part A: Listening

Rejoinders

Directions:

Directions: You will hear several short conversations or parts of conversations followed by four choices, designated A, B, C, and D. Choose the one that continues or completes the conversation in a logical and culturally appropriate manner. After you have decided which of the suggested answers is best, COMPLETELY fill in the corresponding circle on the answer sheet. You will have 5 seconds to answer each question.

(Traditional characters)

1. 男：老師要求我們每個星期在網上跟同學說一個小時的中文，練習口語。
   女：A）那樣的話你的中文水平會提高得很快。
   　　B）我喜歡在網上上課，不喜歡去學校。
   　　C）我漢字寫得很好，不用多練習。
   　　D）在網上學英文，又簡單又方便。
   （學生答題 5 秒）

(Simplified characters)

1. 男：老师要求我们每个星期在网上跟同学说一个小时的中文，练习口语。
   女：A）那样的话你的中文水平会提高得很快。
   　　B）我喜欢在网上上课，不喜欢去学校。
   　　C）我汉字写得很好，不用多练习。
   　　D）在网上学英文，又简单又方便。
   （学生答题 5 秒）

(Traditional characters)

2. 男：你畢業以後打算唸研究生還是找工作？
   女：A）我哥哥正在唸研究生，他學的是醫學。
   　　B）我想先工作掙錢，積累點兒工作經驗。
   　　C）畢業的時候該不該送朋友畢業禮物呢？
   　　D）你爲什麼不想繼續唸研究生，而要工作？
   （學生答題 5 秒）

(Simplified characters)

2. 男：你毕业以后打算念研究生还是找工作？
   女：A）我哥哥正在念研究生，他学的是医学。
   　　B）我想先工作挣钱，积累点儿工作经验。
   　　C）毕业的时候该不该送朋友毕业礼物呢？
   　　D）你为什么不想继续念研究生，而要工作？
   （学生答题 5 秒）

(Traditional characters) | (Simplified characters)

3. 女：你整天都在玩兒遊戲，看起來是玩兒上癮了。

   男：A）我的電腦壞了，用不了了。

   　　B）我的同學都玩兒手機。

   　　C）玩兒遊戲太花時間了，你快別玩兒了！

   　　D）沒那麼嚴重吧？

   （學生答題5秒）

4. 女：我姐姐上個星期跟男朋友分手了。

   男：A）我昨天跟男朋友去看電影。

   　　B）難怪她看起來心情不太好。

   　　C）難怪她的右手受傷了。

   　　D）你想找什麼樣的男朋友？

   （學生答題5秒）

5. 男：下午我想去趟圖書館，你要不要一起去？

   女：A）圖書館寬敞明亮又安靜，是個學習的好地方。

   　　B）好啊，正好我有兩本書該還了。

   　　C）請問，去圖書館怎麼走？

   　　D）我聽說圖書館在招臨時工，你有興趣嗎？

   （學生答題5秒）

6. 女：你的公寓房間住得下兩個人嗎？我能搬去跟你一起住嗎？

   男：A）不行，我的公寓沒有人住。

   　　B）不行，我的房間只住得下一個人。

C）不行，搬家太麻煩了。
D）不行，我家只有兩個臥室。
（學生答題 5 秒）

(Traditional characters)

7. 女：你怎麼從早到晚都在學習？
   男：A）從早到晚學習效果不一定好，休息也很重要。
   B）早上是學習最好的時間。
   C）我的同學都喜歡在晚上學習。
   D）因為我想申請最好的大學。
   （學生答題 5 秒）

(Traditional characters)

8. 女：你週末常常做些什麼?
   男：當然是上網玩兒遊戲，你呢？
   女：A）上網玩兒電腦遊戲很花時間。
   B）我家沒有網絡。
   C）我要麼和朋友微信聊天兒，要麼寫博客。
   D）微信聊天兒、寫博客都沒意思。
   （學生答題 5 秒）

(Traditional characters)

9. 女：你的中文說得真流利。
   男：哪裡，哪裡，我還想繼續提高我的中文水平。
   女：A）你太謙虛了！
   B）你太懶了，你的中文不會進步的。
   C）什麼都不做就能提高中文水平？你太天真了！
   D）多看電視新聞對學英文有幫助。
   （學生答題 5 秒）

C）不行，搬家太麻烦了。
D）不行，我家只有两个卧室。
（学生答题 5 秒）

(Simplified characters)

7. 女：你怎么从早到晚都在学习？
   男：A）从早到晚学习效果不一定好，休息也很重要。
   B）早上是学习最好的时间。
   C）我的同学都喜欢在晚上学习。
   D）因为我想申请最好的大学。
   （学生答题 5 秒）

(Simplified characters)

8. 女：你周末常常做些什么?
   男：当然是上网玩儿游戏，你呢？
   女：A）上网玩儿电脑游戏很花时间。
   B）我家没有网络。
   C）我要么和朋友微信聊天儿，要么写博客。
   D）微信聊天儿、写博客都没意思。
   （学生答题 5 秒）

(Simplified characters)

9. 女：你的中文说得真流利。
   男：哪里，哪里，我还想继续提高我的中文水平。
   女：A）你太谦虚了！
   B）你太懒了，你的中文不会进步的。
   C）什么都不做就能提高中文水平？你太天真了！
   D）多看电视新闻对学英文有帮助。
   （学生答题 5 秒）

10. 男：你買了這麼多魚肉、牛肉，還買了蘋果、西瓜，不買些青菜嗎？
    女：你想吃什麼青菜？
    男：A）中國菜美國菜都可以。
    　　B）我愛吃肉，不吃青菜。
    　　C）小白菜或者芥蘭都可以。
    　　D）青菜都賣完了,想買也買不了了。
    （學生答題 5 秒）

11. 女：你看起來身體很健康。你很注意飲食吧？
    男：是啊，我吃得很清淡，有的時候甚至炒菜不放油。
    女：A）中國菜實在太好吃了。
    　　B）吃清淡一點兒對健康有好處。
    　　C）只要多運動，不用注意飲食。
    　　D）身體好可以吃油一點兒，沒關係。
    （學生答題 5 秒）

12. 男：早上好，你一早就出去散步啊？
    女：是啊，我什麼運動都不會，走路最適合我。
    男：A）你家的小狗真可愛。
    　　B）沒錯，早睡早起身體好。
    　　C）今天是週末，這麼早起床做什麼？
    　　D）沒錯,走路就是最簡單的運動。
    （學生答題 5 秒）

(Simplified characters)

13. 女：你大学想学钢琴专业吗？你的钢琴弹得可真好。

    男：谢谢夸奖！你说对了，我大学就想学钢琴专业，我父母都很支持。

    女：A）真羡慕你啊！我还不知道自己想学什么。

    　　B）钢琴专业毕业后很难找工作，你别学了。

    　　C）这架钢琴是我们店最好的钢琴，您真有眼光！

    　　D）这架钢琴很贵，你父母同意你买吗？

    （学生答题 5 秒）

14. 女：小高，好久不见，你怎么一个人来看电影？

    男：你忘了吗？我现在没有女朋友了，你给我介绍一个吧。

    女：A）一个人看电影也很好呀！

    　　B）这是我的男朋友大卫。

    　　C）没问题啊，你喜欢什么样的？

    　　D）对不起，我忘了你的名字。

    （学生答题 5 秒）

15. 女：谢谢你借给我生物课的笔记，我用完了。我送到你家还给你吧。你家怎么走？

    男：你先在学校门口坐10路公交车，坐两站下车，然后换乘红线地铁，坐两站在平安路北站下车，我家就在地铁口旁边。

女：A）坐公車和地鐵很便宜。
　　B）我沒記住，你可以再說一遍嗎？
　　C）對不起，我把你的筆記本弄丟了。
　　D）你應該走路上學。

（學生答題5秒）

女：A）坐公交车和地铁很便宜。
　　B）我没记住，你可以再说一遍吗？
　　C）对不起，我把你的笔记本弄丢了。
　　D）你应该走路上学。

（学生答题5秒）

Listening Selections

Directions:

You will listen to several selections in Chinese. For each selection, you will be told whether it will be played once or twice. You may take notes as you listen. Your notes will not be graded. After listening to each selection, you will see questions in English. For each question, choose the response that is best according to the selection. You will have 12 seconds to answer each question.

Selection 1: Transportation Announcement

Narrator: Now you will listen twice to a transportation announcement.

Woman:

(Traditional characters)

> 本次列車終點站爲：武漢東站。下一站：中央公園站。請要下車的乘客提前做好準備。中央公園站是換乘站，可換乘2號綫，去往武漢博物館的乘客請在本站下車換乘。請各位乘客從列車前進方向右邊的車門下車，先下後上。

(Simplified characters)

> 本次列车终点站为：武汉东站。下一站：中央公园站。请要下车的乘客提前做好准备。中央公园站是换乘站，可换乘2号线，去往武汉博物馆的乘客请在本站下车换乘。请各位乘客从列车前进方向右边的车门下车，先下后上。

Narrator: Now listen again.

(Repeat)

Narrator: Now answer the questions for this selection.

(12 seconds)

(12 seconds)

Selection 2: Voice Message

Narrator: Now you will listen twice to a voice message.

Man:

(Traditional characters)

> 媽媽，剛纔奶奶的鄰居給我打電話說，奶奶在她家樓下的公園裡騎自行車跌倒了，鄰居已經把她送到醫院去了。奶奶的鄰居給你打電話，你沒有接，你在開會嗎？我跟奶奶通了電話了，她的腳非常疼，但是情緒還不錯。我三點下課以後會直接到醫院去看奶奶，你別擔心。聽到留言後，給我和奶奶打個電話吧！

(Simplified characters)

> 妈妈，刚才奶奶的邻居给我打电话说，奶奶在她家楼下的公园里骑自行车跌倒了，邻居已经把她送到医院去了。奶奶的邻居给你打电话，你没有接，你在开会吗？我跟奶奶通了电话了，她的脚非常疼，但是情绪还不错。我三点下课以后会直接到医院去看奶奶，你别担心。听到留言后，给我和奶奶打个电话吧！

Narrator: Now listen again.

(Repeat)

Narrator: Now answer the questions for this selection.

(12 seconds)

(12 seconds)

(12 seconds)

Selection 3: School Conversation

Narrator: Now you will listen once to a school conversation.

(Traditional characters)

> 女：小林，剛纔老師給我們看的京劇視頻你看得懂嗎？
> 男：看得懂，可是聽不懂。雖然聽不懂，但是能猜出大概的意思。
> 女：我一點兒也聽不清楚唱的是什麼，只是覺得很熱鬧。
> 男：我覺得京劇的音樂特別好，武打動作也很精彩。我也很喜歡京劇的臉譜。
> 女：京劇的服裝也很美。聽說看現場表演，更有趣更精彩。你去劇場看過京劇嗎？
> 男：沒有。下次我們一起去看吧！

(Simplified characters)

女：小林，刚才老师给我们看的京剧视频你看得懂吗？
男：看得懂，可是听不懂。虽然听不懂，但是能猜出大概的意思。
女：我一点儿也听不清楚唱的是什么，只是觉得很热闹。
男：我觉得京剧的音乐特别好，武打动作也很精彩。我也很喜欢京剧的脸谱。
女：京剧的服装也很美。听说看现场表演，更有趣更精彩。你去剧场看过京剧吗？
男：没有。下次我们一起去看吧！

Narrator: Now answer the questions for this selection.

(12 seconds)

(12 seconds)

(12 seconds)

Selection 4: Radio Report

Narrator: Now you will listen once to a radio report.

Man:

(Traditional characters)

歡迎收聽本臺最新新聞。市政府最新消息，爲了減少資源浪費和環境污染，從今年6月1日開始，所有零售業、餐飲業，包括商店、超市、購物中心、餐館兒、飲料店等將停止提供免費塑料袋。在此提醒各位聽衆，購物及購買餐飲時，請自己準備購物袋。

(Simplified characters)

欢迎收听本台最新新闻。市政府最新消息，为了减少资源浪费和环境污染，从今年6月1日开始，所有零售业、餐饮业，包括商店、超市、购物中心、餐馆儿、饮料店等将停止提供免费塑料袋。在此提醒各位听众，购物及购买餐饮时，请自己准备购物袋。

Narrator: Now answer the questions for this selection.

(12 seconds)

(12 seconds)

(12 seconds)

Selection 5: Instructions

Narrator: Now you will listen once to someone giving instructions.

Woman:

(Traditional characters)

女士們、先生們：
　　感謝您在飛行途中對我們工作的支持和配合！現在飛機已經開始下降，請您坐好，繫好安全帶，打開遮陽板，并關閉所有電子設備。謝謝！

(Simplified characters)

女士们、先生们：
　　感谢您在飞行途中对我们工作的支持和配合！现在飞机已经开始下降，请您坐好，系好安全带，打开遮阳板，并关闭所有电子设备。谢谢！

Narrator: Now answer the questions for this selection.

(12 seconds)

(12 seconds)

(12 seconds)

Selection 6: Conversation

Narrator: Now you will listen once to a conversation.

(Traditional characters)

女兒：媽，您看這條紅色的裙子真好看。
媽媽：挺漂亮的，你想買嗎？
女兒：嗯！紅色的裙子很適合過新年穿。
媽媽：可是你的裙子太多了。
女兒：可是這條裙子現在打七折，而且我的生日快到了，您送這條裙子給我當生日禮物，好嗎？
媽媽：你的禮物我早就買好了。再說，你最近已經買了太多新衣服了。
女兒：可是這麼好看的裙子打折以後纔二十塊錢，真的很便宜。
媽媽：不行，我不會給你買的。要是你非買不可，就用你自己的零用錢買。

(Simplified characters)

> 女儿：妈，您看这条红色的裙子真好看。
> 妈妈：挺漂亮的，你想买吗？
> 女儿：嗯！红色的裙子很适合过新年穿。
> 妈妈：可是你的裙子太多了。
> 女儿：可是这条裙子现在打七折，而且我的生日快到了，您送这条裙子给我当生日礼物，好吗？
> 妈妈：你的礼物我早就买好了。再说，你最近已经买了太多新衣服了。
> 女儿：可是这么好看的裙子打折以后才二十块钱，真的很便宜。
> 妈妈：不行，我不会给你买的。要是你非买不可，就用你自己的零用钱买。

Narrator: Now answer the questions for this selection.

(12 seconds)

(12 seconds)

(12 seconds)

(12 seconds)

Section II: Free Response
Part B: Speaking
Recording Scripts
Conversation
Directions:

You will participate in a simulated conversation. Each time it is your turn to speak, you will have 20 seconds to record. You should respond as fully and as appropriately as possible. There will be six times when it is your turn to speak.

You and your friend Tianming are members of the Chinese Culture Club at school. You are having a video chat to discuss plans for the new school year.

(Traditional characters)

> 天明：好久不見，你暑假去北京旅遊最喜歡什麼地方？爲什麼？
> （學生答題20秒）
> 天明：快開學了，我們得討論一下我們中國文化社新學期的活動，你有什麼建議？
> （學生答題20秒）

天明：我們每年都會辦一次中文電影欣賞，你建議選哪一部電影？爲什麽？
（學生答題20秒）

天明：你覺得我們今年的中秋節應該辦什麽活動？爲什麽？
（學生答題20秒）

天明：對感恩節的社區服務，你有什麽看法？我們可以去什麽地方做什麽活動？
（學生答題20秒）

天明：除了社團活動，我們還打算一起出遊，你建議去什麽地方？爲什麽？
（學生答題20秒）

(Simplified characters)

天明：好久不见，你暑假去北京旅游最喜欢什么地方？为什么？
（学生答题20秒）

天明：快开学了，我们得讨论一下我们中国文化社新学期的活动，你有什么建议？
（学生答题20秒）

天明：我们每年都会办一次中文电影欣赏，你建议选一部电影？为什么？
（学生答题20秒）

天明：你觉得我们今年的中秋节应该办什么活动？为什么？
（学生答题20秒）

天明：对感恩节的社区服务，你有什么看法？我们可以去什么地方做什么活动？
（学生答题20秒）

天明：除了社团活动，我们还打算一起出游，你建议去什么地方？为什么？
（学生答题20秒）

Cultural Presentation

Directions:

You will be asked to speak in Chinese on a specific topic. Imagine you are making an oral presentation to your Chinese class. First, you will read and hear the topic for your presentation. You will have 4 minutes to prepare your presentation. Then you will have 2 minutes to record your presentation. Your presentation should be as complete as possible.

Choose ONE example of the use of technology in modern-day China (social media, online shopping, food delivery, mobile pay, bike share, ride share, robot appliances, Smart Homes, satellites, etc.). In your presentation, describe this use of technology and explain its significance.

ANSWER KEYS

TEST SET 1

A: Listening	B: Reading
1. B	1. D
2. C	2. B
3. A	3. A
4. D	4. B
5. C	5. B
6. D	6. A
7. A	7. A
8. B	8. B
9. C	9. B
10. B	10. A
11. C	11. A
12. D	12. B
13. B	13. C
14. C	14. A
15. B	15. C
16. D	16. B
17. D	17. B
18. A	18. D
19. A	19. B
20. B	20. A
21. C	21. B
22. C	22. A
23. C	23. C
24. B	24. C
25. C	25. C
26. A	26. B
27. B	27. C
28. C	28. B
29. B	29. D
30. D	30. B
31. B	31. A
32. B	32. B
33. A	33. C
34. B	34. C
35. B	35. C

TEST SET 2

Part A: Listening	Part B: Reading
1. B	1. B
2. B	2. C
3. A	3. B
4. C	4. B
5. D	5. D
6. A	6. A
7. C	7. B
8. D	8. C
9. B	9. A
10. A	10. B
11. C	11. B
12. A	12. A
13. D	13. A
14. A	14. C
15. C	15. C
16. B	16. C
17. C	17. C
18. B	18. A
19. A	19. D
20. B	20. C
21. C	21. B
22. C	22. D
23. D	23. A
24. B	24. B
25. D	25. D
26. D	26. A
27. B	27. B
28. D	28. B
29. C	29. A
30. B	30. A
31. D	31. C
32. C	32. D
33. C	33. B
34. A	34. A
35. B	35. D

TEST SET 3

A: Listening

1. A
2. C
3. D
4. B
5. B
6. A
7. C
8. D
9. A
10. B
11. C
12. A
13. B
14. C
15. B
16. C
17. C
18. C
19. D
20. B
21. C
22. D
23. C
24. D
25. D
26. B
27. B
28. D
29. B
30. D
31. C
32. B
33. D
34. B
35. C

B: Reading

1. D
2. C
3. C
4. A
5. D
6. A
7. D
8. C
9. D
10. A
11. C
12. D
13. B
14. D
15. A
16. B
17. A
18. C
19. D
20. B
21. B
22. C
23. C
24. A
25. D
26. C
27. B
28. C
29. B
30. C
31. B
32. A
33. A
34. D
35. A

TEST SET 4

Part A: Listening

1. C
2. A
3. B
4. A
5. D
6. D
7. A
8. C
9. C
10. B
11. A
12. C
13. C
14. B
15. D
16. C
17. D
18. B
19. A
20. B
21. A
22. D
23. B
24. C
25. B
26. B
27. D
28. C
29. B
30. C
31. D
32. B
33. A
34. C
35. A

Part B: Reading

1. C
2. D
3. B
4. C
5. A
6. C
7. A
8. C
9. B
10. B
11. B
12. B
13. A
14. D
15. C
16. B
17. C
18. D
19. A
20. B
21. C
22. B
23. A
24. C
25. C
26. C
27. D
28. C
29. A
30. D
31. D
32. B
33. A
34. C
35. B

TEST SET 5

A: Listening	B: Reading
1. C	1. C
2. B	2. D
3. D	3. C
4. B	4. D
5. A	5. D
6. D	6. A
7. A	7. D
8. C	8. D
9. C	9. A
10. C	10. B
11. C	11. D
12. A	12. B
13. A	13. B
14. C	14. A
15. C	15. B
16. C	16. B
17. A	17. A
18. C	18. B
19. C	19. A
20. B	20. C
21. C	21. D
22. B	22. B
23. C	23. C
24. A	24. B
25. D	25. C
26. B	26. B
27. D	27. C
28. B	28. D
29. A	29. C
30. C	30. B
31. D	31. D
32. B	32. A
33. C	33. B
34. C	34. A
35. B	35. C

TEST SET 6

Part A: Listening	Part B: Reading
1. A	1. C
2. C	2. D
3. C	3. B
4. D	4. B
5. C	5. A
6. B	6. C
7. C	7. D
8. D	8. B
9. A	9. A
10. D	10. C
11. C	11. A
12. C	12. C
13. A	13. D
14. C	14. C
15. B	15. B
16. C	16. B
17. B	17. A
18. B	18. D
19. B	19. B
20. D	20. A
21. B	21. D
22. C	22. B
23. A	23. C
24. B	24. B
25. D	25. B
26. A	26. A
27. C	27. C
28. A	28. D
29. B	29. C
30. C	30. A
31. C	31. C
32. B	32. B
33. C	33. D
34. B	34. B
35. D	35. A

TEST SET 7

A: Listening

1. D
2. A
3. C
4. B
5. C
6. B
7. B
8. B
9. C
10. D
11. B
12. A
13. B
14. D
15. B
16. B
17. B
18. A
19. A
20. C
21. C
22. B
23. D
24. B
25. D
26. B
27. C
28. D
29. C
30. B
31. B
32. B
33. A
34. D
35. B

B: Reading

1. A
2. D
3. C
4. B
5. A
6. B
7. D
8. D
9. A
10. D
11. D
12. C
13. C
14. D
15. D
16. D
17. A
18. C
19. B
20. D
21. B
22. A
23. C
24. B
25. C
26. B
27. B
28. D
29. C
30. C
31. B
32. C
33. C
34. C
35. A

TEST SET 8

Part A: Listening

1. A
2. B
3. D
4. B
5. C
6. C
7. A
8. B
9. D
10. C
11. B
12. C
13. A
14. C
15. B
16. C
17. B
18. C
19. D
20. B
21. A
22. C
23. B
24. B
25. C
26. D
27. A
28. A
29. A
30. B
31. D
32. B
33. A
34. B
35. C

Part B: Reading

1. B
2. D
3. A
4. C
5. B
6. C
7. B
8. B
9. A
10. C
11. D
12. C
13. A
14. C
15. C
16. B
17. D
18. B
19. A
20. C
21. B
22. D
23. B
24. C
25. B
26. A
27. D
28. B
29. C
30. D
31. A
32. D
33. A
34. B
35. B

TEST SET 9

A: Listening	B: Reading
1. A	1. A
2. D	2. D
3. A	3. A
4. B	4. A
5. A	5. D
6. D	6. B
7. C	7. A
8. B	8. D
9. A	9. B
10. B	10. A
11. A	11. A
12. C	12. C
13. C	13. D
14. A	14. B
15. B	15. A
16. B	16. B
17. C	17. A
18. A	18. A
19. C	19. C
20. A	20. D
21. B	21. A
22. C	22. D
23. D	23. D
24. B	24. A
25. A	25. B
26. B	26. A
27. B	27. C
28. A	28. D
29. B	29. C
30. A	30. A
31. A	31. D
32. A	32. A
33. A	33. D
	34. C
	35. B
	36. C
	37. D

TEST SET 10

Part A: Listening	Part B: Reading
1. A	1. D
2. B	2. A
3. D	3. B
4. B	4. A
5. B	5. D
6. B	6. A
7. D	7. A
8. C	8. A
9. A	9. B
10. C	10. B
11. B	11. A
12. D	12. C
13. A	13. A
14. C	14. C
15. B	15. A
16. A	16. C
17. D	17. A
18. A	18. C
19. C	19. B
20. B	20. D
21. A	21. B
22. A	22. C
23. D	23. A
24. D	24. C
25. A	25. D
26. D	26. B
27. A	27. D
28. D	28. C
29. B	29. A
30. C	30. C
31. D	31. C
32. D	32. A
33. A	33. C
	34. A
	35. D
	36. A
	37. C